FRENCH

Phrase Book & Dictionary

Philippa Goodrich
Language Consultant: Marie-Laure Vernier

French Phrase Book and Dictionary
Based on the *BBC French Phrase Book* by Carol Stanley and Philippa Goodrich, copyright © Carol Stanley and Philippa Goodrich 1990

Published by BBC Active, an imprint of Educational Publishers LLP, part of the Pearson Education Group. Edinburgh Gate, Harlow, Essex CM20 2JE

Published 2005
Fifth impression 2008

ISBN 978-0-563-51918-8

Managing Editor: Joanna Kirby
Project Editor: Josie Frame
Index Editor: Paula Peebles
Designer: Elizabeth Burns
Concept design: Pentacor Book Design
Cover design: Two Associates
Cover photo copyright © Mike Busselle/ALAMY
Senior Production Controller: Man Fai Lau

Printed and bound in China. CTPSC/05

The Publisher's policy is to use paper manufactured from sustainable forests.

how to use this book

This book is divided into colour-coded sections to help you find the language you need as quickly as possible. You can also refer to the **contents** on pages 4–5, the contents lists at the start of each section or the **index** on page 221.

Along with travel and language tips, each section contains:

 YOU MAY WANT TO SAY...
language you'll need for every situation

 YOU MAY SEE...
words and phrases you'll see on signs or in print

 YOU MAY HEAR... questions, instructions or information people may ask or give you

On page 12 you'll find **essentials**, a list of basic, all-purpose phrases to help you start communicating straight away.

Many of the phrases can be adapted by simply using another word from the dictionary. For instance, take the question Pour aller à l'aéroport? (How do I get to the airport?). If you want to know where the *beach* is, just substitute la plage (beach) for l'aéroport to give Pour aller à la plage?.

The **pronunciation guide** is based on English sounds, and is explained on page 6. If you want some guidance on how the French language works, see **basic grammar** on page 149. The **dictionary** is separated into two sections: English–French (page 159) and French–English (page 199).

We welcome any comments or suggestions about this book, but in the meantime, have a good trip – Bon voyage!

contents

pronunciation guide

✳ pronunciation

You don't need perfect pronunciation to be able to communicate – it's enough to get the sounds approximately right. A pronunciation guide is given with the phrases in this book; the system is based on English sounds, as described below.

Many French consonants are pronounced in a similar way to English. The main differences are with c, g, h, j, ll, q, r, w.

Consonants at the end of words are not normally pronounced, except when followed by another word beginning with a vowel, for example: vous (*voo*) but vous avez (*vooz avay*).

French vowels don't vary as much as English ones, but the way they're pronounced is affected if: (1) there's a written accent; (2) they're followed by an n or m; (3) they're in a combination of vowels.

Vowels followed by n or m have a nasal sound – say them through your nose and mouth at the same time. The n or m itself is not pronounced. In the pronunciation guide the nasal sound is shown by the symbol ñ.

✳ stress

French words are pronounced with almost equal stress on every syllable, so no stresses are shown in this book.

✳ consonants

FRENCH CONSONANTS	APPROX ENGLISH EQUIVALENT	SHOWN IN BOOK AS	EXAMPLE	
b	**b** in 'but'	*b*	bain	*bañ*
c (followed by e or i) and ç	**s** in 'sat'	*s*	citron	*seetrawñ*
			ça	*sa*
ch	**sh** in 'shut'	*sh*	chambre	*shoñbr*
c (otherwise)	**c** in 'can'	*k*	comme	*kom*
d	**d** in 'dog'	*d*	douane	*doo-an*
f	**f** in 'feet'	*f*	français	*froñsay*
g (followed by e or i)	**s** in 'measure'	*j*	gentil	*joñtee*
gn	**ni** in 'onion'	*ny*	oignon	*unyawñ*
g (otherwise)	**g** in 'got'	*g*	grand	*groñ*
h	always silent	–	herbe	*erb*
j	**s** in 'measure'	*j*	je	*juh*
k	**k** in 'kit'	*k*	kilo	*keelo*
l	**l** in 'look'	*l*	livre	*leevr*
ll	**y** in 'yet'	*y*	fille	*feey*
m	**m** in 'mat'	*m*	main	*mañ*
n (but see Vowels below)	**n** in 'not'	*n*	nous	*noo*
p	**p** in 'pack'	*p*	pêche	*pesh*
qu	**k** in 'kit'	*k*	que	*kuh*

r	rolled in the back of the throat	r	rouge	*rooj*
s (between vowels)	z in 'zoo'	z	chose	*shohz*
s (otherwise)	s in 'set'	s	sortie	*sortee*
t	t in 'tin'	t	table	*tabl*
v	v in 'vet'	v	vin	*vañ*
w (except in English words like weekend)	v in 'vet'	v w	wagon	*vagawñ*
x (at end of word)	s in 'six'	s	six	*sees*
x (otherwise)	x in 'six'	x	taxi	*taxee*
y	y in 'yet'	y	payer	*payay*
z	z in 'zoo'	z	douze	*dooz*

✳ vowels

FRENCH VOWELS	APPROX ENGLISH EQUIVALENT	SHOWN IN BOOK AS	EXAMPLE	
a, à, â	between a in 'cat' and 'cart'	a	ami	*amee*
é, er, ez (at end of word)	a in 'gate', but a bit shorter	ay	café avez	*kafay avay*
e, è, ê	e in 'get'	e	cette chèque	*set shek*
e (at end of word)	not pronounced	-	carte	*kart*

e (at end of syllable or in one-syllable word)	**often pronounced weakly, like er in 'other'**	*uh*	petit je, de	*puhtee juh, duh*
i	**ee in 'meet'**	*ee*	ami	*amee*
'weak' i	**y in 'yet'**	*y*	mieux	*myuh*
o	**o in 'lot'**	*o*	opéra	*opayra*
ô	**o in 'note'**	*oh*	hôtel	*ohtel*
u	**to make this sound, shape your lips to say oo, but say ee**	*ew*	une	*ewn*

✳ vowel combinations

FRENCH VOWELS	APPROX ENGLISH EQUIVALENT	SHOWN IN BOOK AS	EXAMPLE	
ai	**a in 'gate'**	*ay*	français	*froñsay*
aî	**e in 'get'**	*e*	fraîche	*fresh*
ail	**i in 'bite'**	*iy*	travail	*traviy*
au, eau	**o in 'note'**	*oh*	cadeau	*kadoh*
ei	**e in 'get'**	*e*	Seine	*sen*
eu, œu	**er in 'other'**	*uh*	peu	*puh*
oi	**wa in 'swam'**	*wa*	moi	*mwa*
oy	**'why'**	*wiy*	voyage	*vwiyaj*
ui	**wee in 'between'**	*wee*	huit	*weet*

✳ nasal vowels

FRENCH VOWELS	APPROX ENGLISH EQUIVALENT	SHOWN IN BOOK AS	EXAMPLE	
an, en	**o** in 'hot' + nasal sound	oñ	banc	boñ
ain, ein, in	**a** in 'cat' + nasal sound	añ	bain	bañ
on	**aw** in 'saw' + nasal sound	awñ	bon	bawñ
un	**u** in 'cut' + nasal sound	uñ	chacun	shakuñ

am.

123

the basics

*essentials

Hello.	Bonjour/Salut.	*bawñjoor/salew*
Goodbye.	Au revoir.	*o revwar*
Yes.	Oui.	*wee*
No.	Non.	*nawñ*
Please.	S'il vous plaît.	*seelvooplay*
Thank you (very much).	Merci (beaucoup).	*mersee (bohkoo)*
I don't know.	Je ne sais pas.	*juh nuh say pa*
I don't understand.	Je ne comprends pas.	*juh nuh kawmproñ pa*
I don't speak much French.	Je ne parle pas bien le français.	*juh ne parl pa byañ luh froñsay*
Do you speak English?	Parlez-vous l'anglais?	*parlay voo loñglay*
Pardon?	Pardon?	*pardawñ*
Could you repeat that, please?	Pourriez-vous répéter, s'il vous plaît?	*pooryay voo raypaytay seelvooplay*
More slowly, please.	Plus lentement.	*plew loñtuhmoñ*
What is it called in French?	Comment ça s'appelle en français?	*komoñ sa sapel oñ froñsay*
Excuse me.	Excusez-moi.	*exkewzsay mwa*
I'm sorry.	Desolé(e).	*dayzolay*
OK, fine.	Bien/D'accord.	*byañ/dakoor*

the basics

Cheers!	À la votre!	*a la vohtr*
I'd like...	Je voudrais...	*juh voodray...*
Do you have...?	Est-ce que vous avez...?	*eskuh vooz avay...*
What's this?	Qu'est-ce que c'est?	*keskuh say*
Is/Are there...?	Est-ce qu'il y a...?	*eskeelya...*
How much is it?	C'est combien?	*say kawmbyañ*
Is it possible to...?	Est-ce qu'on peut...?	*eskawñ puh...*
Where is/are...?	Où se trouve(nt)...?	*oo suh troov...*
How do I/ we get to...?	Pour aller à...?	*poor alay a...*
Can you show me on the map?	Pouvez-vous me montrer sur le plan?	*poovay voo muh mawñtray sewr luh ploñ*
Can you write it down for me?	Pourriez-vous me l'écrire?	*pooryay voo muh laykreer*
Could you...	Pourriez-vous...	*pooryay voo...*
give me...?	me donner...?	*muh donay...*
tell me...?	me dire...?	*muh deer...*
show me...?	me montrer...?	*muh montray...*
help me?	m'aider?	*mayday*
Help!	Au secours!	*oh suhkoor*
Look out!	Attention!	*atoñsyawñ*
It's very urgent!	C'est très urgent!	*say trez ewrjoñ*

the basics

13

✳ numbers

1	un	*uñ*
2	deux	*duh*
3	trois	*trwa*
4	quatre	*katr*
5	cinq	*sañk*
6	six	*sees*
7	sept	*set*
8	huit	*weet*
9	neuf	*nuhf*
10	dix	*dees*
11	onze	*awñz*
12	douze	*dooz*
13	treize	*trez*
14	quatorze	*katorz*
15	quinze	*kañz*
16	seize	*sez*
17	dix-sept	*deeset*
18	dix-huit	*deezweet*
19	dix-neuf	*deeznuhf*
20	vingt	*vañ*
21	vingt et un	*vañteuñ*
22...	vingt-deux	*vañtduh*
30	trente	*troñt*
40	quarante	*karoñt*
50	cinquante	*sañkoñt*
60	soixante	*swasoñt*
70	soixante-dix	*swasoñt dees*
72...	soixante-douze	*swasoñt dooz*
80	quatre-vingts	*katruhvañ*
81...	quatre-vingt-un	*katruhvañ uñ*
90	quatre-vingt-dix	*katruhvañ dees*
93	quatre-vingt-treize	*katruhvañ sez*
97	quatre-vingt-dix-sept	*katruhvañ deeset*
100	cent	*soñ*

101	cent un	*soñuñ*
102...	cent deux	*soñduh*
200	deux cents	*duhsoñ*
201	deux cent un	*duhsoñ uñ*
250	deux cent cinquante	*duh soñ sañkoñt*
300	trois cents	*trwa soñ*
400	quatre cents	*katr soñ*
500	cinq cents	*sañsoñ*
1000	mille	*meel*
100,000	cent mille	*soñ meel*
one million	un million	*uñ meelyawñ*
one and a half million	un million et demi	*uñ meelyawñ e duhmee*

* ordinal numbers

first	premier	*pruhmyay*
second	deuxième	*duhzyem*
third	troisième	*trwazyem*
fourth	quatrième	*katryem*
fifth	cinquième	*sañkyem*
sixth	sixième	*sizyem*
seventh	septième	*setyem*
eighth	huitième	*weetyem*
ninth	neuvième	*nuhvyem*
tenth	dixième	*dizyem*

* fractions

quarter	quart	*kar*
half	moitié	*mwatyay*
three-quarters	trois-quarts	*trwa kar*
a third	tiers	*tyer*
two-thirds	deux-tiers	*duh tyer*

the basics

✳ days

Monday	lundi	*luñdee*
Tuesday	mardi	*mardee*
Wednesday	mercredi	*mercruhdee*
Thursday	jeudi	*juhdee*
Friday	vendredi	*voñdruhdee*
Saturday	samedi	*samuhdee*
Sunday	dimanche	*deemoñsh*

✳ months

January	janvier	*joñvyay*
February	février	*fayvreeyai*
March	mars	*mars*
April	avril	*avreel*
May	mai	*may*
June	juin	*jewañ*
July	juillet	*jeweeye*
August	août	*oot*
September	septembre	*septoñbr*
October	octobre	*octobr*
November	novembre	*novoñbr*
December	décembre	*daysoñbr*

✳ seasons

spring	printemps	*prañtoñ*
summer	été	*aytay*
autumn	automne	*ohton*
winter	hiver	*eever*

the basics

* dates

What day is it today?	Quel jour sommes-nous aujourd'hui?	*kel joor som noo ohjoordwee*
What date is it today?	Quelle est la date d'aujourd'hui?	*kel ay la dat d'ohjoordwee*
What date is... your birthday?	Quelle est la date de... votre anniversaire?	*kel ay la dat duh... votr aneeveser*
(It's) April 15th.	(C'est) le 15 avril.	*(say) luh kañz avreel*
on April 15th	le 15 avril	*luh kañz avreel*

* telling the time
(see **numbers**, page 14)

It is more common in French than in English to use the 24-hour clock. French people write the time using a small 'h' to separate the hours from the minutes. For example, 3.30pm would be written as 15h30 and 4.15am as 4h30. For 12am and 12pm, the French use minuit (midnight) and midi (midday).

What time is it?	Quelle heure est-il?	*kel uhr eteel*
What time does it... open/close? begin/finish?	À quelle heure ça... ouvre/ferme? commence/finit?	*a kel uhr sa... oovr/ferm komoñs/feenee*

the basics

17

- It's....
  - 10 o'clock — Il est... dix heures — *eele... deez uhr*
  - midday — midi — *meedee*
  - midnight — minuit — *meenwee*

English	French	Pronunciation
It's....	Il est...	*eele...*
10 o'clock	dix heures	*deez uhr*
midday	midi	*meedee*
midnight	minuit	*meenwee*
At...	À...	*A...*
half past ten	dix heures et demie	*deez uhr ay duhmee*
quarter past ten	dix heures et quart	*deez uhr ay kar*
quarter to ten	dix heures moins le quart	*deez uhr mwañ luh kar*
twenty past ten	dix heures vingt	*deez uhr vañ*
twenty-five to ten	dix heures moins vingt-cinq	*deez uhr mwañ vañt sañk*
ten on the dot	dix heures pile	*deez uhr peel*
In...	Dans...	*dañz...*
fifteen minutes	un quart d'heure	*uñ kar duhr*
half an hour	une demie heure	*ewn duhmee uhr*
an hour	une heure	*ewn uhr*

✳ time phrases

English	French	Pronunciation
today	aujourd'hui	*ohjoordwee*
tomorrow	demain	*duhmañ*
the day after tomorrow	après-demain	*apreduhmañ*
yesterday	hier	*eeyer*
the day before yesterday	avant-hier	*avoñtyer*
this morning	ce matin	*suh matañ*

this evening	ce soir	*suh swar*
this afternoon	cet après-midi	*set apremeedee*
tonight	ce soir	*suh swar*
on Friday	vendredi	*voñdruhdee*
on Fridays	le vendredi	*luh voñdruhdee*
every Friday	chaque vendredi	*shak voñdruhdee*
for a week	pour une semaine	*poor ewn suhmen*
for two weeks	pour deux semaines	*poor duh suhmen*
next week	la semaine prochaine	*la suhmen proshen*
next month	le mois prochain	*luh mwa prochañ*
next year	l'année prochaine	*lanay proshen*
last night	hier soir	*eeyer swar*
last week	la semaine dernière	*la suhmen dernyer*
last month	le mois dernier	*luh mwa dernyay*
a week ago	il y a une semaine	*eelya ewn suhmen*
a year ago	il y a un an	*eelya uñ oñ*
Since...	Depuis...	*duhpwee...*
last week	la semaine dernière	*la suhmen dernyer*
last month	le mois dernier	*luh mwa dernyay*
last year	l'année dernière	*lanay dernyer*
For...	Pendant...	*poñdoñ...*
two years	deux ans	*duhz oñ*
a month	un mois	*uñ mwa*
I've been here for a month.	Je suis ici depuis un mois.	*juh sweez eecee duhpwee uñ mwa*
I've been learning French for 2 years.	J'apprends le français depuis deux ans.	*japroñ luh froñsay duhpwee duhz oñ*
It's early/late.	C'est tôt/tard.	*say toh/tar*

the basics

19

* measurements

MEASUREMENTS

centimetres	centimètres	soñteemetr
metres	mètres	metr
kilometres	kilomètres	keelometr
millimetres	millimètres	meeleemetr
square metres	mètres carrés	metr karay
a litre	un litre	uñ leetr
25 litres	25 litres	vañtsañk leetr
gramme	gramme	gram
100 grammes	100 grammes	soñ gram
200 grammes	200 grammes	duh soñ gram
kilo	kilo(gramme)	keelo(gram)

CONVERSIONS

10cm = 4 inches

50cm = 19.6 inches

1 metre = 39.37 inches

110 metres = 100 yards

1 inch = 2.45cm

1 foot = 30cm

1 yard = 0.91m

1 mile = 1.61km

1km = 0.62 miles

1 litre = 1.8 pints

100g = 3.5oz

200g = 7oz

½ kilo = 1.1lb

1 kilo = 2.2 lb

1oz = 28g

¼lb = 113g

½lb = 225g

1 lb = 450g

To convert	multiply by	To convert	multiply by
centimetres to inches	0.3937	inches to centimetres	2.54
kilometres to miles	0.6214	miles to kilometres	1.6090
grammes to ounces	0.0353	ounces to grammes	28.35
kilogrammes to pounds	2.2050	pounds to kilogrammes	0.4536

✻ clothes and shoe sizes

WOMEN'S CLOTHES

UK	8	10	12	14	16	18	20
Continent	34	36	38	40	42	44	46

MEN'S CLOTHES

UK	36	38	40	42	44	46	48
Continent	46	48	50	52	54	56	58

MEN'S SHIRTS

UK	14	14½	15	15½	16	16½	17
Continent	36	37	38	39	41	42	43

SHOES

UK	2	3	4	5	6	7	8
Continent	35	36	37	38	39	41	42
UK	9	10	11	12			
Continent	43	44	45	46/47			

✻ false friends

FALSE FRIEND...	NOT TO BE CONFUSED WITH...
attendre à (to wait for)	to attend (assister)
coin (corner)	coin (la pièce)
gentil (nice, kind)	gentle (doux)
grand (big, tall)	grand (éminent, prestigieux)
journée (day)	journey (le voyage, le trajet)
librairie (bookshop)	library (la bibliothèque)
magasin (shop)	magazine (la revue, le périodique)
monnaie (small change)	money (l'argent)
rester (to stay, to remain)	to rest (se reposer)
sympathique (friendly)	sympathetic (compatissant)
travailler (to work)	to travel (voyager)

the basics

21

✳ national holidays and festivals

● If a bank holiday falls on a Sunday, French people take the Monday off instead. For national holidays that fall on Tuesday or Thursday, many people take the Monday or Friday off too. To do this is known as faire le pont (to make a bridge).

Nouvel An	**New Year**	1 Jan *(FBSL)*, 2 Jan *(S)*
Lundi du Carnaval	**Monday before Shrove Tuesday**	*(L)*
Vendredi-Saint	**Good Friday**	*(S)*
Lundi de Pâques	**Easter Monday**	*(FBSL)*
Fête du Travail	**Labour Day**	1 May *(FBSL)*
Fête de la Libération	**VE Day**	8 May *(F)*
Ascension	**Ascension Day**	*(FBSL)*
Lundi de Pentecôte	**Whit Monday**	*(FBSL)*
Fête Nationale	**National Day**	23 June *(L)*
Fête Nationale	**Bastille Day**	14 July *(F)*
Fête Nationale	**National Day**	21 July *(B)*
Fête Nationale	**National Day**	1 August *(S)*
Assomption	**Assumption**	15 August *(FBL)*
Toussaint	**All Saints' Day**	1 November *(FBL)*
Fête des Morts	**All Souls' Day**	2 November *(L)*
Armistice	**Armistice Day**	11 November *(FB)*
Jour de Noël	**Christmas Day**	25 December *(FBSL)*

F = France, B = Belgium, S = Switzerland, L = Luxembourg

general conversation

The word bonjour literally means 'good day' and is used at any time during the day (there's no distinction beween 'good morning' and 'good afternoon'). In the evening, you use bonsoir for 'good evening' and bonne nuit for 'goodnight'.

Au revoir is 'goodbye', but you'll also hear à tout à l'heure and à bientôt (see you later). Salut is a casual greeting, which can be used for both 'hello' and 'goodbye'.

● The French generally shake hands when they meet and when they say goodbye. Women, and men and women, (though not two men) often exchange kisses on both cheeks. The number of kisses given varies from region to region.

● To indicate formality or familiarity, French uses different words to say 'you'. The formal word for 'you' is vous *(voo)* and the informal word is tu *(tew)*. The verb forms are different as well, e.g. you'll hear est-ce que tu veux? instead of est-ce que vous voulez? *(do you want?)*, and tu as instead of vous avez *(you have)*. In this book we have used the more formal way, vous, on the assumption that you will mostly be talking to people you don't know.

✱ greetings

YOU MAY WANT TO SAY...

● **Hello!**
  Hi!
  Bye!

Salut!

salew

● **Good morning.**

Bonjour.

bawñjoor

general conversation

24

● **Good afternoon.**	Bonjour.	*bawñjoor*
● **Good evening.**	Bonsoir.	*bawñswar*
● **Good night.**	Bonne nuit.	*bon nwee*
● **Goodbye.**	Au revoir.	*oh ruhvwar*
● **See you later.**	À tout à l'heure.	*a tootaluhr*
● **How are you?**		
(formal)	Comment allez-vous?	*komoñt alay voo*
(informal)	Comment vas-tu?	*komoñt va tew*
● **How are things?**	Comment ça va?	*komoñ sa va*
● **Fine, thanks.**	Bien, merci.	*byañ mersee*
● **And you?**		
(formal)	Et vous?	*e voo*
(informal)	Et toi?	*e twa*

✳ introductions

YOU MAY WANT TO SAY...

● **My name is...**	Je m'appelle...	*juh mapel...*
● **Pleased to meet you.**	Enchanté(e) de faire votre connaissance.	*oñshoñtay duh fer votr konaysoñs*
● **This is...**	Voici...	*vwasee...*
David Brown	David Brown	*David Brown*
my husband/ partner	mon mari/ partenaire	*mawñ maree/ partuhner*
my wife/ partner	ma femme/ partenaire	*ma fam/ partuhner*

* talking about yourself

- I'm...
  English
  Irish
  Scottish
  Welsh

  Je suis...
  anglais(e)
  irlandais(e)
  écossais(e)
  gallois(e)

  juh swee...
  oñglay(z)
  eerloñday(z)
  aykosay(z)
  galwa(z)

- I come from...
  England
  Ireland
  Scotland
  Wales

  Je viens...
  d'Angleterre
  d'Irlande
  d'Écosse
  du Pays de Galles

  juh vyañ...
  doñgluhter
  deerloñd
  daykos
  dew payee duh gal

- I live in...
  J'habite à...
  jabeet a...

- We live in...
  Newcastle.

  Nous habitons à...
  Newcastle.

  nooz abeetawñ a...
  nyookasuhl

- I'm 25 years old.
  J'ai vingt-cinq ans.
  jay vañtsañk oñ

- He's/She's five
  years old.

  Il/Elle a cinq ans.
  eel/el a sañk oñ

- I'm a...
  web designer
  nurse
  student
  electrician

  Je suis...
  designer web
  infirmier/ère
  étudiant(e)
  électricien/ne

  juh swee...
  dayziynuhr web
  añfeermyay/yer
  aytewdyoñ(t)
  aylektrisyañ/yen

- I work in/for...

  a bank
  a computer firm

  Je travaille dans/
  pour...
  une banque
  une entreprise
  informatique

  juh traviy doñ/poor...

  ewn boñk
  ewn oñtruhpreez
  añformateek

- I'm... / Je suis... / *juh sweez...*
  - unemployed / au chômage / *oh shohmaj*
  - self-employed / à mon compte / *a mawñ kawñt*

- I'm... / Je suis... / *juh swee...*
  - married / marié(e) / *maryay*
  - divorced / divorcé(e) / *deevorsay*
  - separated / séparé(e) / *sayparay*
  - single / célibataire / *sayleebater*

- I have... / J'ai... / *jay...*
  - three children / trois enfants / *trwaz oñfoñ*
  - one sister / une sœur / *ewn suhr*
  - one brother / un frère / *uñ frer*

- I don't have... / Je n'ai pas... / *juh nay pa...*
  - any children / d'enfant / *doñfoñ*
  - a partner / d'ami(e) / *damee*

- I'm on holiday here. / Je suis ici pour les vacances. / *je sweez eesee poor lay vakoñs*

- I'm here on business. / Je suis ici pour les affaires. / *je sweez eesee poor layz afer*

- I'm with my... / Je suis avec... / *je sweez avek...*
  - wife / ma femme / *ma fam*
  - family / ma famille / *ma fameey*
  - colleague / mon/ma collègue / *mawñ/ma koleg*

- My husband is... / Mon mari est... / *mawñ maree ay...*
- My wife is... / Ma femme est... / *ma fam ay...*
- My son is... / Mon fils est... / *mawñ feez ay...*
- My daughter is... / Ma fille est... / *ma feey ay...*
  - an estate agent / agent immobilier / *ajoñ eemobeelyay*

✳ asking about other people

- **Where do you come from?** — D'où venez-vous? — *doo vuhnay voo*

- **What's your name?** — Comment vous appelez-vous? — *komoñ vooz apuhlay voo*

- **Are you married?** — Êtes-vous marié(e)? — *et voo maryay*

- **Do you have...** — Avez-vous... — *avay voo...*
  - **any children?** — des enfants? — *dayz oñfoñ*
  - **any brothers and sisters?** — des frères et sœurs? — *day frer ay day suhr*
  - **a girlfriend/ boyfriend?** — une petite amie/ un petit ami — *ewn puhteet amee/ uñ puhteet amee*

- **How old are they/you?** — Quel âge ont-ils/ avez-vous? — *kel aj awñteel/ avayvoo*

- **Is this your...** — C'est votre... — *say votr...*
  - **husband?** — mari? — *maree*
  - **wife?** — femme? — *fam*
  - **partner?** — partenaire? — *partuhner*
  - **(boy)friend?** — (petit) ami? — *(puhteet) amee*
  - **(girl)friend?** — (petite) amie? — *(puhteet) amee*

- **Where are you going?** — Où allez-vous? — *oo alay voo*

- **Where are you staying?** — Où est-ce que vous logez? — *oo eskuh voo lojay*

- **Where do you live?** — Où est-ce que vous habitez? — *oo eskuh vooz abeetay*

✳ chatting

- **France is very beautiful.** | La France est un beau pays. | *la froñs ay tuñ boh payee*

- **It's the first time I've been to Switzerland.** | C'est la première fois que je viens en Suisse. | *say la pruhmyer fwa kuh juh viañ oñ swees*

- **I often come to Belgium.** | Je viens souvent en Belgique. | *juh viañ soovoñ oñ beljeek*

- **Do you live here?** | Est-ce que vous habitez ici? | *eskuh voo abeetay eesee*

- **Have you ever been to...** | Est-ce que vous êtes déjà allé(e)(s) à... | *eskuh vooz et dayja alay a...*
    London? | Londres? | *lawñdr*
    Edinburgh? | Edimbourg? | *edañboor*

- **Did you like it?** | Ça vous a plu? | *sa vooz a plew*

- Est-ce que vous aimez la France? | *eskuh vooz aymay la froñs* | **Do you like France?**

- Est-ce que vous êtes déjà allé en Belgique? | *eskuh vooz et dayja alay oñ belgeek* | **Have you been to Belgium before?**

- Combien de temps restez-vous? | *kawñbyañ duh toñ restay voo* | **How long are you here for?**

- Vous parlez très bien français. | *voo parlay byañ froñsay* | **Your French is very good.**

general conversation

✳ the weather

- It's a beautiful day/morning! — Quelle belle journée/matinée! — *kel bel joornay/mateenay*
- What fantastic weather! — Quel temps magnifique! — *kel toñ manyfeek*
- It's (very)... — Il fait (très)... — *eel fay (tre)...*
  - hot — chaud — *shoh*
  - cold — froid — *frwa*
- It's windy. — Il y a du vent. — *eelya dew voñ*
- It's cloudy. — C'est nuageux. — *say newajuh*
- It's raining. — Il pleut. — *eel pluh*
- It's snowing. — Il neige. — *eel nej*
- It's humid. — C'est humide. — *say ewmeed*
- What's the forecast? — Quelles sont les prévisions météo? — *kel sawñ lay prayveezyawñ maytayoh*
- It's pouring! — Il pleut des cordes! — *eel pluh day kord*

✳ likes and dislikes

- I like... — J'aime... — *jem...*
  - strawberries — les fraises — *lay frez*
  - beer — la bière — *la byer*
  - dancing — danser — *doñsay*
- I love sailing. — J'adore la voile. — *jador la vwal*

general conversation

● I don't like tomatoes.	Je n'aime pas les tomates.	*juh nem pa lay tomat*
● I don't like her.	Je ne l'aime pas.	*juh nuh lem pa*
● I can't stand him.	Je le déteste.	*juh le daytest*
● I can't stand swimming.	Je déteste nager.	*juh daytest najay*
● Do you like...	Est-ce que vous aimez...	*eskuh vooz aymay...*
ice cream?	la glace?	*la glas*
walking?	marcher?	*marshay*
climbing?	faire de l'escalade?	*fer duh leskalad*
● Do you like him?	Est-ce que vous l'aimez?	*eskuh voo laymay*
● I/We quite like...	J'aime/Nous aimons assez...	*jem/nooz aymawñ asay...*
● I/We really like...	J'aime/Nous aimons vraiment...	*jem/nooz aymawñ vraymoñ*

✳ feelings and opinions

● Are you...	Vous vous sentez...	*voo voo soñtay...*
all right?	bien?	*byañ*
upset?	mal?	*mal*
● Are you (too)...	Vous avez (trop)...	*vooz avay (tro)...*
cold?	froid?	*frwa*
hot?	chaud?	*shoh*
● I'm a bit annoyed.	Je suis un peu contrarié(e)	*juh swee uñ puh kawñtraryay*

I'm (just)...	Je suis (juste)...	juh swee (jewst)...
tired	fatigué(e)	fateegay
sad	triste	treest
embarrassed	gêné(e)	jaynay
What do you think of...?	Que pensez-vous de...?	kuh poñsay voo duh...
I think/We think it's...	Je pense/Nous pensons que c'est...	juh poñs/noo poñsawñ kuh se...
great	super	sewper
pathetic	nul	newl
Did you like it?	Vous avez aimé?	vooz avay aymay
I thought/We thought it was...	J'ai pensé/Nous avons pensé que c'était...	jay poñsay/nooz avawñ poñsay kuh sayte...
beautiful	beau	boh
fantastic	génial	jaynyal
rubbish	nul	newl
Don't you like it?	Vous n'aimez pas ça?	voo naymay pa sa
Don't you like us?	Vous ne nous aimez pas?	voo nuh nooz aymay pa
Don't you like me?	Vous ne m'aimez pas?	voo ne maymay pa
Do you fancy him/her?	Il/Elle vous plaît?	eel/el voo play
Do you fancy me?	Je vous plais?	juh voo play
No way!	Pas du tout!	pa dew too
What's your favourite film?	Quel est votre film préféré?	kel ay votr feelm prayfayray
My favourite (music) is...	Ma (musique) préférée est...	ma mewseek prayfayray e...

✳ making arrangements
(see **telling the time**, page 17)

• What are you doing tonight?	Que fais-tu ce soir?	*kuh fay tew suh swar*
• Would you like... a drink? something to eat? to come with us?	Veux-tu... un verre? quelque chose à manger? venir avec nous?	*vuh tew... uñ ver kelkuh shohz à moñjay vuhneer avek noo*
• Do you fancy... meeting up later? going for a drink?	Veux-tu... qu'on se retrouve plus tard? aller prendre un verre?	*vuh tew... kawñ suh ruhtroov plew tar alay proñdr uñ ver*
• Yes, please.	Oui, avec plaisir.	*wee avek playzeer*
• No, thank you.	Non merci.	*nawñ mersee*
• That'd be great.	Avec plaisir.	*avek playzeer*
• What time shall we meet?	À quelle heure est-ce qu'on se retrouve?	*a kel uhr eskawñ suh ruhtroov*
• Where shall we meet?	Où est-ce qu'on se retrouve?	*oo eskawñ suh ruhtroov*
• See you... later at seven	À... tout à l'heure sept heures	*a... tootaluhr setuhr*
• We're looking forward to it.	Nous attendons ça avec impatience.	*noo zatoñdawñ sa avek añpasioñs*
• I can't wait.	J'ai hâte.	*jay at*

Sorry, we're already doing something.	Désolé, nous avons déjà quelque chose de prévu.	*dayzolay noo zavawñ dayja kelkuh shohz duh prayvew*
I already have plans this evening.	J'ai déjà quelque chose de prévu ce soir.	*jay dayja kelkuh shohz duh prayvew suh swar*
Please go away! (less polite)	Allez-vous en! Va t'en!	*alay voo zoñ va toñ*
Leave us alone!	Laissez-nous tranquilles!	*laysay noo troñkil*

✳ useful expressions
(see **essentials**, page 12)

YOU MAY WANT TO SAY...

Congratulations!	Félicitations!	*fayleeseetasiawñ*
Happy birthday!	Joyeux anniversaire!	*jwiyuh zaneeverser*
Happy Christmas!	Joyeux Noël!	*jwiyuh nohel*
Happy New Year!	Bonne année!	*bon anay*
All the best.	Bonne chance.	*bon shoñs*
That's fantastic!	C'est génial!	*say jaynyal*
What a pity!	Quel dommage!	*kel domaj*
Safe journey!	Bon voyage!	*bawñ vwiyaj*
Enjoy your meal!	Bon appétit!	*bon apaytee*
Thank you, same to you.	Merci, à vous aussi.	*mersee a voo ohsee*
Cheers! (formal) (informal)	À la votre! À la tienne!	*a la vohtr a la tyen*

travel&transport

✳ arriving in the country

● If you're an EU citizen and you arrive by air, road or sea, the formalities (passport control and customs) are quite straightforward; the only document you need is a valid passport. If you come from outside the EU, call the French/Belgian/Swiss/Luxembourg embassy in your country to check what the entry requirements are.

YOU MAY SEE...

Articles à déclarer	**Goods to declare**
Autres passeports	**Non-EU citizens**
Contrôle de passeports	**Passport control**
Douane	**Customs**
Retrait des bagages	**Baggage reclaim**
Sortie	**Exit**
UE	**EU citizens**

YOU MAY WANT TO SAY...

● **I am here...**	Je suis ici...	*juh sweez eesee...*
on holiday	en vacances	*oñ vakañs*
on business	pour affaires	*poor afer*
● **I have...**	J'ai...	*jay...*
this/these	ça	*sa*
two bottles of whisky	deux bouteilles de whisky	*duh bootey duh weeskee*
two cartons of cigarettes	deux cartouches de cigarettes	*duh kartoosh duh seegaret*
a receipt for this	un reçu pour ça	*uñ ruhsew poor sa*

It's for my own personal use.	C'est pour mon usage personnel.	*say poor mawñ ewsaj personel*

YOU MAY HEAR...

Votre passeport, s'il vous plaît.	*votr paspor seelvooplay*	**Your passport, please.**
Vos documents, s'il vous plaît.	*voh dokewmoñ seelvooplay*	**Your documents, please.**
Quel est l'objet de votre visite?	*kel ay lobje duh votr veezeet*	**What is the purpose of your visit?**
Combien de temps restez-vous en France?	*kawñbyañ duh toñ restay voo oñ froñs*	**How long are you going to stay in France?**
Veuillez ouvrir ce sac.	*veryay oovreer suh sac*	**Please open this bag.**
Est-ce que vous avez d'autres bagages?	*eskuh vooz avay dohtr bagaj*	**Do you have any other luggage?**

✳ directions

● To ask the way, simply say pour aller à la/au...? (to go to...?) and add on the name of where you want to go.

YOU MAY SEE...

À la/Au...	**To the...**
Arrêt de bus	**Bus stop**

Arrêt de tramway	Tram stop
Avenue/Boulevard	Avenue
Château	Castle
Église	Church
Galerie d'art	Art gallery
Gare	Station
Gare centrale	Main station
Interdit aux piétons	No pedestrian access
Métro	Underground
Musée	Museum
Passage clouté	Pedestrian crossing
Piétons	Pedestrians
Piste cyclable	Cycle path
Place	Square
Place du marché	Market place
Privé	Private
RER	Suburban underground
Rue piétonnière	Pedestrian precinct

YOU MAY WANT TO SAY...

Excuse me, please.	S'il vous plaît.	seel voo play
Where is...	Où est...	oo ay...
the town centre?	le centre-ville?	luh soñtr veel
the station?	la gare?	la gar
a cashpoint?	le distributeur automatique de billets?	luh deestreebewtuhr ohtomateek duh beeyay
Where are the toilets?	Où sont les toilettes?	oo sawñ lay twalet

How do we get to...	Pour aller à...	poor alay à...
the airport?	l'aéroport?	laayropor
the beach?	la plage?	la plaj
I'm/We're lost.	Je suis/Nous sommes perdu(e)(s).	juh swee/noo som perdew
Is this the right way to...?	Est-ce que c'est le bon chemin pour...?	eskuh say luh bawñ shuhmañ poor...
Can you show me on the map, please?	Pourriez-vous me le montrer sur la carte?	pooreeay voo muh luh mawñtray sewr la kart
Is it far?	C'est loin?	se lwañ
Is there ... near here?	Est-ce qu'il y a ... près d'ici?	eskeelya ... pre deesee
a bank	une banque	ewn boñk
a supermarket	un supermarché	uñ sewpermarshay
an internet café	un cybercafé	uñ seeberkafay
Where is the nearest restaurant/bar?	Où est le restaurant/le bar le plus proche?	oo ay luh restoroñ/ luh bar luh plew prosh

✳ information and tickets
(see **time phrases**, page 18)

(see **time phrases**, page 18)

YOU MAY WANT TO SAY...

Is there a train/bus/boat to Marseilles (today)?	Est-ce qu'il y a un train/bus/bateau pour Marseille (aujourd'hui)?	eskeelya uñ trañ/ bews/batoh poor marsey (ohjoordwee)

travel and transport

39

information and tickets

What time is...	À quelle heure est...	*a kel uhr ay...*
the next train	le prochain train	*luh proshañ trañ*
the last train	le dernier train	*luh dernyay trañ*
the first bus	le premier bus	*luh pruhmyay bews*
...to Lausanne?	...pour Lausanne?	*...poor lohzan*

Do they go often? Est-ce qu'ils sont fréquents? *eskeel sawñ fraykoñ*

What time does it arrive in Bruges? À quelle heure arrive-t-il à Bruges? *a kel uhr areev teel a brewj*

Do I have to change? Est-ce qu'il faut changer? *eskeel foh shoñjay*

Which platform/ bus stop is it for the Eiffel tower? Quel est le quai/ l'arrêt de bus pour la tour Eiffel? *kel ay luh kay/laray duh bews poor la toor efel*

Can I get a ticket on the bus/train/ boat? Est-ce que je peux acheter un billet dans le bus/train/ bateau? *eskuh juh puh ashuhtay uñ beeyay doñ luh bews/trañ/ batoh*

Where can I buy... Où est-ce que je peux acheter... *oo eskuh juh puh ashuhtay...*

a ticket? un billet? *uñ beeyay*

One/Two tickets to ... please. Un/Deux billet(s) pour ... s'il vous plaît. *uñ/duh beeyay poor ... seel voo play*

single aller simple *alay sañpl*

return aller-retour *alay ruhtoor*

for...	pour...	*poor...*
two adults and	deux adultes et	*duh zadewlt ay*
two children	deux enfants	*duh zoñfoñ*
and a car	et une voiture	*ay ewn vwatewr*

40

information and tickets

- **I want to reserve...**   Je voudrais réserver...   *juh voodray rayservay...*
  - a seat   une place   *ewn plas*
  - a cabin   une cabine   *ewn kabeen*

- **Is there...**   Est-ce qu'il y a...   *eskeelya...*
  - a supplement?   un supplément?   *uñ sewplaymoñ*
  - a reduction   une réduction   *ewn raydewcsyawñ*
  - for...   pour...   *poor...*
    - students   les étudiants   *lay zaytewdyoñ*
    - senior citizens?   les personnes âgées?   *lay personzajay*

YOU MAY HEAR...

Il part à...	*eel par a...*	It leaves at...
Il arrive à...	*eel areev a...*	It arrives at...
Il faut changer à Liège.	*eel foh shoñjay a lyej*	You have to change in Liège.
C'est le quai/ l'embarcadère numéro quatre.	*say luh kay/ loñbarkader newmayroh katr*	It's platform/pier number four.
Vous pouvez acheter un billet dans le bus/train/ bateau.	*voo poovay ashuhtay uñ beeyay doñ luh bews/trañ/batoh*	You can buy a ticket on the bus/train/boat.
Aller simple ou aller-retour?	*alay sañpl oo alay ruhtoor*	Single or return?
Fumeur ou non fumeur?	*fewmuhr oo nawñ fewmuhr*	Smoking or non-smoking?

travel and transport

✳ trains

(see **information and tickets**, page 39)

● You can get rail information from the following websites:
France – www.sncf.com; Switzerland – www.cff.ch;
Luxembourg – www.lcto.lu; Belgium – www.b-rail.be/E

YOU MAY SEE...

Accès aux quais/trains	To the platforms/trains
Arrivées	Arrivals
Billets	Tickets
Bureau des objets trouvés	Lost property office
Consigne	Left luggage
Consigne automatique	Luggage lockers
Départs	Departures
Destination	Destination
Dimanche et jours fériés	Sundays and holidays
Eau non potable	Water not for drinking
Entrée	Entrance
Fumeurs/Non fumeurs	Smoking/Non-smoking
Guichet	Ticket office
Horaires des trains	Train timetables
Il est interdit de se pencher	Do not lean out
Objets trouvés	Lost property
Quai	Platform
Renseignements	Information
Salle d'attente	Waiting room
Sauf le dimanche	Except Sundays
Sonnette d'alarme	Alarm
Sortie (de secours)	(Emergency) Exit
Wagon-lit	Sleeping-car

I'd like a single/return ticket to Lille, please.	Je voudrais un aller simple/aller-retour pour Lille, s'il vous plaît.	juh voodray uñ alay sañpl/alay ruhtoor poor leel seelvooplay
Is there a lift to the platform?	Est-ce qu'il y a un ascenseur pour aller sur le quai?	eskeelya uñ asoñsuhr poor alay syoor luh kay
Can I take my bicycle on the train?	Est-ce que je peux emporter mon vélo dans le train?	eskuh juh puh oñportay mawñ vayloh doñ luh trañ
Does this train go to...?	Est-ce que ce train va à...?	eskuh suh trañ va a...
Excuse me, I've reserved...	Pardon, j'ai réservé...	pardawñ jay rayservay...
that seat	cette place	set plas
a couchette	une couchette	ewn kooshet
Is this seat free?	C'est libre?	say leebr
May I...	Puis-je...	pweej...
open the window?	ouvrir la fenêtre?	oovreer la fuhnetr
sit here?	m'asseoir ici?	maswar eesee
Where are we?	Où sommes-nous?	oo som noo
How long does the train stop here?	Combien de temps est-ce que le train s'arrête ici?	kawñbyañ duh toñ eskuh luh trañ saret eesee
Can you tell me when we get to...?	Pourriez-vous m'avertir quand nous arriverons à...?	pooryay voo maverteer koñ nooz areevuhrawñ a...

✴ buses and coaches
(see **information and tickets**, page 39)

(see **information and tickets**, page 39)

YOU MAY SEE...

Arrêt de bus	Bus stop
Arrêt fixe	Obligatory bus stop
Arrêt sur demande	Request stop
Conservez votre billet	Keep your ticket
Défense de fumer	No smoking
Défense d'entrer	No entry
Défense de parler au conducteur	Do not talk to the driver
Défense de sortir	No exit
Entrée	Entrance
Entrez par la porte de devant/derrière	Enter by the front/back door
Gare routière	Bus station
Sortez par la porte avant/arrière	Exit by the front/back door
Sortie (de secours)	(Emergency) Exit

YOU MAY WANT TO SAY...

- **Where does the bus to the town centre leave from?**
  D'où part le bus pour le centre-ville?
  doo par luh bews poor luh soñtr veel

- **Does the bus to the airport leave from here?**
  Est-ce que le bus pour l'aéroport part d'ici?
  eskuh luh bews poor laayropor par deesee

- **What number is it?**
  C'est quel numéro?
  se kel newmayroh

- **Does this bus go...** Est-ce que ce bus va... *eskuh suh bews va...*
  to the lake? au lac? *oh lac*
  to the station? à la gare? *a la gar*

- **Can you tell me** Pourriez-vous me *pooryay voo muh*
  where to get off, dire où descendre, *deer oo desoñdr*
  please? s'il vous plaît? *seelvooplay*

- **The next stop,** Le prochain arrêt, *luh proshañ aray*
  please. s'il vous plaît. *seelvooplay*

- **Can you open the** Pourriez-vous ouvrir *pooryay voo oovreer*
  doors, please? la porte, s'il vous *la port seelvooplay*
  plaît?

✳ underground
(see **information and tickets**, page 39)

- The underground is called le métro, and there are systems in Paris, Lyons, Marseilles, Toulouse, Rennes, Lille and Brussels.

- In Paris, you can buy a tourist pass (Paris Visite) for one, two, three or five consecutive days. For more information, visit www.ratp.fr. Most of the other métro systems also have special one-day and tourist passes – consult local tourist offices for more information.

YOU MAY SEE...

Entrée	Entrance
Métro	Underground
RATP	Paris transport authority

travel and transport

45

boats and ferries

RER	Suburban underground
Sortie	Exit

- **Can I have a book of tickets, please?** — Puis-je avoir un carnet de tickets, s'il vous plaît? — *pweej avwar uñ karnay duh teekay seelvooplay*

- **Do you have a map of the underground?** — Est-ce que vous avez un plan du métro? — *eskuh vooz avay uñ ploñ dew maytroh*

- **Which line is it for...?** — C'est quelle ligne pour...? — *say kel leenyuh poor...*

- **Which stop is it for Notre-Dame cathedral?** — C'est quel arrêt pour la cathédrale Notre-Dame? — *say kel aray poor la kataydral notr dam*

- **Is this the right stop for the Louvre?** — Est-ce que c'est le bon arrêt pour le Louvre? — *eskuh say luh bawñ aray poor luh loovr*

- **Does this train go to Versailles?** — Est-ce que ce train va à Versailles? — *eskuh suh trañ va a versiy*

✻ boats and ferries
(see **information and tickets**, page 39)

As well as car ferry and hovercraft services across the Channel, there are ferries and hydrofoils to and from the Channel Islands and car ferry services to Corsica (la Corse) from Marseilles, Nice and Toulon.

YOU MAY SEE...

Aéroglisseur	Hovercraft
Aller-retour	Round trip
Bateau à vapeur	Steamer
Bateau mouche	Riverboat, pleasure boat
Bateaux	Boats
Ceinture de sauvetage	Lifebelt
Croisières (du lac)	Cruises (on the lake)
Embarcadère	Pier
Hydroptère	Hydrofoil
Pont	Deck
Pont autos	Car deck

YOU MAY WANT TO SAY...

- **Is there a boat to ... today?** — Est-ce qu'il y a un bateau pour ... aujourd'hui? — *eskeelya uñ batoh poor ... ohjoordwee*

- **Are there any boat trips on the river?** — Est-ce qu'il y a des excursions sur la rivière? — *eskeelya dayz exkewrsyawñ sewr la rivyer*

- **How long is the cruise?** — Combien de temps dure la croisière? — *kawñbyañ duh toñ dewr la krwasyer*

- **Where do the boats leave from?** — D'où partent les bateaux? — *doo part lay batoh*

- **Is there wheelchair access?** — Est-ce qu'il y a un accès pour les fauteuils roulants? — *eskeelya uñ axe poor lay fohtuhy rooloñ*

- **What's the sea like today?** — Comment est la mer aujourd'hui? — *komoñ ay la mer ohjoordwee*

travel and transport

47

Can I/we go out on deck?	Est-ce que je peux/ nous pouvons sortir sur le pont?	*eskuh juh puh/noo poovawñ sorteer sewr luh pawñ*

YOU MAY HEAR...

Les bateaux partent...	*lay batoh part...*	Boats go on ...
le mardi et le vendredi	*luh mardee ay luh voñdruhdee*	Tuesdays and Fridays
tous les deux jours	*too lay duh joor*	every other day
La mer est...	*la mer ay...*	The sea is...
calme	*kalm*	calm
agitée	*ajeetay*	choppy

✳ air travel
(see **information and tickets**, page 39)

YOU MAY SEE...

Arrivées	Arrivals
Articles à déclarer	Goods to declare
Attachez votre ceinture	Fasten your seatbelt
Autres passeports	Other passports
Autres terminaux	Other terminals
Bagages (à main)	(Hand) Luggage
Départ nationaux	Domestic departures
Départs	Departures
Départs internationaux	International departures

Enregistrement (des bagages)	**Check-in**
Location de voitures	**Car hire**
Prière de garder vos bagages avec vous	**Do not leave luggage unattended**
Retard	**Delay**
Retrait des bagages	**Luggage reclaim**
Salle des départs/d'arrivée	**Departure lounge/Arrival hall**
Sortie (de secours)	**(Emergency) Exit**
Vol	**Flight**

YOU MAY WANT TO SAY...

● **I want to change/ cancel my ticket.** Je voudrais changer/ annuler mon billet. *juh voodray shoñjay/anewlay mawñ beeyay*

● **What time do I/ we have to check in?** À quelle heure faut-il enregistrer ses bagages? *a kel uhr fohteel oñruhjeestray say bagaj*

● **Is there a delay?** Est-ce qu'il y a du retard? *eskeelya dew ruhtar*

● **Which gate is it?** Quelle porte est-ce? *kel port es*

● **Have you got a wheelchair?** Avez-vous un fauteuil roulant? *avay voo uñ fohtuhy rooloñ*

● **My luggage hasn't arrived.** Mes bagages ne sont pas là. *may bagaj nuh sawñ pa la*

● **Is there a bus/ train to the centre of town?** Est-ce qu'il y a un bus/train pour le centre-ville? *ekeelya uñ bews/trañ poor luh soñtr veel*

WORDS TO LISTEN OUT FOR... ⓘ

annonce	*anawñs*	call
vol	*vol*	flight
porte	*port*	gate
dernier appel	*dernyay apel*	last call
retard	*ruhtar*	delay
annulé	*anewlay*	cancelled

✳ taxis
(see **information and tickets**, page 39)

● You can hail taxis in the street, or find them at a taxi rank (station de taxi). Taxis available for hire have a light on.

● Taxis have meters, but you may be charged extra for luggage, airport pick-ups, etc. A tip of 10% or so is usual (in Switzerland it's sometimes included in the fare).

YOU MAY WANT TO SAY... 💬

● **Is there a taxi rank round here?**
Est-ce qu'il y a une station de taxi par ici?
eskeelya ewn stasyawñ duh taxee par eesee

● **Can you order me a taxi?**
Pouvez-vous m'appeler un taxi?
poovay voo mapuhlay uñ taxee

● **To this address, please.**
À cette adresse, s'il vous plaît.
a set adres seelvooplay

● **How much will it cost?**
Combien ça va coûter?
kawñbyañ sa va kootay

- **Can you put it on the meter, please?** — Pourriez-vous le mettre sur le compteur, s'il vous plaît? — *pooryay voo luh metr sewr luh kawñtuhr seelvooplay*

- **I'm in a hurry.** — Je suis pressé(e). — *juh swee presay*

- **Stop here, please.** — Arrêtez-vous ici, s'il vous plaît. — *aretay voo eesee seelvooplay*

- **Can you wait for me, please?** — Pourriez-vous m'attendre, s'il vous plaît? — *pooryay voo matoñdr seelvooplay*

- **I think there's a mistake.** — Je crois qu'il y a une erreur. — *juh krwa keelya ewn eruhr*

- **Keep the change.** — C'est bon, merci. — *say bawñ mersee*

- **Can you give me a receipt...** — Pourriez-vous me donner un reçu... — *pooryay voo muh donay uñ ruhsew...*
  - **for ten euros?** — pour dix euros? — *poor deez uhroh*

YOU MAY HEAR...

- C'est à dix kilomètres. — *seta dee keelometr* — It's ten kilometres away.

- Il y a un supplément... — *eelya uñ sewplaymoñ...* — There's a supplement...
  - pour les bagages — *poor lay bagaj* — for the luggage
  - pour chaque valise — *poor shak valeez* — for each suitcase
  - pour le trajet à l'aéroport — *poor luh trajay a laayropor* — for the journey to the airport

✳ hiring cars and bicycles

YOU MAY WANT TO SAY...

- I'd like to hire...
  Je voudrais louer...
  juh voodray looay...
  - two bicycles
    deux vélos
    duh vayloh
  - a small car
    une petite
    voiture
    *ewn puhteet
    vwatewr*
  - an automatic
    car
    une voiture
    automatique
    *ewn vwatewr
    ohtohmateek*

- For...
  Pour...
  poor...
  - the day
    la journée
    la joornay
  - a week
    la semaine
    la suhmen
  - two weeks
    deux semaines
    duh suhmen

- How much is it...
  C'est combien pour...
  se kawñbyañ poor...
  - per day?
    la journée?
    la joornay
  - per week?
    la semaine?
    la suhmen

- Is mileage
  included?
  Le kilométrage est-il
  compris?
  *luh keelomaytraj eetel
  kawñpree*

- Is insurance
  included?
  L'assurance est-elle
  comprise?
  *lasewroñs etel
  kawñpreez*

- My partner wants
  to drive too.
  Mon partenaire
  voudrait conduire
  aussi.
  *mawñ partuhner
  voodre kawñdweer
  ohsee*

- Is there a deposit
  to pay?
  Est-ce qu'il y a une
  caution?
  *eskeelya ewn
  kohsyawñ*

- Do you take...
  Vous prenez...
  voo pruhnay...
  - credit cards?
    les cartes de
    crédit?
    *lay kart duh
    craydee*
  - travellers'
    cheques?
    les chèques de
    voyage?
    *lay shek duh
    vwiyaj*

Quel genre de voiture/vélo souhaitez-vous?	*kel goñr de vvatewr/vayloh sooaytay voo*	What kind of car/bicycle do you want?
Pour combien de temps?	*poor kawñbyañ duh toñ*	For how long?
Votre permis de conduire, s'il vous plaît.	*votr permee duh kawñdweer seelvooplay*	Your driving licence, please.
Il y a une caution de 100 euros.	*eelya ewn kohsyawñ duh soñ uhroh*	There's a deposit of 100 euros.
Avez-vous une carte de crédit?	*avay voo ewn kart duh kraydee*	Have you got a credit card?
Rendez la voiture après avoir fait le plein s'il vous plaît.	*roñday la vvatewr aprez avvar fay luh plañ seelvooplay*	Please return the car with a full tank.
Rendez la voiture/ le vélo avant six heures.	*roñday la vvatewr/ luh vayloh avoñ sees uhr*	Please return the car/bicycle before six o'clock.

✳ driving
(see mechanical problems, page 56)

● You drive on the right. Traffic from the right generally has priority on roads. This does not apply on roundabouts in France, where traffic already on the roundabout has priority, or where there are signs indicating otherwise (a yellow diamond sign shows that there is no priority for traffic from the right, and a diamond sign with a black bar through it indicates that it has been reinstated). Seatbelts are compulsory in the front and in the back, as are crash helmets for both drivers and passengers of motorbikes and scooters.

● Speed limits in France are 50km per hour in built-up areas, 90kph on normal roads, 110kph on dual carriageways and 130kph on motorways. In Belgium and Luxembourg they are 50kph in built-up areas, 90kph on normal roads and 120kph on motorways. Swiss speed limits are 50kph in built-up areas, 80kph on normal roads and 120kph on motorways.

● Main roads are labelled as follows:
A (autoroute) – motorway
N (route nationale) – national highway
D (route départementale) – provincial or secondary road

YOU MAY SEE...

Accès réservé aux riverains	**Residents only**
Allumez vos phares	**Use headlights**
Attention	**Caution**
Autoroute	**Motorway**
Carrefour dangereux	**Dangerous crossroads**
Cédez le passage	**Give way**
Centre-ville	**Town centre**
Chaussée déformée	**Uneven road surface**
Chutes de pierres	**Falling rocks**
Circulation sur les deux voies	**Two-way traffic**

Col (fermé)	Mountain pass (closed)
Croisement de piste cyclable	Cycle path crossing
Dernière station essence avant l'autoroute	Last petrol station before the motorway
École	School
Garage	Car repairs/Garage
Impasse	No through road
Interdiction de doubler	No overtaking
Interdiction de s'arrêter	No stopping
Passage interdit	No entry
Péage	Toll
Piétons	Pedestrians
Piste cyclable	Cycle path
Ralentir	Slow
Route barrée	Road closed
Rue piétonnière	Pedestrian precinct
Sens unique	One-way street
Sortie	Exit
Stationnement interdit	Parking prohibited
Travaux	Road works
Traversée interdite	No through traffic
Verglas	Black ice

YOU MAY WANT TO SAY...

- **Where is the nearest petrol station?** | Où est la station d'essence la plus proche? | *oo ay la stasyawñ desoñs la plew prosh*

travel and transport

mechanical problems

- **Fill it up with...**
  unleaded
  diesel
  ...please.

  Le plein de...
  sans plomb
  gasoil
  ...s'il vous plaît.

  luh plañ duh...
  soñ plawñ
  gazwal
  ...seelvooplay

- **30 euros' worth**
  of unleaded,
  please.

  30 euros de sans
  plomb, s'il vous plaît.

  troñt uhroh duh soñ
  plawñ seelvooplay

- **20 litres of**
  unleaded, please.

  20 litres de sans
  plomb, s'il vous plaît.

  vañ leetr duh soñ
  plawñ seelvooplay

- **A litre of oil,**
  please.

  Un litre d'huile,
  s'il vous plaît.

  uñ leetr dweel
  seelvooplay

- **A can of oil,**
  please.

  Un bidon d'huile,
  s'il vous plaît.

  uñ beedawñ dweel
  seelvooplay

- **Can you check**
  the tyre pressure,
  please.

  Pourriez-vous
  vérifier la pression
  des pneus, s'il vous
  plaît?

  pooryay voo
  vayreefyay la
  presyawñ day pnuh
  seelvooplay

- **Can you change**
  the tyre, please?

  Pourriez-vous
  changer le pneu,
  s'il vous plaît?

  pooryay voo shoñjay
  luh pnuh seelvooplay

- **Where is the air,**
  please?

  Où est la pompe
  à air, s'il vous plaît?

  oo ay la pawñp
  a er seelvooplay

* mechanical problems
(see **car parts**, page 58)

YOU MAY WANT TO SAY...

- **My car has**
  broken down.

  Ma voiture est en
  panne.

  ma vwatewr ay
  toñ pan

● I've run out of petrol.	Je suis en panne d'essence.	*juh sweez oñ pan desoñs*
● I have a puncture.	J'ai un pneu crevé.	*jay uñ pnuh kruhvay*
● Can you telephone a garage?	Pourriez-vous appeler un garage?	*pooryay voo apuhlay uñ garaj*
● Do you do repairs?	Est-ce que vous faites les réparations?	*eskuh voo fet lay rayparasyawñ*
● I don't know what's wrong.	Je ne sais pas ce qui ne marche pas.	*juh nuh say pas suh kee nuh marsh pa*
● I need a...	J'ai besoin de...	*jay buhswañ duh...*
● The ... doesn't work.	Le ... ne marche pas.	*luh ... nuh marsh pa*
● Is it serious?	C'est grave?	*say grav*
● Can you repair it today?	Pouvez-vous la réparer aujourd'hui?	*poovay voo la rayparay ohjoordwee*
● When will it be ready?	Ce sera prêt quand?	*suh suhra pre koñ*
● How much will it cost?	Ça va coûter combien?	*sa va kootay cawñbiañ*

YOU MAY HEAR...

● Ce sera prêt...	*suh suhra pre...*	It'll be ready...	
dans une heure	*doñz ewn uhr*	in an hour	
lundi	*luñdee*	on Monday	
● Ça va coûter 100 euros.	*sa va kootay soñ uhroh*	It'll cost a hundred euros.	

✳ car parts

accelerator	l'accélérateur	laxaylayratuhr
alternator	l'alternateur	lalternatuhr
battery	la batterie	la batree
bonnet	le capot	luh kapo
boot	le coffre	luh kofr
brakes	les freins	lay frañ
carburettor	le carburateur	luh karbewratuhr
distributor	le distributeur	luh deestreebewtuhr
engine	le moteur	luh motuhr
exhaust pipe	le pot d'échappement	luh poh dayshapmoñ
fanbelt	la courroie de ventilateur	la koorwa duh voñteelatuhr
fuel pump	la pompe à essence	la pawñp a esoñs
gearbox	la boîte à vitesses	la bwat a veetes
gears	les vitesses	lay veetess
hazard lights	les feux de détresse	lay fuh duh daytres
headlights	les phares	lay far
ignition	l'allumage	lalewmaj
indicators	les clignotants	lay kleenyotoñ
points	les contacts	lay kawñtakt
radiator	le radiateur	luh radyatuhr
rear lights	les feux arrières	lay fuh aryer
reversing lights	les feux de marche arrière	lay fuh duh marsh aryer
side lights	les feux latéraux	lay fuh latayroh
spare wheel	la roue de secours	la roo duh suhkoor
spark plugs	les bougies	lay boojee
starter motor	le démarreur	luh daymaruhr

accommodation

YOU MAY SEE...

Ascenseur	Lift
Auberge de jeunesse	Youth hostel
Blanchisserie	Laundry
Camping	Campsite
Camping interdit	No camping
Caravanes interdites	No caravans
Chambre d'hôte	Bed and breakfast
Chambres à louer	Rooms vacant
Complet	Full up
Demi-pension	Half-board
Deuxième étage	Second floor
Douches	Showers
Eau potable	Drinking water
Hôtel	Hotel
Issue de secours	Emergency exit
Ordures	Rubbish
Pension complète	Full board
Pension de famille	Guesthouse
Premier étage	First floor
Prière de ne pas jeter d'ordures	Do not dump rubbish
Relais	Inn
Rez-de-chaussée	Ground floor
Salle à manger	Dining room
Salle de bains	Bathroom
Salon	Lounge
Sonnez, s'il vous plaît	Please ring the bell
Sortie (de secours)	(Emergency) exit

✳ booking in advance

● Many regions in France have a service called Loisir-Accueil that can book local accommodation. This service is free. There are also Accueil de France offices in some towns. These provide hotel booking facilities for a small fee.

● **Do you have...**	Est-ce que vous avez une chambre...	*eskuh vooz avay ewn shoñbr...*
a single room?	pour une personne?	*poor ewn person*
a double room?	pour deux personnes?	*poor duh person*
a twin-bedded room?	avec lits jumeaux?	*avek lee jewmoh*
● **Do you have space for...**	Est-ce que vous avez de la place pour...	*eskuh vooz avay duh la plas poor...*
a tent?	une tente?	*ewn toñt*
a caravan?	une caravane?	*ewn karavan*
● **I'd like to rent...**	Je voudrais louer...	*juh voodray looay...*
an apartment	un appartement	*uñ apartuhmoñ*
a holiday home	une maison de vacances	*ewn maysawñ duh vakoñs*
● **For...**	Pour...	*poor...*
tonight	ce soir	*suh swar*
one night	une nuit	*ewn nwee*
two nights	deux nuits	*duh nwee*
a week	une semaine	*ewn suhmen*
● **From ... to...**	Du ... au...	*dew... oh...*
● **with bath/shower**	avec baignoire/douche	*avek baynywar/doosh*

accommodation

61

It's a two-person tent.	C'est une tente deux places.	*set ewn toñt duh plas*
How much is it...	C'est combien...	*say kawñbyañ...*
per night?	par nuit?	*par nwee*
per week?	par semaine?	*par suhmen*
Is breakfast included?	Est-ce que le petit déjeuner est compris?	*eskuh luh puhtee dayjuhnay ay kawñpree*
Is there...	Est-ce qu'il y a...	*eskeelya...*
a reduction for children?	une réduction pour les enfants?	*ewn raydewxyawñ poor layz oñfoñ*
a single room supplement?	un supplément pour une chambre simple?	*uñ sewplaymoñ poor ewn shoñbr sampl*
wheelchair access?	un accès pour les fauteuils roulants?	*uñ axay poor lay fohtuhy rooloñ*
Can I pay by...	Puis-je payer avec...	*pweej payyay avek...*
credit card?	une carte de crédit?	*ewn kart duh craydee*
travellers' cheque?	des chèques de voyage?	*day shek duh vwiyaj*
Can I book online?	Puis-je réserver en ligne?	*pweej rayservay oñ leeny*
What's the address?	Quelle est l'adresse?	*kel ay ladres*
Can you recommend anywhere else?	Pourriez-vous me recommander un autre endroit?	*pooryay voo muh ruhkomoñday uñ ohtr oñdrwa*

YOU MAY HEAR...

Vous désirez?	*voo dayzeeray*	Can I help you?
Pour combien de nuits?	*poor kawñbyañ duh nwee*	For how many nights?
Pour combien de personnes?	*poor kawñbyañ duh person*	For how many people?
Pour une personne ou deux personnes?	*poor ewn person oo duh person*	Single or double room?
Voulez-vous un grand lit?	*voolay voo uñ groñ lee*	Do you want a double bed?
Avec... baignoire? douche?	*avek... baynywar doosh*	With... bath? shower?
Votre nom, s'il vous plaît?	*votr nawñ seelvooplay*	What's your name, please?
Avez-vous une carte de crédit?	*avay voo ewn kart duh craydee*	Do you have a credit card?
Je suis désolé(e), nous sommes complets.	*juh swee dayzolay noo som kawñplay*	I'm sorry, we're full.

✳ checking in

● When you book in somewhere you will usually be asked for your passport and to fill in a registration card.

REGISTRATION CARD INFORMATION

Prénom	First name

accommodation

63

Nom	Surname
Adresse/rue/numéro	Home address/ street/number
Code postal	Postcode
Nationalité	Nationality
Profession	Occupation
Date de naissance	Date of birth
Lieu de naissance	Place of birth
Numéro de passeport	Passport number
En partance de/à destination de	Coming from/ going to
Délivré à	Issued in
Date	Date
Signature	Signature

YOU MAY WANT TO SAY...

- I have a reservation for...
  - tonight
  - two nights
  - a week

  J'ai réservé pour...
  - ce soir
  - deux nuits
  - une semaine

  jay rayzervay poor...
  - suh swar
  - duh nwee
  - ewn suhmen

- It's in the name of...

  Au nom de...

  oh nawñ duh...

- Here's my passport.

  Voici mon passeport.

  vwasee mawñ paspor

- I'm paying by credit card.

  Je règle avec une carte de crédit.

  juh regl avek ewn kart de credee

YOU MAY HEAR... ?

Avez-vous réservé une chambre/un emplacement?	*avay voo rayzervay ewn shoñbr/uñ oñplasmoñ*	Have you reserved a room/space?
Pour combien de nuits?	*poor kawñbyañ duh nwee*	For how many nights?
Votre passeport, s'il vous plaît?	*votr paspor seelvooplay*	Can I have your passport, please?
Comment allez-vous régler?	*komoñ alay voo rayglay*	How are you going to pay?

* hotels, B&Bs and hostels

● French hotels are graded from one to four stars. Logis de France and Auberges de France are small, family-run hotels, mainly one- or two-star. There are more than 5,000 of them all over France. A guide to these is available from the French National Tourist Office (www.franceguide.com).

YOU MAY WANT TO SAY...

Where can I/we park?	Où est-ce qu'on peut stationner?	*oo eskawñ puh stasyonay*
Can I/we see the room, please?	On peut voir la chambre, s'il vous plaît?	*awñ puh vwar la shoñbr seelvooplay*
Do you have...	Est-ce que vous avez...	*eskuh vooz avay...*
a room with a view?	une chambre avec vue?	*ewn shoñbr avek vew*
a bigger room?	une plus grande chambre?	*ewn plew groñd shoñbr*

accommodation

65

a cot for the baby?	un berceau pour le bébé?	*uñ bersoh poor luh baybay*
Is breakfast included?	Est-ce que le petit déjeuner est compris?	*eskuh luh puhtee dayjuhnay ay kawñpree*
What time...	À quelle heure vous...	*a kel uhr voo...*
is breakfast?	servez le petit déjeuner?	*servay luh puhtee dayjuhnay*
do you lock the front door?	fermez la porte?	*fermay la port*
Where is...	Où est...	*oo e...*
the dining room?	la salle à manger?	*la sal a moñjay*
the bar?	le bar?	*luh bar*
Is there...	Est-ce qu'il y a...	*eskeelya...*
24 hour room service?	un service en chambre vingt-quatre heures sur vingt-quatre?	*uñ servees oñ shoñbr vañt katr uhr sewr vañt katr*
an internet connection here?	une connexion internet ici?	*ewn konexyawñ añternet eesee*
a business centre here?	un centre d'affaires ici?	*uñ soñtr dafer eesee*

accommodation

Le petit déjeuner est servi de ... à...	*luh puhtee dayjuhnay ay servee duh ... a...*	**Breakfast is from ... to...**
Nous fermons la porte à...	*noo fermawñ la port a...*	**We shut the front door at...**
Il y a un service en chambre de ... à...	*eelya uñ servees oñ shoñbr duh ... a...*	**There's room service from ... to...**

* camping and caravanning
(see **directions**, page 37)

● There are many campsites across France. They are often quite luxurious, and like hotels they are rated from one to four stars according to facilities. Many have tents and caravans on site. It is advisable to book places at campsites in advance, especially during the summer.

YOU MAY WANT TO SAY...

● **Is there a campsite round here?**	Est-ce qu'il y a un camping par ici?	*eskeelya uñ koñpeeng par eesee*
● **Can we camp here?**	Est-ce qu'on peut camper ici?	*eskawñ puh koñpay eesee*
● **Can we park our caravan here?**	Est-ce qu'on peut stationner notre caravane ici?	*eskawñ puh stasyonay notr karavan eesee*
● **It's a two/four person tent.**	C'est une tente pour deux/quatre personnes.	*say ewn toñt poor duh/katr person*

camping and caravanning

Where are...	Où sont...	*oo sawñ...*
the toilets?	les toilettes?	*lay twalet*
the showers?	les douches?	*lay doosh*
the dustbins?	les poubelles?	*lay poobel*
Do we pay extra for the showers?	Est-ce qu'il y a un supplément pour les douches?	*eskeelya uñ sewplaymoñ poor lay doosh*
Is the water OK for drinking?	Est-ce que l'eau est potable?	*eskuh loh ay potabl*
Where's the electricity?	Où est l'électricité?	*oo ay laylektreeseetay*

YOU MAY HEAR...

Le camping le plus proche est...	*luh koñpeeng luh plew prosh e...*	The nearest camp-site/caravan site is...
à cinq kilomètres	*a sañk keelometr*	5km away
dans le village voisin	*doñ luh veelaj vwazañ*	in the next village
Avez-vous une carte?	*avay voo ewn kart*	Have you got a map?
Vous ne pouvez pas camper ici.	*voo nuh poovay pa koñpay eesee*	You can't camp here.
Les douches sont gratuites.	*lay doosh sawñ gratweet*	The showers are free.
C'est ... euros par douche.	*say ... uhroh par doosh*	It's ... euros for a shower.
L'électricité est là-bas.	*laylektreeseetay ay la ba*	The electricity is over there.

* requests and queries

- **Are there any messages for me?** Est-ce qu'il y a des messages pour moi? *eskeelya day mesaj poor mwa*

- **I'm expecting...** J'attends... *jatoñ...*
  - a phone call   un appel   *uñ apel*
  - a fax   un fax   *uñ fax*

- **Can I...** Puis-je... *pweej...*
  - leave this in the safe?   mettre ça dans le coffre?   *metr sa doñ luh kofr*
  - charge it to my room?   mettre ça sur la chambre?   *metr sa sewr la shoñbr*

- **Can you...** Pouvez-vous... *poovay voo...*
  - give me my things from the safe?   me donner mes affaires qui sont dans le coffre?   *muh donay mayz afer kee sawñ doñ luh kofr*
  - wake me up at eight o'clock?   me réveiller à huit heures?   *muh rayveyay a weet uhr*
  - order me a taxi?   me commander un taxi?   *muh komoñday uñ taxee*

- **Do you have...** Avez-vous... *avay voo...*
  - a babysitting service?   un service de garde d'enfants?   *uñ servees duh gard doñfoñ*
  - a baby alarm?   une alarme pour bébé?   *ewn alarm poor baybay*

- **I need...** J'ai besoin... *jay buhswañ...*
  - another pillow   d'un autre oreiller   *duñ ohtr orayay*
  - an adaptor   d'un adaptateur   *duñ adaptatuhr*
  - a new key   d'une nouvelle clé   *dewn noovel klay*

- **I've lost my key.** J'ai perdu ma clé. *jay perdew ma klay*

| I've left my key in the room. | J'ai laissé ma clé dans la chambre. | *jay laysay ma klay doñ la shoñbr* |

* problems and complaints

YOU MAY WANT TO SAY...

Excuse me...	Pardon...	*Pardawñ...*
The room is too...	Il fait trop ... dans la chambre.	*eel fay troh ... doñ la shoñbr*
hot	chaud	*shoh*
cold	froid	*frwa*
The room is too small.	La chambre est trop petite.	*la shoñbr ay troh puhteet*
There isn't any...	Il n'y a pas...	*eelnya pa...*
toilet paper	de papier hygiénique	*duh papyay eejeneek*
hot water	d'eau chaude	*doh shohd*
electricity	d'électricité	*daylektreeseetay*
There aren't any...	Il n'y a pas...	*eelnya pa...*
towels	de serviettes	*duh servyet*
I can't...	Je ne peux pas...	*juh nuh puh pa...*
open the window	ouvrir la fenêtre	*oovreer la fuhnetr*
turn the tap off	fermer le robinet	*fermay le robeenay*
work the TV	faire marcher la télé	*fer marshay la taylay*
The bed is uncomfortable.	Le lit n'est pas confortable.	*luh lee ne pa kawñfortabl*
The bathroom is dirty.	La salle de bains est sale.	*la sal duh bañ ay sal*

- **The toilets are dirty.** — Les toilettes sont sales. — *lay twalet sawñ sal*

- **It's very noisy.** — C'est très bruyant. — *say tre brweeyoñ*

- **The key doesn't work.** — La clé ne marche pas. — *La klay nuh marsh pa*

- **The microwave...** — Le micro-ondes... — *luh meekroawñd*
  The shower... — La douche... — *la doosh*
  The TV remote... — La télécommande... — *la taylaykomoñd*
  ...is broken. — ...est cassé(e). — *...ay kasay*

- **I can smell gas.** — Ça sent le gaz. — *sa soñ luh gaz*

- **I want to see the manager!** — Je veux voir le responsable! — *juh vuh vwar luh respawñsabl*

* checking out

- **The bill, please.** — La note, s'il vous plaît. — *la noht seelvooplay*

- **What time is check out?** — À quelle heure doit-on quitter la chambre? — *a kel uhr dwatawñ keetay la shoñbr*

- **Can I...** — Puis-je... — *pweej...*
  have a late check out? — quitter la chambre plus tard? — *keetay la shoñbr plew tar*
  leave my bags here? — laisser mes sacs ici? — *laysay may sak eesee*

- **I'd like to...** — Je voudrais... — *juh voodray...*
  check out — régler ma note — *rayglay ma not*
  stay another night — rester une nuit supplémentaire — *restay ewn nwee sewplaymoñter*

- **There's a mistake on the bill.** | Il y a une erreur dans la note. | *eelya ewn eruhr doñ la not*

- **I/We've had a great time here.** | On a passé un très bon séjour. | *awñ na pasay uñ tre bawñ sayjoor*

YOU MAY HEAR...

- Il faut quitter la chambre à... | *eel foh keetay la shoñbr a...* | Check out is at...

- Vous pouvez garder la chambre jusqu'à... | *voo poovay garday la shoñbr jewska...* | You can have the room till...

- Combien de sacs? | *kawñbyañ duh sak* | How many bags?

- Laissez-les ici. | *laysay lay eesee* | Leave them here.

- Laissez-moi vérifier. | *laysay mwa vayreefyay* | Let me check it.

* self-catering/second homes
(see **directions**, page 37; **problems and complaints**, page 70)

Gîtes are a type of self-catering accommodation in rural areas of France in country cottages, parts of farmhouses, mills, etc. They can be booked via Gîtes de France Ltd: www.gites-de-france.fr (details also available from local French tourist offices).

Belgium also has a broad range of gîtes (Landelijke in Flemish). For more information go to www.visitbelgium.com.

accommodation

I've rented...	J'ai loué...	jay looay...
a chalet	un chalet	uñ shalay
an apartment	un appartement	uñ apartuhmoñ
My name is...	Je m'appelle...	juh mapel...
We're in number...	Nous sommes dans la chambre numéro...	noo som doñ la shañbr newmayroh...
Can you give me the key, please?	Pouvez-vous me donner la clé, s'il vous plaît?	poovay voo muh donay la klay seelvooplay
Where is...	Où est...	oo e...
the fusebox?	la boîte à fusibles?	la bwat a fewseebl
the stopcock?	le robinet d'arrêt?	luh robeenay daray
How does the ... work?	Comment marche...	komoñ marsh...
cooker	la cuisinière?	la kweeseenyer
hot water	le chauffe-eau?	luh shohfoh
Is there...	Est-ce qu'il y a...	eskeelya...
air-conditioning?	la climatisation?	la kleemateezasyawñ
another gas bottle?	une autre bouteille de gaz?	ewn ohtr bootey duh gaz
Where does the rubbish go?	Où est-ce qu'on met les ordures?	oo eskawñ may layz ordewr
When does the cleaner come?	Quel jour est fait le ménage?	kel joor ay fay luh maynaj

accommodation

73

- **Can I borrow...** Est-ce qu'on peut emprunter... *eskawñ puh oñpruñtay...*

  a drill? une perceuse? *ewn persuhz*

  a corkscrew? un tire-bouchon? *uñ teerbooshawñ*

- **We need...** Nous avons besoin... *nooz avoñ buhswañ...*

  an (emergency) plumber d'un plombier (d'urgence) *duñ plawñbyay (dewrjoñs)*

  an electrician d'un électricien *duñ naylektreesyañ*

  help d'aide *dayd*

- **What shall we do with the key when we leave?** Qu'est-ce qu'on fait de la clé quand on part? *keskawñ fay duh la klay koñ tawñ par*

YOU MAY HEAR...

- Ça marche comme ça. *sa marsh com sa* **It works like this.**

- Appuyez sur ce bouton/cet interrupteur. *apweeyay sew suh bootawñ/set añterewptuhr* **Press this button/ switch.**

- Mettez vos ordures... *metay voz ordewr...* **Put the rubbish...**

  dans la poubelle *doñ la poobel* **in the dustbin**

  dans la rue *doñ la rew* **on the street**

- La femme de ménage vient le... *la fam duh maynaj vyañ luh...* **The cleaner comes on...**

- Laissez la clé chez le voisin. *laysay la klay shay luh vwazañ* **Leave the key with the neighbour.**

accommodation

74

food&drink

- Restaurants often have a set menu (menu à prix fixe or menu touristique), as well as à la carte. Some have a menu gastronomique featuring local specialities.

- In France especially, Sunday lunch is a traditional time for families to eat out, so booking is advisable if you want to eat out then. Many restaurants are not open on Sunday evenings.

YOU MAY SEE...

Auberge	Inn
Bar	Bar
Brasserie	Large café/restaurant
Buffet	Station restaurant
Carnotzet	Cellar restaurant found in Switzerland serving local dishes and cheese
Cave viticole	Wine cellar
Dégustation de vins	Wine-tasting
Glacier	Ice-cream parlour
Libre-service	Self-service
Nous acceptons les cartes de crédit	We take credit cards
Plat du jour	Dish of the day
Plats à emporter	Take-away meals
Relais (de campagne)	Country inn
Restaurant de routiers	Roadside diner
Rôtisserie	Restaurant, grill
Salle à manger	Dining-room
Salon de thé	Tea-room

✳ making bookings
(see **time phrases**, page 18)

(see **time phrases**, page 18)

YOU MAY WANT TO SAY...

I'd like to reserve a table for...	Je voudrais réserver une table pour...	*juh voodray rayzervay ewn tabl poor...*
two people	deux personnes	*duh person*
tomorrow night	demain soir	*duhmañ swar*
this evening (at 7 o'clock)	ce soir (à sept heures)	*suh swar (a set uhr)*
My name is...	Je m'appelle...	*juh mapel...*
My (mobile) phone number is...	Mon numéro de téléphone (portable) est le...	*mawñ newmayroh duh taylayfon (portabl) ay luh...*

YOU MAY HEAR...

Pour quelle heure désirez-vous la table?	*poor kel uhr dayzeeray voo la tabl*	What time would you like the table for?
Pour combien de personnes?	*poor kawñbyañ duh person*	For how many people?
Quel est votre nom?	*kel ay votr nawñ*	What's your name?
Je suis désolé, nous sommes complets.	*juh swee dayzolay noo som kawñplay*	I'm sorry, we're fully booked.

✳ at the restaurant

YOU MAY WANT TO SAY...

I've booked a table.	J'ai réservé une table.	*jay rayzervay ewn tabl*

food and drink

77

ordering your food

● **My name is...**	Je m'appelle...	*juh mapel...*
● **We haven't booked.**	Nous n'avons pas réservé.	*noo navawñ pa rayzervay*
● **Have you got a table for four?**	Avez-vous une table pour quatre personnes?	*avay voo ewn tabl poor katr person*
● **Smoking**	Fumeur	*fewmuhr*
● **Non-smoking**	Non fumeur	*nawñ fewmuhr*
● **Have you got a high chair?**	Avez-vous une chaise pour bébés?	*avay voo ewn shez poor baybay*
● **How long's the wait?**	Combien de temps faut-il attendre?	*kawñbyañ duh toñ fohteel atoñdr*
● **Do you take credit cards?**	Vous acceptez les cartes de crédit?	*vooz axeptay lay kart duh craydee*

YOU MAY HEAR...

Vous avez réservé?	*vooz avay rayzervay*	**Have you reserved?**
Fumeur ou non fumeur?	*fewmuhr oo nawñ fewmuhr*	**Smoking or non-smoking?**
Voulez-vous attendre?	*voolay voo atoñdr*	**Would you like to wait?**

✴ ordering your food

● To order something, all you need to do is name it, and say 'please' (s'il vous plaît), adding 'for me' (pour moi), 'for him' (pour lui) or 'for her' (pour elle) if you're ordering for several people to show who wants what.

food and drink

78

YOU MAY WANT TO SAY...

- Excuse me! — Pardon! — *pardawñ*

- The menu, please. — La carte, s'il vous plaît. — *la kart seelvooplay*

- Do you have... — Avez-vous un menu... — *avay voo uñ muhnew...*
  - a kids' menu? — enfant? — *oñfoñ*
  - a tourist menu? — touristique? — *tooristeek*
  - an à la carte menu? — à la carte? — *a la kart*

- Is it self-service? — C'est un libre-service? — *set uñ leebr servees*

- We're ready to order. — Nous sommes prêts à commander. — *noo som pre a komoñday*

- Can I have...? — Puis-je avoir...? — *pweej avwar*

- As a ... I'd like... — Comme ... je voudrais... — *kom ... juh voodray...*
  - starter — entrée — *oñtray*
  - main course — plat — *pla*
  - dessert — dessert — *deser*

- Does that come with vegetables? — Est-ce que c'est servi avec des légumes? — *eskuh say servee avek day laygewm*

- What's this? — Qu'est-ce que c'est? — *keskuh say*

- What are your specials today? — Quel est le plat du jour aujourd'hui? — *kel ay luh pla dew joor ohjoordwee*

- What's the local speciality? — Quelle est la spécialité locale? — *kel ay la spaysyaleetay lokal*

- What cheeses do you have? — Qu'est-ce que vous avez comme fromages? — *keskuh vooz avay kom fromaj*

- I'll have the same as him. — Je vais prendre la même chose que lui. — *juh vay proñdruh la mem shohz kuh lwee*

- **I'd like it rare/ medium/well done.** Je le veux saignant/ à point/bien cuit. *juh luh vuh saynyoñ/ a pwañ/byañ kwee*

YOU MAY HEAR...

Avez-vous choisi?	*avay voo shwazee*	Have you decided?
Nous vous recommandons...	*noo voo rekomoñdawñ...*	We recommend...
Je suis désolé, nous n'en avons plus.	*juh swee dayzolay noo noñ navawñ plew*	I'm sorry, that's run out.
Autre chose?	*ohtr shohz*	Anything else?
Quelle cuisson?	*kel kweesawñ*	How would you like it cooked?

✱ ordering your drinks

YOU MAY WANT TO SAY...

- **Can I/we see the wine list, please?** Est-ce qu'on pourrait avoir la carte des vins, s'il vous plaît? *eskawñ pooray avwar la kart day vañ seelvooplay*

- **A (half) bottle of ... please.** Une (demi-)bouteille de ... s'il vous plaît. *ewn (duhmee) bootey duh ... seelvooplay*

- **A glass of...** Un verre de... *uñ ver duh...*

- **We'll have the house red/white, please.** Nous allons prendre le rouge/blanc cuvée maison, s'il vous plaît. *nooz alawñ proñdr luh rooj/bloñ kewway maysawñ seelvooplay*

- **What beers do you have?** Quelles bières avez-vous? *kel byer avay voo*

food and drink

80

- **Can I have...** Je voudrais... *juh voodray...*
  - **a whisky** un whisky *uñ weeskee*
  - **a vodka and coke** une vodka coca *ewñ vodka koka*

- **Do you have any liqueurs?** Avez-vous des liqueurs? *avay voo day leekuhr*

- **A bottle of mineral water, please.** Une bouteille d'eau minérale, s'il vous plaît. *ewn bootey doh meenayral seelvooplay*

- **What soft drinks do you have?** Qu'est-ce que vous avez comme boissons non-alcoolisées? *keskuh vooz avay kom bwasawñ nawñ alkoleezay*

✳ bars, cafés and snack bars

- **I'll have...** Je vais prendre... *juh vay proñdr...*
  - **a coffee** un café *uñ kafay*
  - **a coffee with cream** un café crème *uñ kafay crem*
  - **a white coffee** un café au lait *uñ kafay oh lay*
  - **a black coffee** un café noir *uñ kafay nwar*
  - **a tea** un thé *uñ tay*
  - **a herbal tea** une tisane *ewn teezan*

- **with milk/lemon** avec du lait/du citron *avek dew lay/dew seetrawñ*

- **A glass of...** Un verre... *uñ ver...*
  - **tap water** d'eau du robinet *doh dew robeenay*
  - **wine** de vin *duh vañ*
  - **apple juice** de jus de pomme *duh jew duh pom*
  - **...please** ...s'il vous plaît *...seelvooplay*

food and drink

81

No ice, thanks.	Pas de glaçons, merci.	*pa duh glasawñ mersee*
A bottle of water, please.	Une bouteille d'eau, s'il vous plaît.	*ewn bootey doh seelvooplay*
What kind of ... do you have?	Quel ... avez-vous?	*kel ... avay voo*
How much is that?	C'est combien?	*say kawñbyañ*

YOU MAY HEAR...

Vous désirez?	*voo dayzeeray*	What would you like?
Une petite ou une grande?	*ewn puhteet oo ewn groñd*	Large or small?
Gazeuse ou plate?	*gazuhz oo plat*	Sparkling or still?
Avec des glaçons?	*avek day glasawñ*	With ice?

✱ comments and requests

YOU MAY WANT TO SAY...

This is delicious.	C'est délicieux.	*say dayleesyuh*
Can I/we have more...	Est-ce qu'on peut avoir...	*eskawñ puh avwar...*
bread	plus de pain	*plews duh pañ*
water	de l'eau	*duh loh*
...please?	...s'il vous plaît?	*...seelvooplay*

food and drink

Can I/we have another...	Est-ce qu'on peut avoir...	*eskawñ puh avwar...*
bottle of wine?	une autre bouteille de vin?	*ewn ohtr bootey duh vañ*
glass?	un autre verre?	*uñ ohtr ver*
I can't eat another thing.	Je n'en peux plus.	*juh noñ puh plew*

✳ special requirements

I'm diabetic.	Je suis diabétique.	*juh swee dyabayteek*
I'm allergic to...	Je suis allergique...	*juh swee alerjeek...*
nuts	aux noix	*oh nwa*
cow's milk	au lait de vache	*oh lay duh vash*
MSG	au glutamate	*oh glewtamat*
shellfish	aux fruits de mer	*oh frwee duh mayr*
I'm...	Je suis...	*juh swee...*
vegetarian	végétarien(ne)	*vayjaytaryañ/yen*
vegan	végétalien(ne)	*vayjaytalyañ/yen*
I can't eat ... products.	Je ne peux pas manger de produits...	*juh nuh puh pa moñjay duh prodwee...*
dairy	laitiers	*laytyay*
wheat	à base de blé	*a baz duh blay*
Do you have ... food?	Est-ce que vous avez de la nourriture...	*eskuh vooz avay duh la nooreetewr...*
halal	halal?	*alal*
kosher	kasher?	*kasher*
low sodium	pauvre en sodium?	*pohvr oñ sodyom*
low fat	allégée?	*alayjay*
organic	biologique?	*byolojeek*

food and drink

83

- **Do you have anything without...** Vous avez quelque chose sans... *vooz avay kelkuh shohz soñ...*
  - **meat?** viande? *vyoñd*

- **Does that have ... in it?** Est-ce que ça contient... *eskuh sa kawñtyañ*
  - **nuts** des noix? *day nwa*

YOU MAY HEAR...

- Je vais vérifier en cuisine. *juh vay vayreefyay oñ kweezeen* I'll check with the kitchen.

- Tout est préparé avec... *too te prayparay avek...* It's all got ... in it.
  - du beurre *dew buhr* butter

---

* problems and complaints

- **Excuse me.** Pardon. *pardawñ*

- **This is...** C'est... *say...*
  - **cold** froid *frwa*
  - **burnt** brûlé *brewlay*

- **This is underdone.** Ce n'est pas cuit. *suh ne pa kwee*

- **I didn't order this.** Je n'ai pas commandé ça. *juh nay pa komoñday sa*

- **I ordered the...** J'ai commandé... *jay komoñday...*

- **Is our food coming soon?** Est-ce que notre commande arrive bientôt? *eskuh notr komoñd areev byañtoh*

* paying the bill

- **The bill, please.** L'addition, s'il vous plaît. *ladeesyawñ seelvooplay*

- **Is service included?** Est-ce que le service est compris? *eskuh luh servees ay kawñpree*

- **There's a mistake here.** Il y a une erreur ici. *eelya ewn eruhr eesee*

- **That was fantastic, thank you.** C'était excellent, merci. *sayte exeloñ mersee*

YOU MAY HEAR...

- Le service n'est pas compris. *luh servees ne pa kawñpree* **Service isn't included.**

- Désolé, nous n'acceptons que les paiements en espèces. *dayzolay noo naxeptawñ kuh lay paymoñ oñ espes* **Sorry, we only accept cash.**

* buying food

- **I'd like...** Je voudrais... *juh voodray...*
  some of that un peu de ça *uñ puh duh sa*
  a kilo (of...) un kilo (de...) *uñ keeloh (duh...)*
  two hundred grammes (of...) deux cents grammes (de...) *duh soñ gram (duh...)*
  a piece (of...) un morceau (de...) *uñ morsoh (duh...)*
  two slices (of...) deux tranches (de...) *duh troñsh (duh...)*

food and drink

85

● **How much is that?**	Combien ça coûte?	*kawñbyañ sa koot*
● **How much is a kilo of cheese?**	Combien coûte un kilo de fromage?	*kawñbyañ koot uñ keeloh duh fromaj*
● **What's that?**	Qu'est-ce que c'est?	*keskuh say*
● **Have you got... any bread?**	Vous avez... du pain?	*vooz avay... dew pañ*
● **Have you got any more?**	Vous en avez encore?	*vooz oñ avay oñkor*
● **A bit more/less, please.**	Un peu plus/moins, s'il vous plaît.	*uñ puh plews/mwuñ seelvooplay*
● **That's all, thank you.**	C'est tout, merci.	*say too mersee*
● **I'm looking for the ... section.**	Je cherche le rayon des...	*juh shersh luh rayyawñ day...*
frozen food	surgelés	*sewrjuhlay*
dairy	produits laitiers	*prodwee laytyay*
fruit and veg	fruits et légumes	*frwee ay laygewm*
● **Can I have a bag, please?**	Puis-je avoir un sac, s'il vous plaît?	*pweej avwar uñ sak seelvooplay*

food and drink

menu reader

DRINKS

Appellation d'origine contrôlée
(AOC) guarantee of origin and
quality of wine
armagnac brandy from Armagnac region
bière beer
   blonde light, lager
   brune dark, bitter
   pression draught
   sans alcool alcohol-free
blanc de blancs white wine made
   from white grapes
blanc limé white wine with lemonade
bouteille bottle
brut very dry
cacao cocoa
café coffee
   au lait white
   crème with cream
   décaféiné decaffeinated
   filtre filter
   frappé iced
   noir black
calvados apple brandy
camomille camomile tea
carafe carafe, jug
cassis blackcurrant liqueur
chambré(e) at room temperature
champagne champagne
chocolat (chaud/froid) chocolate
   (hot/cold)
   grande tasse large hot
   chocolate
diabolo menthe mint cordial
   and lemonade
cidre (brut/doux) cider (dry/sweet)

citron pressé freshly squeezed lemon
cognac cognac, brandy
cru: grand cru, Premier cru vintage wine
cuvée du patron house wine
demi draught beer (France); half litre
   of wine (Switzerland)
doux/douce sweet
eau water
eau de Seltz soda water
eau de vie brandy
eau minérale (gazeuse/plate) mineral
   water (sparkling/still)
frappé iced, milk shake
gin gin
   gin-tonic gin and tonic
grand crème large white coffee
infusion herbal tea
jus de fruit fruit juice
   de pomme apple juice
   d'orange orange juice
   de tomate tomato juice
   de raisin grape juice
   de fraise strawberry juice
   de framboise raspberry juice
   de pamplemousse grapefruit juice
   de poire pear juice
   de banane banana juice
   de mangue mango juice
kir kir (with white wine)
kir royal kir (with champagne)
kirsch cherry brandy
lait (chaud/froid) milk (hot/cold)
limonade lemonade
madère Madeira
marc grape brandy

marc de framboise **raspberry brandy**
menthe **mint; peppermint**
mirabelle **plum brandy**
muscat **moscatel**
orange pressée **freshly squeezed orange**
panaché **shandy**
pastis **aniseed flavoured aperitif**
    Ricard **brand of above**
pichet **jug, pitcher**
porto **port**
pression **draught beer**
quetsche **plum brandy**
rhum **rum**
réserve du patron **house wine**
rouge limé **red wine with lemonade**
Schweppes **tonic water**
sec/sèche **dry**
sirop **cordial, syrup**
soda **fizzy drink**
    à l'orange **fizzy orange, orangeade**

thé **tea**
    à la menthe **mint tea**
    au lait/citron **with milk/lemon**
    glacé **iced**
tilleul **lime tea**
tisane **herbal tea**
vermouth **vermouth**
verveine **verbena tea**
vin **wine**
    blanc **white**
    chaud **mulled wine**
    de table **table**
    de pays **local**
    mousseux **sparkling**
    ordinaire **ordinary**
    rosé **rosé**
    rouge **red**
vodka **vodka**
whisky **whisky**
xérès **sherry**

FOOD

A

abricot **apricot**
agneau **lamb**
aiglefin **haddock**
aigre **sour**
    à l'aigre-doux **sweet and sour**
ail **garlic**
    à l'ail **with garlic**
aïoli **garlic mayonnaise**
amandes **almonds**
ananas **pineapple**
anchois **anchovies**
andouille, andouillette **(smaller)**
    chitterling sausage
anguille **eel**

à point **medium (steak)**
cacahuètes **peanuts**
asperges **asparagus**
assiette anglaise **assorted cold roast meats**
assiette de... **plate of...**
artichaut **artichoke**
aubergine **aubergine**
avocat **avocado**

B

baba au rhum **rum baba**
banane **banana**
bar **bass**
barbue **brill**
barquette **small boat-shaped pastry**
basilic **basil**

bavaroise type of light mousse
bavette à l'échalote beef with shallots
beignet type of doughnut or fritter
betterave beetroot
beurre butter
    maître d'hôtel parsley butter
    noir black butter
bien cuit well done (steak)
bifteck steak
    tartare minced raw steak with raw egg, onion, tartare or Worcestershire sauce
biscuit de savoie sponge cake
bisque seafood soup, chowder
blanquette de veau stewed veal in white sauce
bleu very rare (steak)
bœuf beef
bœuf bourguignon beef braised with red wine and vegetables
bois: des bois wild
bolets boletus mushrooms
bouchée à la reine chicken vol-au-vent
boudin blanc white pudding
boudin noir black pudding
bouillabaisse fish soup, speciality of the South of France
bouilli(e) boiled
bouillon broth
boulettes meatballs
bouquet rose prawn
bourride fish stew
braisé(e) braised
brandade (de morue) poached cod with cream, parsley and garlic
brioche type of bun
broche: à la broche spit-roasted
brochet pike
brochette kebab
brugnon nectarine

C

cabillaud cod
cabri kid
cacahouètes peanuts
caille quail
calmar squid
campagne: de campagne country-style
canard duck
    à l'orange in orange sauce
    sauvage sauvage
caneton duckling
cannelle cinnamon
câpres capers
carbonnade de bœuf beef stewed in beer with onions
carottes carrots
    râpées grated carrots with vinaigrette
    vichy cooked with butter and sugar
carpe carp
carré d'agneau rack of lamb
carrelet plaice
cassis blackcurrant
cassoulet casserole of haricot beans, mutton, pork, goose and sausage, speciality of the Toulouse region
céleri celeriac/celery
    remoulade celeriac in mustard dressing
cèpes boletus mushrooms
cerises cherries
cervelas type of sausage
cervelle brains
champignons mushrooms
    à la grecque in olive oil, herbs and tomato
charcuterie assorted cold meats
charlotte dessert of cream with fruit and biscuits
chateaubriand large fillet steak
chaud(e) hot
chausson aux pommes apple turnover

food and drink

chef: du chef **chef's own/special**

chevreuil **venison**

chicorée **endive**

chips **crisps**

chocolat **chocolate**

chou **cabbage**

chou à la crème **cream puff**

choucroute (garnie) **sauerkraut served with smoked ham, sausages, etc**

chou-fleur **cauliflower**

chou-rave **kohlrabi**

choux de Bruxelles **Brussels sprouts**

citron **lemon**

civet de lapin/lièvre **jugged rabbit/hare**

clafoutis **fruit (usually black cherries) cooked in batter**

cochon de lait **sucking pig**

cocotte: en cocotte **casseroled**

cœurs d'artichaut **artichoke hearts**

coing **quince**

colin **hake**

compote **stewed fruit**

concombre **cucumber**

confit d'oie **goose preserved in fat**

confiture **jam**

consommé **consommé, clear soup**

à l'œuf **with raw egg**

au porto **with port**

coq au vin **chicken in wine, bacon, onions and mushrooms**

coque **cockle**

coque: à la coque **soft-boiled (egg)**

coquilles St Jacques **scallops, served in a cream sauce in their shells**

corbeille **basket**

cornichon **gherkin**

côte de bœuf **chop, cutlet rib of beef**

côtelette **chop, cutlet**

coulis **sauce**

coupe **cup**

de fruits **fruit salad**

glacée **ice-cream sundae**

courgette **courgette**

court-bouillon **stock**

couscous **north African speciality, steamed semolina served with meat and vegetables**

couvert **cover charge**

crabe **crab**

crème **cream**

à la crème **in cream sauce**

anglaise **custard**

caramel **cream caramel**

chantilly **whipped cream**

Dubarry **cream of cauliflower soup**

pâtissière **confectioner's custard**

renversée **moulded cream dessert**

vichyssoise **cream of leek and potato soup, served cold**

crêpe **thin pancake**

à la confiture **with jam**

au sucre **sprinkled with sugar**

Suzette **with orange sauce and flamed with brandy or liqueur**

cresson **watercress**

crevettes **prawns, shrimps**

croque-madame **toasted ham and cheese sandwich with a fried egg on top**

croque-monsieur **toasted ham and cheese sandwich**

croustade **pastry shell**

croûte: en croûte **in a pastry crust**

crudités **assorted raw vegetables**

cuisses de grenouille **frogs' legs**

D

darne **thick fish steak**

dattes **dates**

daube: en daube **casseroled**

daurade **sea bream**

déjeuner **lunch**

diable: à la diable **devilled**

dinde **turkey**
dîner **dinner**
douzaine **dozen**

E

échalotes **shallots**
écrevisses **crayfish**
endives **chicory**
entrecôte **entrecote (rib) steak**
épaule d'agneau **shoulder of lamb**
épinards **spinach**
escalope **escalope**
  de veau **veal**
  milanaise **breaded veal with**
    tomato sauce
  panée/viennoise **breaded**
escargots **snails**
  à la bourguignonne **in garlic butter**
estragon **tarragon**

F

faisan **pheasant**
farci(e) **stuffed**
faux-filet **sirloin**
fenouil **fennel**
fèves **broad beans**
figue **fig**
filet **fillet**
  mignon **small fillet**
fines herbes **herbs**
flageolets **small kidney beans**
flambé(e) **sprinkled with brandy or**
  other spirit and ignited
flan **crème caramel**
flétan **halibut**
foie **liver**
  de volaille **chicken liver**
  gras **goose (or duck) liver pâté**
fondue bourguignonne **meat fondue:**
  pieces of raw meat on forks cooked
  by diners in pot of hot oil
fondue au chocolat **chocolate fondue:**
  pieces of fruit (banana, pear, apple,

etc) dipped in hot melted chocolate
fondue au fromage **pot of melted cheese**
  with white wine, into which diners dip
  pieces of bread on a fork
fouetté(e) **whipped**
four: au four **baked**
frais, fraîche **fresh**
fraise **strawberry**
framboise **raspberry**
francfort (saucisse de) **frankfurter**
  (sausage)
fricassé(e) **stewed**
frisée **curly endive**
frit(e) **fried**
frites **chips**
froid(e) **cold**
fromage **cheese**
  blanc **soft cream cheese**
  de chèvre **goat's cheese**
  demi-sel **soft cream cheese,**
    slightly salted
  fumé(e) **smoked**

G

galantine **cold poultry or game in**
  aspic or gelatine
galette **pancake made with**
  buckwheat flour
garbure **thick cabbage soup**
garni(e) **garnished, with vegetables**
gâteau **cake, gateau**
gaufre **wafer, waffle**
gelée **jelly**
  en gelée **in aspic, jellied**
germes de soja **beansprouts**
gigot (d'agneau) **leg of lamb**
gingembre **ginger**
girolle **chanterelle mushroom**
glace **ice cream**
  au praliné **with crushed almonds**
    and burnt sugar
goujon **gudgeon**

granité water-ice
gras-double tripe
   à la lyonnaise with onions and wine
gratin: au gratin with cheese topping,
   in cheese sauce
gratin dauphinois sliced potatoes
   baked with milk, cream and cheese
grillé(e) grilled
groseilles (blanches/rouges) currants
   (white/red)
   à maquereau gooseberries

H

hachis Parmentier minced meat,
   hash type of cottage pie
hareng herring
haricot de mouton mutton stew with
   haricot beans
haricots beans
   blancs haricot beans
   rouges red kidney beans
   verts green/French beans
herbes herbs
homard lobster
   à l'américaine/armoricaine in wine,
   tomatoes, shallots and brandy
   Thermidor with white wine, mushrooms
   and spices, flamed with brandy
hors-d'œuvre variés mixed hors-d'œuvres
huile oil
   d'arachide groundnut
   d'olive olive
huîtres oysters

I

iles flottantes floating islands: whisked
   egg whites floating in custard

J

jambon ham
   cru raw cured
   cuit cooked

de Bayonne type of raw cured ham
jardinière: à la jardinière with mixed
   vegetables
jarret knuckle, shin
jour: du jour of the day
julienne soup of shredded vegetables

L

laitue lettuce
langouste crayfish
langoustines scampi
langue tongue
lapin rabbit
   aux pruneaux casseroled in red wine
   with prunes
   chasseur with white wine and herbs
lard bacon, fat
lardons strips of bacon
légume vegetable
lentilles lentils
   en salade in vinaigrette
lièvre hare
limande lemon sole
longe loin
lotte burbot
lotte de mer angler fish
loup sea bass

M

macédoine de fruits fruit salad
macédoine de légumes mixed vegetables
magret de canard breast of duck
maïs sweetcorn
maison (eg tarte maison) house speciality,
   home-made
maquereau mackerel
marchand de vin red wine sauce with
   shallots
mariné(e) marinated
marrons chestnuts
   glacés candied
massepain marzipan

matelote d'anguilles **eel stew with wine**
médaillons **medallions, tenderloin steak**
melon **melon**
menthe **mint**
menu du jour **menu of the day**
merguez **spicy sausage, from North Africa**
merlan **whiting**
meunière, à la meunière **fried in butter,**
  with lemon juice and parsley
miel **honey**
mille feuille **cream slice**
morilles **morel mushrooms**
mortadelle **mortadella, Bologna sausage**
morue **salt cod**
moules **mussels**
  marinières **in their shells with white**
  wine, shallots and parsley
mousse **mousse**
  au chocolat **chocolate mousse**
  au jambon **light ham mousse**
moutarde **mustard**
  à la moutarde **in mustard sauce**
mouton **mutton**
mûres **blackberries**
myrtilles **bilberries, blueberries**

N

nature, au naturel **plain**
navarin d'agneau **lamb stew with**
  vegetables
navet **turnip**
noisette d'agneau **small boneless**
  round of lamb
noisettes **hazelnuts**
noix **walnuts**
noix de coco **coconut**
normande: à la normande **in cream sauce**
nouilles **noodles**

O

œuf(s) **egg(s)**
  à la coque **soft-boiled**

à la neige **floating islands, whisked**
  egg whites floating in custard
au/sur le plat **fried**
brouillés **scrambled**
dur **hard-boiled**
dur mayonnaise **egg mayonnaise**
(dur) mimosa **stuffed hard-boiled egg**
oie **goose**
oignon **onion**
olive **olive**
  farcie **stuffed**
  noire **black**
  verte **green**
omelette **omelette**
  aux fines herbes **with herbs**
  norvégienne **baked Alaska**
  paysanne **with potatoes and bacon**
orange **orange**
  givrée **orange sorbet served in**
  scooped-out orange
oseille **sorrel**
oursin **sea urchin**

P

pain **bread**
  d'épices **gingerbread**
  grillé **toast**
palourdes **clams**
pamplemousse **grapefruit**
pané(e) **breaded**
papillote: en papillote **baked in paper**
  or foil
passé(e) au four **finished in the oven**
pastèque **water melon**
pâté **pâté**
  de campagne **coarse pork pâté**
  de foie **liver pâté**
paupiettes de veau **rolled and stuffed**
  slices of veal
pêche **peach**
  Melba **with vanilla ice cream,**
  raspberry sauce and whipped cream

perche **perch**
perdrix **partridge**
persil **parsley**
petit déjeuner **breakfast**
petite friture **whitebait**
petit pain **roll**
petits pois **peas**
petit suisse **fresh cream cheese**
pieds de porc **pig's trotters**
pigeon **pigeon**
pintade **guinea fowl**
piperade **egg dish with tomatoes and peppers**
pissaladière **onion tart with black olives and anchovies**
pistache **pistachio**
plateau de fromages **cheese board**
plats du jour **specials**
poché(e) **poached**
pointes d'asperges **asparagus tips**
poire **pear**
  belle Hélène **pear with vanilla ice cream and chocolate sauce**
poireau **leek**
pois chiches **chickpeas**
poisson **fish**
poivre **pepper**
  noir **black**
  vert **green**
poivron **sweet pepper**
pomme **apple**
  bonne femme **baked**
pommes (de terre) **potatoes**
  à l'huile **fried**
  allumettes **matchstick**
  dauphine **croquettes of potato mashed with butter and egg yolks and deep-fried**
  duchesse **mashed with butter and egg yolks**
  en robe de chambre/des champs **jacket**
  frites **chips**

mousseline **mashed**
nature, vapeur **boiled, steamed**
porc **pork**
pot: au pot **stewed**
potage **thick vegetable soup**
  bonne femme **potato and leek**
  crécy **carrot**
  parmentier **potato**
  printanier **mixed vegetables**
pot-au-feu **beef and vegetable stew**
potée **hotpot**
poule **chicken**
  au pot **boiled with vegetables**
poulet **chicken**
  à l'estragon **in tarragon sauce**
  au sang **jugged**
  basquaise **basque-style, in sauce of ham, tomatoes, onions and peppers**
  chasseur **in wine, mushroom and tomato sauce**
  frites **and chips**
  marengo **with white wine, tomatoes, garlic, shallots and mushrooms**
poulpe **octopus**
poussin **spring chicken**
praline **burnt-sugar almond**
pressé(e) (eg orange pressée) **freshly squeezed juice**
profiteroles **small choux pastry puffs filled with cream or confectioner's custard**
provençale: à la provençale **with tomatoes, garlic and herbs**
prune **plum**
pruneau **prune**
purée **mashed potatoes**

Q

quenelle **type of fish or meat dumpling**
queue de bœuf **oxtail**
quiche lorraine **bacon, egg and cheese flan**

R

raclette Swiss speciality, hot melted
  cheese eaten with potatoes and
  pickles
radis radish
ragoût meat stew
raie skate
raisins grapes
  secs raisins
rascasse scorpion fish (used in
  bouillabaisse)
ratatouille mixture of courgettes,
  peppers, aubergine and tomatoes
  cooked in olive oil
reine-claude greengage
rillettes (de porc) potted pork
rillettes de saumon potted salmon
ris de veau veal sweetbreads
riz rice
  au lait pudding
rognons kidneys
romarin rosemary
rosbif roast beef
rôti(e) roast
rouget red mullet

S

sabayon dessert of whipped egg yolks
  with wine and sugar
saignant rare (steak)
saint-Honoré gateau of choux pastry
  puffs and cream
saison: de saison in season
salade salad
  composée mixed
  de tomates tomatoes with oil and
  vinegar and sometimes garlic
  en salade in vinaigrette
  mixte mixed
  niçoise green beans, tuna,
  anchovies, tomatoes and black olives
  russe russian salad, diced cooked

  vegetables in mayonnaise
  verte green
salmis ragout of game in wine and
  vegetable sauce
sandwich sandwich, made with French
  bread
sanglier wild boar
sardine sardine
sauce sauce
  aurore white sauce with tomato purée
  béarnaise butter, egg yolks, shallots,
  vinegar and herbs
  béchamel white
  bigarade brown sauce with oranges
  blanche white
  bordelaise mushrooms, red wine
  and shallots
  chasseur white wine, shallots,
  tomatoes and mushrooms
  gribiche vinaigrette with hard-boiled
  eggs and capers
  hollandaise egg yolks, butter and
  vinegar
  mornay cheese
  provençale tomatoes, garlic and herbs
  rémoulade mayonnaise with mustard
  and herbs
saucisse sausage
saucisson cold sausage, salami
  à l'ail garlic sausage
saumon salmon
sauté(e) sautéed
savarin type of rum baba
sec dried
sel salt
selle d'agneau saddle of lamb
service compris service included
sole sole
  bonne femme in white wine with
  mushrooms
sorbet sorbet

soufflé **soufflé**
  au Grand Marnier **in Grand Marnier**
soupe **soup**
  à l'oignon **French onion soup, topped with slice of bread with cheese on**
  au pistou **thick soup of potatoes, courgettes, beans and herbs, from Provence**
spaghettis **spaghetti**
  à la bolognaise **bolognese**
  à l'italienne **with tomato sauce**
stea(c)k **steak**
  au poivre **with peppercorns**
  frites **steak and chips**
  haché **minced meat, hamburger**
  tartare **raw minced steak with a raw egg**
sucre **sugar**
suprême de volaille **chicken breast in cream sauce**

T

tarte **tart, flan**
  frangipane **almond cream tart**
  tatin **apple tart**
tartelette **small tart**
tartine **slice of bread and butter**
terrine **terrine, pâté**
tête de veau **calf's head**
thon **tuna**
tomate **tomato**
topinambour **Jerusalem artichoke**
tournedos **thick fillet steak**
  rossini **with foie gras and truffles, in Madeira sauce**

tourte **layer cake**
tranche **slice**
tripes **tripe**
  à la mode de Caen **cooked in cider and Calvados with vegetables and herbs**
truffe **truffle**
truffé(e) **with truffles**
truite **trout**
  au bleu **poached**
  aux amandes **with butter and almonds**
turbot **turbot**
TVA incluse **VAT included**

V

vacherin glacé **ice cream and meringue gateau**
vanille **vanilla**
vapeur, (cuit) à la vapeur **steamed, boiled**
veau **veal**
velouté **cream (soup)**
vinaigre **vinegar**
vinaigrette **French dressing**
volaille **poultry, chicken**

W

waterzoi de poulet **chicken in wine and cream sauce with vegetables**

Y

yaourt **yoghurt (plain, eaten as part of cheese course)**

sightseeing
&activities

✳ at the tourist office

YOU MAY WANT TO SAY...

- **Do you speak English?** — Parlez-vous anglais? — *parlay voo oñglay*

- **Do you have...** — Avez-vous... — *avay voo...*
  - a map of the town? — un plan de la ville? — *uñ ploñ duh la veel*
  - a list of hotels? — une liste des hôtels? — *ewn leest dayz otel*

- **Can you recommend...** — Pouvez-vous recommander... — *poovay voo ruhkomoñday...*
  - a cheap hotel? — un hôtel bon marché? — *uñ notel bawñ marshay*
  - a good campsite? — un bon terrain de camping? — *uñ bawñ terañ duh koñpeeng*
  - a traditional restaurant? — un restaurant typique? — *uñ restohroñ teepeek*

- **Do you have information...** — Avez-vous des informations... — *avay voo dayz añformasyawñ...*
  - in English? — en anglais? — *oñ oñglay*
  - about opening times? — sur les heures d'ouverture? — *sewr layz uhr doovertewr*

Can you book...	Pouvez-vous réserver...	poovay voo rayzervay...
a hotel room for me?	une chambre d'hôtel pour moi?	ewn shoñbr dotel poor mwa
this day trip for me?	cette excursion pour moi?	set exkewrsyawñ poor mwa
Where is...	Où est...	oo ay...
the old town?	la vieille ville?	la vyey veel
the art gallery?	la galerie d'art?	la galuhree dar
the Grévin museum?	le musée Grévin?	luh mewsay grayvañ
Is there...	Est-ce qu'il y a...	eskeelya...
a swimming pool?	une piscine?	ewn peeseen
a bank?	une banque?	ewn boñk
Is there a post office near here?	Est-ce qu'il y a un bureau de poste par ici?	eskeelya uñ bewroh duh post par eesee
Can you show me on the map?	Pouvez-vous me montrer sur le plan?	poovay voo muh mawñtray sewr luh ploñ

✱ opening times
(see **telling the time**, page 17)

● Most museums in France, and some in other countries, are closed on Mondays or Tuesdays.

YOU MAY WANT TO SAY...

What time does the museum/ palace open/close?	À quelle heure ouvre/ferme le musée/palais?	a kel uhr oovr/ferm luh mewsay/palay

99

- **When does the exhibition open?** — À quelle heure ouvre l'exposition? — *a kel uhr oovr lexpohzeesyawñ*

- **Is it open...** — C'est ouvert... — *set oover...*
  - **on Mondays?** — le lundi? — *luh luñdee*
  - **at the weekend?** — le week-end? — *luh weekend*

- **Can I/we visit...** — Peut-on visiter... — *puhtawñ veezeetay...*
  - **the monastery?** — le monastère? — *luh monaster*

- **Is it open to the public?** — Est-ce que c'est ouvert au public? — *eskuh set oover oh pewbleek*

YOU MAY HEAR...

- C'est ouvert tous les jours sauf le... — *Set oover too lay joor sohf luh...* — It's open every day except...

- C'est ouvert de ... à... — *Set oover duh ... a ...* — It's open from ... to ...

- C'est fermé le... — *say fermay luh...* — It's closed on...

- C'est fermé... — *say fermay...* — It's closed for...
  - l'hiver — *leever* — the winter
  - pour cause de travaux — *poor kohz duh travoh* — repairs

* visiting places

YOU MAY SEE...

Défense d'entrer	No entry
Défense de toucher	Do not touch
Fermé (pour cause de travaux)	Closed (for restoration)
Heures d'ouverture	Opening hours

Interdiction de prendre des photos avec le flash	**No flash photography**
Ouvert	**Open**
Privé	**Private**
Visites organisées	**Guided tours**

How much does it cost to get in?	Combien coûte l'entrée?	kawñbyañ koot loñtray
One adult, please.	Un adulte, s'il vous plaît.	uñ adewlt seelvooplay
Two adults, please.	Deux adultes, s'il vous plaît.	duhz adewlt seelvooplay
One adult and two children, please.	Un adulte et deux enfants, s'il vous plaît.	uñ adewlt ay duhz oñfoñ seelvooplay
A family ticket, please.	Un billet familial, s'il vous plaît.	uñ beeyay fameelyal seelvooplay
Is there a reduction for...	Est-ce qu'il y a une réduction pour...	eskeelya ewn raydewksyawñ poor...
students?	les étudiants?	layz aytewdyoñ
pensioners?	les retraités?	lay ruhtretay
children?	les enfants?	layz oñfoñ
people with disabilities?	les personnes handicapées?	lay person oñdeekapay
Is there...	Est-ce qu'il y a...	eskeelya...
wheelchair access?	un accès pour les fauteuils roulants?	uñ axe poor lay fohtuhy rooloñ
an audio tour?	une visite audio?	ewn veezeet ohdyoh
a picnic area?	une aire de pique-nique?	ewn er duh peekneek

- **Are there guided tours (in English)?** — Est-ce qu'il y a des visites guidées (en anglais)? — *eskeelya day veezeet geeday (oñ oñglay)*

- **Can I/we take photos?** — Est-ce qu'on peut prendre des photos? — *eskawñ puh proñdr day fohtoh*

YOU MAY HEAR...

- Ça coûte ... euros par personne. — *sa koot ... uhroh par person* — **It costs ... euros per person.**

- Il y a une réduction pour les étudiants/ les personnes âgées. — *eelya ewn raydewksyawñ poor layz aytewdyoñ/lay person zajay* — **There's a reduction for students/senior citizens.**

- Il y a des rampes d'accès pour les fauteuils roulants. — *eelya day roñp daxe poor lay fohtuhy rooloñ* — **There are wheelchair ramps.**

- Je suis désolé, ce n'est pas conçu pour les fauteuils roulants. — *juh swee dayzolay suh ne pa kawñsew poor lay fohtuhy rooloñ* — **I'm sorry, it's not suitable for wheelchairs.**

✳ going on tours and trips

YOU MAY WANT TO SAY...

- **I/We'd like to join the tour to...** — On voudrait participer à la visite de... — *awñ voodray parteeseepay a la veezeet duh...*

- **What time...** — À quelle heure... — *a kel uhr...*
  - **does it leave?** — ça commence? — *sa komoñs*
  - **does it get back?** — ça se termine? — *sa suh termeen*

How long is it?	Elle dure combien de temps?	*el dewr kawñbyañ duh toñ*
Where does it leave from?	Elle part d'où?	*el par doo*
Does the guide speak English?	Est-ce que le guide parle anglais?	*eskuh luh geed parl oñglay*
How much is it?	Combien ça coûte?	*kawñbyañ sa koot*
Is lunch/ accommodation included?	Est-ce que le déjeuner/ l'hébergement est compris?	*eskuh luh dayjuhnay/ layberjuhmoñ ay kawñpree*
When's the next...	Quand a lieu la prochaine...	*koñ a lyuh la proshen...*
boat trip?	excursion en bateau?	*exkewrsyawñ oñ batoh*
day trip?	excursion?	*exkewrsyawñ*
Can we hire...	Est-ce qu'on peut réserver...	*eskawñ puh rayzervay...*
a guide?	un guide?	*uñ geed*
an English-speaking guide?	un guide anglophone?	*uñ geed oñglofon*
How much is it (per day)?	C'est combien (par jour)?	*say kawñbyañ (par joor)*
I/We'd like to see...	On voudrait voir...	*awñ voodray vwar...*
I'm with a group.	Je suis dans un groupe.	*juh swee doñz uñ groop*
I've lost my group.	J'ai perdu mon groupe.	*jay perdew mawñ groop*

sightseeing and activities

103

YOU MAY HEAR...

Elle part à...	el par a...	It leaves at...
Elle revient à...	el ruhvyañ a...	It gets back at...
Elle part de...	el par duh...	It leaves from...
Ne soyez pas en retard!	nuh swayay paz oñ ruhtar	Don't be late!
Il/Elle demande ... par jour.	eel/el duhmoñd ... par joor	He/She charges ... per day.
Comment s'appelle votre groupe?	komoñ sapel votr groop	What's the name of your group?

✳ entertainment
(see **time phrases**, page 18)

Many American and British films are shown at the cinema, sometimes subtitled (sous-titré) but mostly dubbed (doublé). Unless a foreign film is labelled VO (version originale), it is dubbed.

YOU MAY SEE...

Balcon	Dress circle
Billets pour les représentations d'aujourd'hui	Tickets for today's performance
Cinéma	Cinema
Cirque	Circus
Complet	Sold out

Discothèque	Disco
Entrée	Entry
Fauteuil d'orchestre	Orchestra stalls
Hippodrome	Racecourse
Interdit aux moins de 18 ans	No admittance to under-18s
Les spectateurs ne sont pas admis après le début de la séance/représentation	No entry once the performance has begun
Loges	Boxes
Matinée	Matinee
Opéra	Opera house
Orchestre	Stalls
Permanent	Continuous performance
Rang	Row, tier
Réservation anticipée	Advance booking
Salle de concert	Concert hall
Sans entracte	No intervals
Soirée	Evening performance
Théâtre	Theatre
Tribune	Stand, grandstand

YOU MAY WANT TO SAY...

● Is there anything for children?	Est-ce qu'il y a quelque chose pour les enfants?	eskeelya kelkuh shohz poor layz oñfoñ
● Is there...	Est-ce qu'il y a...	eskeelya...
a cinema round here?	un cinéma par ici?	uñ seenayma par eesee
a good club round here?	une bonne discothèque par ici?	ewn bon deeskotek par eesee

What's on...	Qu'est-ce qu'il y a...	*keskeelya...*
tonight?	ce soir?	*suh swar*
tomorrow?	demain?	*duhmañ*
at the theatre?	au théâtre?	*oh tayatr*
at the cinema?	au cinéma?	*oh seenayma*
When does the game/performance start?	À quelle heure commence le match/la représentation?	*a kel uhr komoñs luh matsh/la ruhprayzoñtasyawñ*
What time does it finish?	À quelle heure ça se termine?	*a kel uhr sa suh termeen*
Do we need to book?	Est-ce qu'il faut réserver?	*eskeel foh rayzevay*
Where can I/we get tickets?	Où peut-on acheter des billets?	*oo puhtawñ ashuhtay day beeyay*
Is it suitable for children?	Est-ce que les enfants sont autorisés?	*eskuh layz oñfoñ sawñ ohtohreezay*
Has the film got subtitles?	Est-ce que le film est sous-titré?	*eskuh luh feelm ay sooteetray*
Is it dubbed?	Est-ce que le film est doublé?	*eskuh luh feelm ay dooblay*

sightseeing and activities

Vous pouvez acheter les billets ici.	*voo poovay ashuhtay lay beeyay eesee*	You can buy tickets here.
Ça commence à...	*sa komoñs a...*	It starts at...
Ça fini à...	*sa finee a...*	It finishes at...

Il vaut mieux réserver à l'avance.	*eel voh myuh rayzervay a lavoñs*	**It's best to book in advance.**
C'est doublé.	*se dooblay*	**It's dubbed.**
Il y a des sous-titres (anglais).	*eelya day sooteetr (oñglay)*	**It's got (English) subtitles.**
C'est avec...	*set avek*	**It stars...**

* booking tickets

Have you got tickets for...	Avez-vous des billets pour...	*avay voo day beeyay poor...*
the ballet?	le ballet?	*luh balay*
the football match?	le match de foot?	*luh matsh duh foot*
the theatre?	le théâtre?	*luh tayatr*
Are there any seats left for Saturday?	Est-ce qu'il y a encore des places pour samedi?	*eskeelya oñkor day plas poor samuhdee*
I'd like to book...	Je voudrais réserver...	*juh voodray rayzervay...*
a box	une loge	*ewn loj*
two seats	deux places	*duh plas*
in the stalls	à l'orchestre	*a lorkestr*
in the dress circle	au balcon	*oh balkawñ*
Do you have anything cheaper?	Est-ce que vous avez quelque chose de moins cher?	*eskuh vooz avay kelkuh shohz duh mwañ sher*
Is there wheelchair access?	Est-ce qu'il y a un accès pour les fauteuils roulants?	*eskeelya uñ axe poor lay fohtuhy roolon*

at the show

YOU MAY HEAR...

Combien?	*kawñbyañ*	How many?
Pour quand?	*poor koñ*	When for?
Avez-vous une carte de crédit?	*avay voo ewn kart duh craydee*	Do you have a credit card?
Pouvez-vous me donner le numéro de votre carte?	*poovez voo muh donay luh newmayroh duh votr kart*	Can you give me your credit card number?
Je suis désolé(e), c'est complet ce soir/ce jour-là.	*juh swee dayzolay say kawñplay suh swar/suh joor la*	I'm sorry, we're sold out that night/day.

✱ at the show

YOU MAY WANT TO SAY...

What film/play/opera is on tonight?	Quel film/quelle pièce/quel opéra se joue ce soir?	*kel feelm/kel pyes/kel opayra se joo suh swar*
Two for tonight's performance, please.	Deux places pour la représentation de ce soir, s'il vous plaît.	*duh plass poor la ruhprayzoñtasyawñ duh suh swar, seelvooplay*
One adult and two children, please.	Un adulte et deux enfants, s'il vous plaît.	*uñ adewlt ay duhz oñfoñ seelvooplay*
How much is that?	C'est combien?	*se kawñbyañ*

sightseeing and activities

- **We'd like to sit...** Nous voudrions être... *noo voodreeawñ etr...*
  - **at the front** devant *duhvoñ*
  - **at the back** au fond *oh fawñ*
  - **in the middle** au milieu *oh meelyuh*

- **We've reserved seats.** Nous avons réservé des places. *nooz avawñ rayzervay day plas*

- **My name is...** Je m'appelle... *juh mapel...*

- **Is there an interval?** Est-ce qu'il y a un entracte? *eskeelya uñ oñtrakt*

- **Where's...** Où est... *oo ay...*
  - **the dress circle?** le balcon? *luh balkawñ*
  - **the bar?** le bar? *luh bar*

- **Where are the toilets?** Où sont les toilettes? *oo sawñ lay twalet*

- **Can you stop talking, please?** Vous pouvez vous taire, s'il vous plaît? *voo poovay voo ter seelvooplay*

✳ sports and activities

Baignade interdite	No swimming
Centre sportif	Sports centre
Chasse gardée	Hunting reserve
Court de tennis	Tennis court
Danger d'avalanches	Danger of avalanches
Défense d'entrer sous peine de poursuites	Trespassers will be prosecuted
École de ski	Ski school
Équitation	Horse-riding

sports and activities

Location de skis	Ski hire
Pêche interdite	No fishing
Pétanque	Petanque *(similar to bowls)*
Piscine couverte	Indoor swimming pool
Piscine en plein air	Outdoor swimming pool
Piste	Course, track, ski-run
Plage	Beach
Plage privée	Private beach
Planche à voile	Windsurfing
Premiers secours	First aid
Randonnées	Walks, rambles
Salle de sport	Sports hall
Ski de fond	Cross-country skiing
Ski nautique	Water-skiing
Téléphérique	Cable car
Télésiège	Chair lift
Téléski	Ski lift
Terrain de football	Football pitch
Terrain de golf	Golf course

YOU MAY WANT TO SAY...

- **Can I/we...** Est-ce qu'on peut... *eskawñ puh...*
  - **go riding?** monter à cheval? *mawñtay a shuhval*
  - **go fishing?** pêcher? *payshay*
  - **go skiing?** skier? *skeeay*
  - **go swimming?** nager? *najay*

- **Where can I/we...** Où est-ce qu'on peut... *oo eskawñ puh...*
  - **play tennis?** jouer au tennis? *jooay oh tenees*
  - **play golf?** jouer au golf? *jooay oh golf*

- I'm...
  a beginner
  quite good

  Je suis...
  débutant(e)
  assez bon(ne)

  juh swee...
  daybewtoñ(t)
  asay bawñ/bon

- How much
  does it cost...
  per hour?
  per day?
  per week?
  per round?

  C'est combien...

  de l'heure?
  pour la journée?
  pour la semaine?
  pour un tour?

  say kawñbyañ...

  duh luhr
  poor la joornay
  poor la suhmen
  poor uñ toor

- Can I/we hire...

  equipment?
  clubs?
  rackets?

  Est-ce qu'on peut
  louer...
  l'équipement?
  des clubs?
  des raquettes?

  eskawñ puh
  looay...
  laykeepmoñ
  day kluhb
  day raket

- Can I/we have
  lessons?

  Est-ce qu'on
  peut prendre des
  cours?

  eskawñ puh
  proñdr day koor

- Do I/we have
  to be a member?

  Est-ce qu'il faut
  être membre?

  eskeel foh etr
  moñbr

- Can children do
  it too?

  Est-ce que les
  enfants ont le droit
  d'en faire?

  eskuh layz oñfoñ awñ
  luh drwa doñ fer

- Is there a
  reduction for
  children?

  Est-ce qu'il y a une
  réduction pour les
  enfants?

  eskeelya ewn
  raydewksyawñ
  poor layz oñfoñ

- What's...
  the water like?
  the snow like?

  Comment est...
  l'eau?
  la neige?

  komoñ ay...
  loh
  la nej

YOU MAY HEAR...

C'est ... euros de l'heure.	*say ... uhroh duh luhr*	It costs ... euros per hour.
Il y a une caution remboursable de ... euros.	*eelya ewn kohsyawñ roñboorsabl duh ... uhroh*	There's a refundable deposit of ... euros.
C'est complet pour le moment.	*say kawñplay poor luh momoñ*	We're booked up at the moment.
Nous avons de la place demain.	*nooz avawñ duh la plas duhmañ*	We've got places tomorrow.
Quelle taille faites-vous?	*kel tiy fet voo*	What size are you?

✳ at the beach, river or pool

YOU MAY WANT TO SAY...

Can I/we... swim here? swim in the river?	Est-ce qu'on peut... nager ici? nager dans la rivière?	*eskawñ puh... najay eesee najay doñ la reevyer*
Is it dangerous?	Est-ce que c'est dangereux?	*eskuh say doñjruh*
Is it safe for children?	Est-ce que c'est sans danger pour les enfants?	*eskuh say soñ doñjay poor layz oñfoñ*
When is high tide?	À quelle heure est la marée haute?	*a kel uhr e la maray oht*
Is the water clean?	Est-ce que l'eau est propre?	*eskuh loh ay propr*

shops&services

* shopping

If you pay with a credit card, you may be asked to provide some ID for security reasons (a passport or photo driving licence will do).

Chemists have a green cross sign outside. They sell mainly medicines, baby and health products (see **at the chemist's**, page 136). For toiletries and cosmetics, you need to go to a parfumerie.

YOU MAY SEE...

Alimentation	Groceries
Aliments diététiques	Health foods
Antiquités/Antiquaires	Antiques
Appareils électriques	Electrical goods
Articles de cuir	Leather goods
Bijouterie	Jeweller's
Boucherie	Butcher's
Boulangerie	Baker's
Bureau de poste	Post office
Cabine d'essayage	Fitting rooms
Caisse	Cashier
Cave	Wine merchant
Centre commercial	Shopping centre
Charcuterie	Delicatessen
Chaussures	Shoes
Coiffeur	Hairdresser's
Confiserie	Sweet shop
Défense d'entrer	No entry

shops and services

Défense de sortir	No exit
Disques	Records
Droguerie	Toiletries and household items
En promotion	On offer
Entrée	Entrance
Entrée gratuite/libre	Free admission (no obligation to buy)
Épicerie	Grocer's
Épicerie fine	Delicatessen
Fermé	Closed
Grand magasin	Department store
Heures d'ouverture	Business hours
Hypermarché	Hypermarket
Jouets	Toys
Laverie automatique	Launderette
Légumes	Vegetables
Librairie	Bookshop
Libre-service	Self-service shop
Liquidation avant fermeture	Closing down sale
Magasin de photo	Film processing shop
Magasin de vins et spiritueux	Off-licence (wine shop)
Marchand de journaux	Newsagent's
Marché	Market
Meubles	Furniture
Modes	Fashions
Opticien	Optician's
Ouvert	Open
Papeterie	Stationer's
Parfumerie	Perfumery

shopping

Pâtisserie	Cake shop
Pharmacie	Chemist's
Pharmacie de garde	Duty chemist's
Poissonnerie	Fishmonger's
Poste	Post office
Pressing/Teinturerie	Dry cleaner's
Primeurs	Greengrocer's
Quincaillerie	Hardware
Soldes	Sale
Sortie (de secours)	(Emergency) exit
Tabac	Tobacconist's
Timbres	Stamps
Vêtements	Clothes

YOU MAY WANT TO SAY...

- Where is...
  the main shopping street?
  the post office?

  Où est...
  la principale rue commerçante?
  la poste?

  oo ay...
  la prañseepal rew komersoñt
  la post

- Where can I buy...
  a map?

  Où est-ce que je peux acheter...
  une carte?

  oo eskuh juh puh ashuhtay...
  ewn kart

- I'd like...
  that one there
  this one here

  Je voudrais...
  celui-là
  celui-ci

  juh voodray ...
  suhlweela
  suhlweesee

- I'd like two of those, please.

  J'en voudrais deux, s'il vous plaît.

  joñ voodray duh seelvooplay

shops and services

116

- **Have you got...?** Est-ce que vous avez...? *eskuh vooz avay...*

- **How much...** Combien... *kawñbyañ...*
  does it cost? ça coûte? *sa koot*
  do they cost? coûtent-ils? *kooteel*

- **Can you write it down, please?** Pouvez-vous l'écrire, s'il vous plaît? *poovay voo laykreer seelvooplay*

- **I'm just looking.** Je regarde. *juh ruhgard*

- **I'll take it.** Je vais le prendre. *juh vay luh proñdr*

- **Is there a guarantee?** Est-ce qu'il y a une garantie? *eskeelya ewn garoñtee*

- **Can you ... for me?** Est-ce que vous pouvez ... pour moi? *eskuh voo poovay ... poor mwa*
  keep it le garder *luh garday*
  order it le commander *luh komoñday*

- **I need to think about it.** Je vais réfléchir. *juh vay rayflaysheer*

- Je peux vous aider? *juh puh vooz eday* Can I help you?

- C'est ... euros. *say ... uhroh* It costs ... euros.

- Je suis désolée, notre stock est épuisé. *juh swee dayzolay notr stok ay aypweezay* I'm sorry, we've sold out.

- Nous pouvons le commander pour vous. *noo poovawñ luh komoñday poor voo* We can order it for you.

* paying

- **Where do I pay?** Où est-ce qu'on paie? *oo eskawñ pay*

- **Do you take credit cards?** Est-ce que vous acceptez les cartes de crédit? *eskuh vooz axeptay lay kart duh craydee*

- **Can you wrap it, please?** Pourriez-vous l'emballer, s'il vous plaît? *pooryay voo loñbalay seelvooplay*

- **Can I have...** Puis-je avoir... *pweej avwar...*
  - **the receipt?** un reçu? *uñ ruhsew*
  - **a bag?** un sac? *uñ sak*
  - **my change?** ma monnaie? *ma monay*

- **Sorry, I haven't got any change.** Désolé(e), je n'ai pas de monnaie. *dayzolay juh nay pa duh monay*

- Est-ce que vous voulez un paquet? *eskuh voo voolay uñ pakay* **Do you want it wrapped?**

- Est-ce que vous voulez un sac? *eskuh voo voolay uñ sak* **Do you want a bag?**

- Puis-je voir votre carte d'identité, s'il vous plaît? *pweej vwar votr kart deedoñteetay seelvooplay* **Can I see some ID, please?**

- Vous n'avez rien de plus petit? *voo navay ryañ duh plew puhtee* **Have you got anything smaller?** *(money)*

shops and services

118

clothes and shoes, changing rooms

✱ buying clothes and shoes
(see **clothes and shoe sizes**, page 21)

Have you got...	Est-ce que vous avez...	eskuh vooz avay...
the next size up/down?	la taille au dessus/ en dessous?	la tiy oh duhsew/ oñ duhsoo
another colour?	une autre couleur?	ewn ohtr kooluhr
What size is this in British sizes?	C'est quelle taille en taille britannique?	say kel tiy oñ tiy breetaneek
I'm size...	Je fais du...	juh fe dew...
I'm looking for...	Je cherche...	juh shersh...
a shirt	une chemise	ewn shuhmeez
a pair of jeans	un jean	uñ djeen
a jumper	un pull	uñ pewl
a jacket	une veste	ewn vest
A pair of...	Une paire de...	ewn per duh...
trainers	baskets	basket
shoes	chaussures	shohsewr
sandals	sandales	soñdal
Where are the changing rooms, please?	Où sont les cabines d'essayage, s'il vous plaît?	oo sawñ lay kabeen desayyaj seelvooplay

✱ changing rooms

Can I try this on, please?	Est-ce que je peux l'essayer, s'il vous plaît?	eskuh juh puh lesayyay seelvooplay

shops and services

119

changing things

- **It doesn't fit.** Ça ne va pas. *sa nuh va pa*
- **It's too big/small.** C'est trop grand/ *se tro groñ/puhtee* petit.
- **It doesn't suit me.** Ça ne me va pas. *sa nuh muh va pa*

- Est-ce que vous voulez l'essayer/ les essayer? *eskuh voo voolay lesayyay/layz esayyay* Would you like to try it/them on?

- Quelle taille faites-vous? *kel tiy fet voo* What size are you?

- Je vais vous en chercher une autre. *juh vay vooz oñ shershay uñ nohtr* I'll get you another one.

- Désolé(e), c'est le dernier. *dayzolay say luh dernyay* Sorry, that's the last one.

- Il vous va/Ils vous vont bien. *eel voo va/eel voo vawñ byañ* It suits/They suit you.

✳ changing things

- **Excuse me...** Pardon... *pardawñ...*
  this is faulty il y a un défaut *eelya uñ dayfoh*
  this doesn't fit ça ne va pas *sa nuh va pa*

- **I'd like...** Je voudrais... *juh voodray...*
  a refund un remboursement *uñ romborsemoñ*
  a new one un neuf *uñ nuhf*

- I'd like... | Je voudrais... | *juh voodray...*
  - to return this | vous rendre ça | *voo roñdr sa*
  - to change this | échanger ça | *ayshoñjay sa*

YOU MAY HEAR...

- Est-ce que vous avez... | *eskuh vooz avay...* | Have you got...
  - le reçu? | *luh resew* | the receipt?
  - la garantie? | *la garoñtee* | the guarantee?
- Désolé(e), nous ne faisons pas de remboursement. | *dayzolay noo nuh fuhsawñ pa duh romborsemoñ* | Sorry, we don't give refunds.

* bargaining

YOU MAY WANT TO SAY...

- Is this your best price? | Est-ce que c'est votre meilleur prix? | *eskuh say votr mayyuhr pree*

- It's too expensive. | C'est trop cher. | *say tro sher*

- Is there a reduction for cash? | Vous faites une réduction si on paie en espèces? | *voo fet ewn raydewxyawñ see awñ pay oñ espes*

- I'll give you... | Je vous offre... | *juh vooz ofr...*

- That's my final offer. | C'est mon dernier prix. | *say mawñ dernyay pree*

✳ at the drugstore
(see **at the chemist's**, page 136)

● Although you may find some toiletries and cosmetics at the chemist's, these are usually medicated or for special conditions. For toiletries and cosmetics, perfumes, creams, etc. you need a parfumerie or droguerie.

YOU MAY WANT TO SAY...

● I need...
shampoo
shower gel
deodorant
moisturising
cream
toothpaste
tampons
sanitary towels

toilet paper

aftersun
some mascara

Je voudrais...
du shampooing
du gel douche
du déodorant
de la crème
hydratante
du dentifrice
des tampons
des serviettes
hygiéniques
du papier
hygiénique
du lait après-soleil
du mascara

juh voodray...
dew shoñpwañ
dew jel doosh
dew dayodoroñ
duh la krem
eedratoñt
dew doñteefrees
day tompoñ
day servyet
eejyayneek
dew papyay
eejyayneek
dew lay apresolay
dew mascara

● I am looking for...
perfume
(pink) nail
varnish

Je cherche...
du parfum
du vernis à ongles
(rose)

juh shersh...
dew parfuñ
dew vernee a awñgl
(rohz)

● I'd like some...
foundation
make-up
remover

Je voudrais...
du fond de teint
du démaquillant

juh voodray...
dew foñ duh tañ
dew daymakeeyoñ

* photography

- **Can you develop this film for me?** — Est-ce que vous pouvez développer cette pellicule? — *eskuh voo poovay dayvuhlopay set peleekewl*

- **I have a digital camera.** — J'ai un appareil photo numérique. — *jay uñ naparayy fohtoh newmayreek*

- **Can you print from this memory card?** — Est-ce que vous pouvez imprimer à partir de cette carte mémoire? — *eskuh voo poovay añpreemay a parteer duh set kart maymwar*

- **When will it be ready?** — Quand est-ce que ce sera prêt? — *koñteskuh suh suhra pre*

- **When will they be ready?** — Quand est-ce qu'elles seront prêtes? — *koñteskel suhrawñ pret*

- **Do you have an express service?** — Est-ce que vous avez un service rapide? — *eskuh vooz avay uñ servees rapeed*

- **Does it cost extra?** — Est-ce que ça coûte plus cher? — *eskuh sa koot plew sher*

- **How much does it cost...** — Combien ça coûte... — *kawñbyañ sa koot...*
  - per film? — par pellicule? — *par peleekewl*
  - per print? — par tirage? — *par teeraj*

- **I need...** — J'ai besoin... — *jay buhswañ...*
  - a colour film — d'une pellicule couleur — *dewn peleekewl kooluhr*
  - a black and white film — d'une pellicule noir et blanc — *dewn peleekewl nwar ay bloñ*
  - a memory card — d'une carte mémoire — *dewn kart maymwar*

photography

- **I'd like a ... film.** — Je voudrais une pellicule... — *juh voodray ewn peleekewl...*

  24 exposure — 24 poses — *vañt katr pohz*
  36 exposure — 36 poses — *troñt see pohz*

- **I'd like to buy a disposable camera, please.** — Je voudrais un appareil jetable, s'il vous plaît. — *juh voodray uñ naparayy juhtabl seelvooplay*

- **My camera is broken.** — Mon appareil est cassé. — *mawñ naparayy ay kasay*

- **Do you do repairs?** — Est-ce que vous faites des réparations? — *eskuh voo fet day rayparasyawñ*

YOU MAY HEAR...

- En quel format voulez-vous vos tirages? — *oñ kel forma voolay voo voh teeraj* — **What size do you want your prints?**

- Est-ce que vous les voulez mats ou brillants? — *eskuh voo lay voolay mat oo breeyoñ* — **Do you want them matt or gloss?**

- Revenez... — *ruhvuhnay...* — **Come back...**
  demain — *duhmañ* — tomorrow
  dans une heure — *doñz ewn uhr* — in an hour

- Combien de poses voulez-vous? — *kawñbyañ duh pohz voolay voo* — **How many exposures do you want?**

- Quelle vitesse de pellicule voulez-vous? — *kel veetes duh peleekewl voolay voo* — **What speed film do you want?**

✱ at the tobacconist's

● Cigarettes and tobacco are sold in bureaux de tabac – they have the sign Tabac (and a red sign outside, usually lit). (You can also get cigarettes from Bar-tabac.) Bureaux de tabac also sell stamps, magazines, phone cards (both for telephone boxes and pay-as-you-go mobile phones), and sometimes bus tickets.

YOU MAY WANT TO SAY...

● **Can I have...** — Je voudrais... — *juh voodray...*
a packet of... — un paquet de... — *uñ pakay duh...*
two cartons of... — deux cartouches de... — *duh kartoosh duh...*

● **Do you have matches/lighters?** — Est-ce que vous avez des allumettes/des briquets? — *eskuh vooz avay dayz alewmet/day breekay*

● **Do you have any cigars?** — Avez-vous des cigares? — *avay voo day seegar*

● **One stamp for...** — Un timbre pour... — *uñ tañbr poor...*
Five stamps for... — Cinq timbres pour... — *sañk tañbr poor...*
Great Britain — la Grande-Bretagne — *la groñd bruhtany*
America — les États-Unis — *layz aytazewnee*

✱ at the post office

● Post offices in the various countries are open all day, Monday to Friday. In Belgium, opening hours are 9am to 5pm; in Luxembourg, 8am to 5pm; and in Switzerland, 7.30am to 6.30pm (Saturdays till 11am). Post boxes are painted yellow in all the countries except Belgium, where they're red.

at the post office

YOU MAY WANT TO SAY...

- **One stamp for...** Un timbre pour... *uñ tañbr poor...*
  Five stamps for... Cinq timbres pour... *sañk tañbr poor...*
  Great Britain la Grande-Bretagne *la groñd bruhtany*
  America les États-Unis *layz aytazewnee*
  for postcards/ pour cartes *poor kart postal/*
  letters postales/lettres *letr*

- **Can I send this...** Est-ce que je peux *eskuh juh puh*
  envoyer ça... *oñvwayay sa...*
  registered? en recommandé? *oñ ruhkomoñday*
  airmail? par avion? *par avyawñ*

- **It contains...** Il contient... *eel kawñtyañ...*

- **Do you change** Est-ce que vous *eskuh voo shoñjay*
  money here? changez l'argent ici? *larjoñ eesee*

- **Can I have a** Est-ce que je peux *eskuh juh puh*
  receipt, please? avoir un reçu, s'il *avwar uñ ruhsew*
  vous plaît? *seelvooplay*

YOU MAY HEAR...

- Pour cartes *poor kart postal oo* **For postcards or**
  postales ou lettres? *letr* **letters?**

- Mettez-le sur la *metay luh sewr la* **Put it on the scales,**
  balance, s'il vous *baloñs seelvooplay* **please.**
  plaît.

- Qu'est-ce qu'il *keskeel kawñtyañ* **What's in it?**
  contient?

- Veuillez remplir *vuhyay roñpleer* **Please fill in this**
  ce formulaire de *suh formewler duh* **customs declaration**
  déclaration en *dayklarasyawñ oñ* **form.**
  douane. *dwan*

✳ at the bank

● The unit of currency in France, Belgium and Luxembourg is the euro, and in Switzerland it's the Swiss franc.

● Most cash dispensers will offer you a choice of languages. You may have to pay a fee to use them.

YOU MAY WANT TO SAY...

Where's the foreign exchange counter, please?	Pardon, où est le comptoir de change?	pardawñ oo ay luh kawñtwar duh shoñj
Is there a cashpoint machine here?	Est-ce qu'il y a un distributeur de billets par ici?	eskeelya uñ deestreebewtuhr duh beeyay par eesee
The cashpoint machine has eaten my card.	Le distributeur de billets a avalé ma carte.	luh deestreebewtuhr duh beeyay a avalay ma kart
I've forgotten my PIN.	J'ai oublié mon code secret.	jay oobleeay mawñ kod suhkray
Can I check my account, please?	Est-ce que je peux vérifier mon compte, s'il vous plaît?	eskuh juh puh vayreefyay mawñ kawñt seelvooplay
My account number is...	Mon numéro de compte est le...	mawñ newmayroh duh kawñt ay luh...
My name is...	Je m'appelle...	juh mapel...
I'd like to...	Je voudrais...	juh voodray...
withdraw some money	retirer de l'argent	ruhteeray duh larjoñ
pay some money in	déposer de l'argent sur mon compte	daypohzay duh larjoñ sewr mawñ kawñt
cash this cheque	encaisser ce chèque	oñkesay suh shek

shops and services

127

changing money

Has my money arrived yet?	Est-ce que mon argent est arrivé?	*eskuh mawñ narjoñ et areevay*

YOU MAY HEAR...

Votre carte d'identité, s'il vous plaît.	*votr kart deedoñteetay seelvooplay*	**Your ID, please.**
Votre passeport, s'il vous plaît.	*votr paspor seelvooplay*	**Your passport, please.**
Votre solde est...	*vohtr sohld ay...*	**Your balance is...**
Vous avez un découvert de...	*vooz avay uñ daykoover duh...*	**You're overdrawn by...**

✳ changing money

● You can change travellers' cheques and money in banks, post offices and bureaux de change.

YOU MAY WANT TO SAY...

● **I'd like to change...**	Je voudrais changer...	*juh voodray shoñjay...*
these travellers' cheques	ces chèques de voyage	*say shek duh vwayaj*
£100	cent livres	*soñ leevr*
● **Could I have...**	Est-ce que je pourrais avoir...	*eskuh juh pooray avwar...*
small notes	des petites coupures?	*day puhteet koopewr*
new notes	des billets neufs?	*day beeyay nuhf*
some change?	de la monnaie?	*duh la monay*

● **Can I get money out on my credit card?**	Est-ce que je peux retirer de l'argent avec ma carte de crédit?	*eskuh juh puh ruhteeray duh larjoñ avek ma kart duh craydee*
● **What's the rate today for...**	Quel est le taux d'aujourd'hui pour...	*kel ay luh toh dohjoordwee poor...*
the pound?	la livre?	*la leevr*
the dollar?	le dollar?	*luh dolar*
the euro?	l'euro?	*luhroh*

YOU MAY HEAR...

● Combien?	*kawñbyañ*	**How much?**
● Votre passeport, s'il vous plaît.	*votr paspor seelvooplay*	**Your passport, please.**
● Signez ici, s'il vous plaît.	*seenyay eesee seelvooplay*	**Sign here, please.**
● C'est ... euros pour une livre.	*se ... uhroh poor ewn leevr*	**It's ... euros to the pound.**

✴ telephones

● To call abroad, first dial 00, then the code for the country – for the UK it's 44. Follow this with the town code minus the 0 and then the number you want. For example: for a central London number, dial 00 44 207, then the number.

EMERGENCY TELEPHONE NUMBERS

Country	Police	Fire	Ambulance
France	17	18	15
Belgium	101	100	100
Luxembourg	113	112	112
Switzerland	117	118	144

YOU MAY WANT TO SAY...

- Where's the (nearest) phone?
  Où est la cabine téléphonique (la plus proche)?
  oo ay la kabeen taylayfoneek (la plew prosh)

- Is there a public phone?
  Est-ce qu'il y a une cabine téléphonique?
  eskeelya ewn kabeen taylayfoneek

- Have you got change for the phone, please?
  Est-ce que vous avez de la monnaie pour le téléphone, s'il vous plaît?
  eskuh vooz avay duh la monay poor luh taylayfon seelvooplay

- I'd like to...
  Je voudrais...
  juh voodray...
  - buy a phone card
    acheter une carte de téléphone
    ashuhtay ewn kart duh taylayfon
  - call England
    appeler l'Angleterre
    aplay loñgluhter
  - make a reverse charge call
    appeler en PCV
    aplay oñ paysayvay

- The number is...
  Le numéro est le...
  luh newmayroh ay luh...

- How much does it cost per minute?
  C'est combien la minute?
  say kawñbyañ la meenewt

telephones

What's the ... for?	Quel est l'indicatif...	*kel ay lañdeekateef...*
area code	de zone pour...?	*duh zohn poor...*
country code	national pour...?	*nasyonal poor...*
How do I get an outside line?	Qu'est-ce que je dois faire pour avoir une ligne externe?	*keskuh juh dwa fer poor avvwar ewn leeny extern*
Hello.	Âllo.	*aloh*
It's ... speaking.	C'est ... à l'appareil.	*say ... a laparey*
Can I have extension ... please?	Puis-je avoir le poste ... s'il vous plaît?	*pweej avwar luh post ... seelvooplay*
Can I speak to...?	Puis-je parler à...?	*pweej parlay a...*
When will he/she be back?	Quand est-ce qu'il/elle sera de retour?	*koñteskeel/el suhra duh ruhtoor*
I'll ring back.	Je rappellerai.	*juh rapelray*
Can I leave a message?	Puis-je laisser un message?	*pweej laysay uñ mesaj*
Can you say ... called?	Pouvez-vous dire que ... a appelé?	*poovay voo deer kuh ... a aplay*
My number is...	Mon numéro est le...	*mawñ newmayroh ay le...*
Sorry, I've got the wrong number.	Désolé(e), je me suis trompé(e) de numéro.	*dayzolay juh muh swee trawñpay duh newmayroh*
It's a bad line.	La ligne est mauvaise.	*la liny ay movez*
I've been cut off.	J'ai été coupé(e).	*jay aytay koopay*

YOU MAY HEAR...

Âllo.	*aloh*	Hello.
C'est moi.	*say mwa*	Speaking.
Qui est-ce?	*kee es*	Who's calling?
Désolé(e), il/elle n'est pas là.	*dayzolay eel/el ne pa la*	Sorry, he/she's not here.
Patientez un instant.	*pasyoñtay uñ nañstoñ*	Hang on a minute.
C'est occupé.	*say tokewpay*	It's engaged.
Est-ce que vous voulez patienter?	*eskuh voo voolay pasyoñtay*	Do you want to hold?
Désolé(e), vous vous êtes trompé(e) de numéro.	*dayzolay voo vooz et trawñpay duh newmayroh*	Sorry, you've got the wrong number.

* mobiles

If your phone is not barred for international use (check with your service provider before leaving the UK), you should not have any problem using your mobile in France. Some UK companies also operate in France, so you may be able to use your usual service provider. Otherwise your mobile will connect to one of the local networks.

YOU MAY WANT TO SAY...

Have you got... a charger for this phone?	Est-ce que vous avez... un chargeur pour ce téléphone?	*eskuh vooz avay... uñ sharjuhr poor suh taylayfon*

a SIM card for the local network?	une carte SIM pour le réseau local?	ewn kart seem poor luh rayzoh lokal
a pay-as-you-go phone?	un téléphone à carte?	uñ taylayfon a kart
Can I hire a mobile?	Est-ce je peux louer un téléphone portable?	eskuh juh puh looay uñ taylayfon portabl
What's the tariff?	Quel est le tarif?	kel ay luh tareef
Are text messages included?	Est-ce que les SMS sont inclus?	eskuh layz esemes sawñ tañklew
How do you make a local call?	Comment est-ce qu'on fait un appel local?	komoñ eskawñ fay uñ napel lokal
Is there a code?	Est-ce qu'il y a un code?	eskeelya uñ kod
How do you send text messages?	Comment est-ce qu'on envoie un SMS?	komoñ eskawñ noñvwa uñ esemes

* the internet

YOU MAY WANT TO SAY...

Is there an internet café near here?	Est-ce qu'il y a un cybercafé par ici?	eskeelya uñ seeberkafay par eesee
I'd like to... log on check my emails	Je voudrais... me connecter vérifier mes e-mails	juh voodray... muh konektay vayreefyay mayz eemel

shops and services

133

- How much is it per minute?
C'est combien la minute?
say kawñbyañ la meenewt

- I can't...
get in
log on
Je ne peux pas...
entrer
me connecter
*juh nuh puh pa...
oñtray
muh konektay*

- It's not connecting.
Il n'y a pas de connexion.
eelnya pa duh konexyawñ

- It's very slow.
C'est très lent.
say tre loñ

- Can you...

print this?
scan this?
Est-ce que vous pouvez...
imprimer ça?
numériser ça?
*eskuh voo poovay...
añpreemay sa
newmayreezay sa*

- Do you have...

a CD rom?
a zip drive?
a UBS lead?
Est-ce que vous avez...
un CD-ROM?
un lecteur ZIP?
un câble USB?
*eskuh vooz avay...
uñ saydayrom
uñ lektuhr zeep
uñ kabl ewesbay*

* faxes

YOU MAY WANT TO SAY...

- What's your fax number?
Quel est votre numéro de fax?
kel ay votr newmayroh duh fax

- Can you send this fax for me, please?
Est-ce que vous pouvez envoyer ce fax pour moi, s'il vous plaît?
eskuh voo poovay oñvwayay suh fax poor mwa seelvooplay

- How much is it?
C'est combien?
say kawñbyañ

health&safety

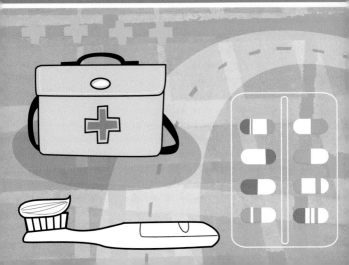

✳ at the chemist's
(see **at the drugstore**, page 122)

● Pharmacies (pharmacie) have a green cross sign outside. They sell mainly medicines, baby and health products. For toiletries and cosmetics, go to a perfumerie or droguerie.

YOU MAY WANT TO SAY...

● **Have you got something for...**	Est-ce que vous avez quelque chose pour...	*eskuh vooz avay kelkuh shohz poor...*
sunburn?	les coups de soleil?	*lay koo duh soley*
diarrhoea?	la diarrhée?	*la dyaray*
headaches?	les maux de tête?	*lay moh duh tet*
stomach ache?	les maux d'estomac?	*lay moh destoma*
a sore throat?	les maux de gorge?	*lay moh duh gorj*
● **I need some...**	J'ai besoin...	*jay buhswañ...*
aspirin	d'aspirine	*daspeereen*
plasters	de pansements	*duh poñsmoñ*
painkillers	de calmants	*duh kalmoñ*
suntan lotion	de lait solaire	*duh lay soler*
condoms	de préservatifs	*duh prayzervateef*
tampons	de tampons	*duh toñpawñ*
sanitary towels	de serviettes hygiéniques	*duh servyet eejyayneek*
● **Can you make up this prescription?**	Est-ce que vous pouvez me faire cette ordonnance?	*eskuh voo poovay muh fer set ordonoñs*

Est-ce que vous avez déjà pris ça avant?	*eskuh vooz avay dayja pree sa avoñ*	**Have you taken this before?**
Est-ce que vous avez une ordonnance?	*eskuh vooz avay ewn ordonoñs*	**Have you got a prescription?**

✳ at the doctor's

YOU MAY WANT TO SAY...

I need a doctor (who speaks English).	J'ai besoin d'un médecin (qui parle anglais).	*jay buhswañ duñ maydsañ (kee parl oñglay)*
Can I make an appointment?	Est-ce que je pourrais avoir un rendez-vous?	*eskuh juh pooray avwar uñ roñdayvoo*
I've run out of my medication.	Je n'ai plus de médicament.	*juh nay plew duh maydeekamoñ*
I'm on medication for...	Je suis un traitement pour...	*juh swee uñ tretmoñ poor...*
I've had a ... jab	J'ai été vacciné(e) contre...	*jay aytay vaxeenay kawñtr...*
tetanus	le tétanos	*luh taytanohs*
typhoid	la typhoïde	*la teefoeed*
rabies	la rage	*la raj*
polio	la polio	*la polyo*
measles	la rougeole	*la roujol*
mumps	les oreillons	*layz oreyawñ*
Can I have a receipt for my health insurance, please?	Est-ce que je pourrais avoir un reçu pour mon assurance médicale, s'il vous plaît?	*eskuh juh pooray avwar uñ ruhsew poor mawñ asewroñs maydeekal seelvooplay*

* describing your symptoms

● To indicate where a pain is, you can simply point and say 'it hurts here' (j'ai mal là). Otherwise, look up the French for the appropriate part of the body on page 141.

YOU MAY WANT TO SAY...

● I don't feel well.	Je ne me sens pas bien.	*juh nuh muh soñ pa byañ*
● It's my...	C'est mon/ma/mes...	*say mawñ/ma/may...*
● It hurts here.	J'ai mal là.	*jay mal la*
● My ... hurt(s).	J'ai mal...	*jay mal...*
stomach	à l'estomac	*a lestoma*
head	à la tête	*a la tet*
ears	aux oreilles	*ohz orey*
feet	aux pieds	*oh pyay*
● I feel...	J'ai...	*jay...*
sick	la nausée	*la nohzay*
dizzy	la tête qui tourne	*la tet kee toorn*
● I can't ...	Je ne peux pas ...	*juh nuh puh pa ...*
properly.	correctement.	*korektuhmoñ*
breathe	respirer	*respeeray*
sleep	dormir	*dormeer*
swallow	avaler	*avalay*
● I've cut myself.	Je me suis coupé(e).	*juh muh swee koopay*
● I've burnt myself.	Je me suis brûlé(e).	*juh muh swee brewlay*
● I've been sick.	J'ai vomi.	*jay vomee*

* medical complaints and conditions

I am...	Je suis...	*juh swee...*
asthmatic	asthmatique	*asmateek*
diabetic	diabétique	*dyabayteek*
epileptic	épileptique	*aypeelepteek*
HIV positive	séropositif/ve	*sayrohpohseeteef/v*
arthritic	arthritique	*artreeteek*
pregnant	enceinte	*oñsañt*
blind	aveugle	*avuhgl*
deaf	sourd(e)	*soor(d)*
I am a wheelchair user.	J'utilise un fauteuil roulant.	*jewteeleez uñ fohtuhy rooloñ*
I have high/low blood pressure.	J'ai une tension élevée/basse.	*jay ewn toñsyawñ aylvay/bas*
I have difficulty walking.	J'ai des problèmes pour marcher.	*jay day problem poor marshay*
I have a heart condition.	J'ai des problèmes de cœur.	*jay day problem duh kuhr*
I am allergic to...	Je suis allergique...	*juh sweez alergeek...*
nuts	aux noix	*oh nwa*
milk	au lait	*oh lay*
antibiotics	aux antibiotiques	*ohz oñteebyoteek*
cortisone	à la cortisone	*a la korteezon*
I suffer from...	Je souffre...	*juh soofr...*
hayfever	du rhume des foins	*dew rewm day fwañ*
angina	d'angine de poitrine	*doñjeen duh pwatreen*

YOU MAY HEAR...

Où avez-vous mal?	*oo avay voo mal*	Where does it hurt?
Vous suivez un traitement?	*voo sweevay uñ tretmoñ*	Are you on medication?
Vous êtes allergique à quelque chose?	*vooz et alerjeek a kelkuh shohz*	Are you allergic to anything?
Déshabillez-vous, s'il vous plaît.	*dayzabeeyay voo seelvooplay*	Get undressed, please.
Ce n'est pas grave.	*suh ne pa grav*	It's nothing serious.
Vous avez une infection.	*vooz avay ewn añfexyawñ*	You've got an infection.
J'ai besoin d'un prélèvement... de sang	*jay buhswañ duñ praylevmoñ... duh soñ*	I need a ... sample. blood
Vous devez faire une radio.	*voo duhvay fer ewn radyoh*	You need an X-ray.
Je vais vous faire... une piqûre	*juh vay voo fer... ewn peekewr*	I'm going to give you... an injection
Prenez ça (trois) fois par jour.	*pruhnay sa (trwa) fwa par joor*	Take this (three) times a day.
Vous devez aller à l'hôpital.	*voo duhvay alay a lopeetal*	You need to go to hospital.
Vous vous êtes... foulé(e)... cassé(e)...	*voo vooz et... foolay... kasay...*	You've ... your... sprained broken
Vous avez... l'appendicite	*vooz avay... lapañdeeseet*	You've got... appendicitis

C'est une crise cardiaque.	*say tewn kreez kardyak*	**It's a heart attack.**

* parts of the body

ankle	la cheville	*la shuhveey*
appendix	l'appendice	*lapañdees*
arm	le bras	*luh bra*
artery	l'artère	*larter*
back	le dos	*luh doh*
bladder	la vessie	*la vesee*
blood	le sang	*luh soñ*
body	le corps	*luh kor*
bone	l'os	*los*
bottom	le derrière	*luh deryer*
bowels	l'intestin	*lañtestañ*
breast	le sein	*luh sañ*
buttock	la fesse	*la fess*
cartilage	le cartilage	*luh karteelaj*
chest	la poitrine	*la pwatreen*
chin	le menton	*luh moñtawñ*
collar bone	la clavicule	*la klaveekewl*
ear	l'oreille	*lorey*
elbow	le coude	*luh kood*
eye	l'œil	*luhy*
face	le visage	*luh veezaj*
finger	le doigt	*luh dwa*
foot	le pied	*luh pyay*
genitals	les organes génitaux	*lorgan jayneetoh*
gland	la glande	*la gloñd*
hair	les cheveux	*lay shuhvuh*

health and safety

hand	la main	la mañ
head	la tête	la tet
heart	le cœur	luh kuhr
heel	le talon	luh talawñ
hip	la hanche	la oñsh
jaw	la mâchoire	la mashwar
joint	l'articulation	larteekewlasyawñ
kidney	le rein	luh rañ
knee	le genou	luh juhnoo
leg	la jambe	la joñb
ligament	le ligament	luh leegamoñ
lip	la lèvre	la levr
liver	le foie	luh fwa
lung	le poumon	luh poomawñ
mouth	la bouche	la boosh
muscle	le muscle	luh mewskl
nail	l'ongle	lawñgl
neck	le cou	luh koo
nerve	le nerf	luh ner
nose	le nez	luh nay
penis	le pénis	luh paynees
rib	la côte	la koht
shoulder	l'épaule	laypohl
skin	la peau	la poh
spine	la colonne vertébrale	la kolon vertaybral
stomach	l'estomac	lestoma
tendon	le tendon	luh toñdawñ
testicle	le testicule	luh testeekewl
throat	la gorge	la gorj
thumb	le pouce	luh poos
toe	le doigt de pied	luh dwa duh pyay
tongue	la langue	la loñg
tonsils	les amygdales	lay ameedal

tooth	la dent	*la doñ*
vagina	le vagin	*luh vajañ*
wrist	le poignet	*luh pwanye*

✱ at the dentist's

I've got toothache.	J'ai mal aux dents.	*jay mal oh doñ*
It really hurts.	Ça fait très mal.	*sa fay tre mal*
It's my wisdom tooth.	C'est ma dent de sagesse.	*say ma doñ duh sajes*
I've lost... a filling a crown/cap	J'ai perdu... un plombage une couronne	*jay perdew... uñ plawñbaj ewn kooron*
I've broken a tooth.	Je me suis cassé(e) une dent.	*juh muh swee kasay ewn doñ*
Can you fix it temporarily?	Pourriez-vous le réparer provisoirement?	*pooryay voo luh rayparay proveeswarmoñ*

Ouvrez grand.	*oovray groñ*	Open wide.
Mordez.	*morday*	Bite your jaws together.
Vous avez besoin d'un plombage.	*vooz avay buhswañ duñ plawñbaj*	You need a filling.

health and safety

143

emergencies

Il faut que je l'arrache.	*eel foh kuh juh larash*	I'll have to take it out.
Je vais vous...	*juh vay voo...*	I'm going to...
faire une piqûre	*fer ewn peekewr*	give you an injection
faire un plombage provisoire	*fer uñ plawñbaj proveeswar*	give you a temporary filling
mettre une couronne provisoire	*metr ewn kooron proveeswar*	give you a temporary crown

* emergencies

EMERGENCY TELEPHONE NUMBERS

Country	Police	Fire	Ambulance
France	17	18	15
Belgium	101	100	100
Luxembourg	113	112	112
Switzerland	117	118	144

YOU MAY WANT TO SAY...

I need...	J'ai besoin...	*jay buhswañ...*
a doctor	d'un médecin	*duñ maydsañ*
an ambulance	d'une ambulance	*dewn oñbewloñs*
the fire brigade	des pompiers	*day pawñpyay*
the police	de la police	*duh la polees*
Immediately!	Immédiatement!	*eemaydyatmoñ*
It's very urgent!	C'est très urgent!	*say trez ewrjoñ*

health and safety

Help!	À l'aide!	*a led*
Please help me/us.	Aidez-moi/nous, s'il vous plaît.	*eday mwa/noo seelvooplay*
There's a fire.	Il y a le feu.	*eelya luh fuh*
There's been an accident.	Il y a eu un accident.	*eelya ew uñ axeedoñ*
It's...	C'est...	*say...*
my wife	ma femme	*ma fam*
my husband	mon mari	*mawñ maree*
my son	mon fils	*mawñ fees*
my daughter	ma fille	*ma feey*
my friend	mon ami(e)	*mawñ namee*
I've been attacked/mugged.	On m'a attaqué(e)/agressé(e).	*awñ ma atakay/agressay*
I have to use the phone.	Il faut que je téléphone.	*eel foh kuh juh taylayfon*
I'm lost.	Je suis perdu(e).	*juh swee perdew*
I've lost...	J'ai perdu...	*jay perdew...*
my son	mon fils	*mawñ fees*
my daughter	ma fille	*ma feey*
my friends	mes amis	*mayz amee*
Stop!	Arrêtez!	*araytay*

YOU MAY HEAR...

Où êtes-vous?	*oo et voo*	**Where are you?**
Quelle est votre adresse?	*kel ay votr adres*	**What's your address?**

health and safety

145

✳ police

YOU MAY WANT TO SAY...

- **Sorry, I didn't realise it was against the law.** Désolé(e), je ne savais pas que c'était illégal. *dayzolay juh nuh savay pa kuh saytay teelaygal*

- **I haven't got my passport on me.** Je n'ai pas mon passeport sur moi. *juh nay pa mawñ paspor sewr mwa*

- **I don't understand.** Je ne comprends pas. *juh nuh kawñproñ pa*

- **I'm innocent.** Je suis innocent(e). *juh sweez eenosoñ(t)*

- **I need a lawyer (who speaks English).** J'ai besoin d'un avocat (qui parle anglais). *jay buhswañ duñ avoka (kee parl oñglay)*

- **I want to contact my embassy/consulate.** Je veux contacter mon ambassade/consulat. *juh vuh kawñtaktay mawñ oñbasad/kawñsewla*

- **Give me back my passport/our passports, please.** Rendez-moi mon passeport/nos passeports, s'il vous plaît. *roñday mwa mawñ paspor/noh paspor seelvooplay*

YOU MAY HEAR...

- Vous devez payer une amende. *voo duhvay payyay ewn amoñd* You have to pay a fine.

- Vos papiers, s'il vous plaît. *voh papyay seelvooplay* Your documents, please.

- Vous êtes en état d'arrestation. *vooz et oñ ayta darestasyawñ* You're under arrest.

✳ reporting crime

Where's the (nearest) police station?	Où est le poste de police (le plus proche)?	oo ay luh post duh polees (luh plew prosh)
I want to report a theft.	Je voudrais déclarer un vol.	juh voodray dayklaray uñ vol
My ... has been stolen.	On m'a volé(e) mon...	awñ ma volay mawñ...
purse	porte-monnaie	portuhmonay
wallet	portefeuille	portuhfuhy
passport	passeport	paspor
bag	sac	sak
Our car has been stolen.	On a volé notre voiture.	awñ na volay notr vwatewr
Our car has been broken into.	On a fracturé notre voiture.	awñ na fraktewray notr vwatewr
I've lost my...	J'ai perdu mes...	jay perdew may...
credit cards	cartes de crédit	kart duh kraydee
luggage	bagages	bagaj
I've been...	On m'a...	awñ ma...
mugged	volé(e)	volay
attacked	attaqué(e)	atakay

Ça s'est passé quand?	sa say pasay koñ	When did it happen?
Où?	oo	Where?

health and safety

reporting crime

Qu'est-ce qui s'est passé?	keskee say pasay	**What happened?**
Vous devrez remplir ce formulaire.	voo duhvray roñpleer suh formewler	**You'll have to fill in this form.**
À quoi il/elle ressemblait?	a kwa eel/el ruhsoñblay	**What did he/she look like?**
À quoi ils ressemblaient?	a kwa eel ruhsoñblay	**What did they look like?**

YOU MAY WANT TO SAY...

It happened...	Ça s'est passé...	sa say pasay...
just now	à l'instant	a lañstoñ
by the (cathedral)	près de (la cathédrale)	pre duh (la kataydral)
on the beach	sur la plage	sewr la plaj
He/She had...	Il/Elle avait...	eel/el avay...
dark/blonde hair	les cheveux foncés/blonds	lay shuhvuh fawñsay/blawñ
a knife	un couteau	uñ kootoh
He/She was...	Il/Elle était...	eel/el aytay...
tall	grand(e)	gran(d)
young	jeune	juhn
short	petit(e)	puhtee(t)
He/She was wearing...	Il/Elle portait...	eel/el portay...
jeans	un jean	uñ djeen
a denim jacket	une veste en jean	ewn vest oñ djeen
a (red) shirt	une chemise (rouge)	ewn shuhmeez (rooj)

basic grammar

✳ nouns

All French nouns have a gender – masculine or feminine.
It's best to learn the gender of each new noun as you
come across it. However, there are some clues to help you
remember:

Most nouns ending in -age, -ment or -oir are masculine.
Most nouns ending in -ance, -ence, -té and -ion are feminine.

For others, it's probably best to check in a dictionary.

Some nouns can be both masculine and feminine. Some
nouns add an e to the masculine form to make the feminine,
e.g. ami (male friend), amie (female friend).

A masculine plural noun can refer to a mixture of masculine
and feminine, e.g.
amis (male friends, or male and female friends)
les Français (French men or the French)

✳ plurals

Nouns are generally made plural by adding s. The s is not
pronounced, so there is no difference in the sound of the
word between singular and plural, e.g.
livre – livres (both pronounced *leevr*)
voiture – voitures (both pronounced *vwatewr*)

The same applies to adjectives, e.g.
blanc – blancs   bleu – bleus

Some nouns add x in the plural, e.g. bateau – bateaux. The x
is not pronounced. Nouns ending in -s, -x or -z do not change.
Nouns ending in -al change to -aux, e.g. animal – animaux.

articles (a, an, the)

The French indefinite article (the equivalent of 'a' or 'an') has different forms: un is used with masculine nouns, une with feminine ones, e.g. un livre, une voiture.

The definite article ('the') has different forms for masculine and feminine singular, but only one form for the plural:

	MASCULINE	FEMININE
singular	le	la
plural	les	les
example:	le livre	la voiture
	les livres	les voitures

Le and la are shortened to l' before any noun beginning with a vowel or h, e.g. l'aspirine, l'hôtel.

In the dictionaries on pages 159 and 199, nouns are marked to show their gender: (m) for masculine and (f) for feminine.

✳ 'à' and 'de'

When à (at, to) and de (of) are followed by the articles le or les, they change:

à + le = au   de + le = du
à + les = aux   de + les = des
e.g. au centre, le pont du Gard

De becomes d' before a word beginning with a vowel or h.

✳ adjectives

Adjectives 'agree' with the nouns they are describing – they have different endings for masculine and feminine, singular and plural. Plurals are formed as described on page 149.

Most adjectives add e to the masculine singular to give the feminine form, e.g.

bleu – bleue   grand – grande   petit – petite

Some adjectives have only one ending for the singular, both masculine and feminine, e.g.

un sac rouge   une voiture rouge

Some adjectives double the final consonant and then add e, e.g. bon – bonne   gros – grosse

Adjectives ending in -f change to -ve for the feminine; and -x changes to -se. e.g.

vif – vive   heureux – heureuse

In the dictionaries on pages 159 and 199, both masculine and feminine forms are shown.

✳ position of adjectives

Most adjectives come after the noun, e.g.

vin blanc   le menu touristique   une chemise bleue

Autre (other) and chaque (each, every) always come before the noun, as do premier/première (first) and other numerical adjectives, e.g.

une autre personne   chaque année   la première fois

✳ comparatives and superlatives
(more, the most)

'More' is plus and 'less' is moins. Both come before the adjective, e.g.

plus intéressant (more interesting)
plus grand (bigger); plus jeune (younger)
moins important (less important)
moins compliqué (less complicated)

The comparatives of 'good' and 'bad' are meilleur (better) and pire (worse).

'Than', as in 'more than' and 'less than', is que, e.g. cette voiture est plus grande que l'autre (this car is bigger than the other).

To say 'the most' or 'the least', put the definite article le or la before plus or moins, e.g.
la région la plus intéressante (the most interesting region)
le/la plus grand(e) du monde (the biggest in the world).

✳ possessives (my, your, his, her, etc.)

Like other adjectives, possessive adjectives 'agree' with the noun they are describing. The forms are:

	SINGULAR		PLURAL
	(m)	(f)	(m/f)
my	mon	ma	mes
your	ton	ta	tes
his/her	son	sa	ses
our	notre		nos
your	votre		vos
their	leur		leurs

e.g. mon frère (my brother), notre maison (our house).

To indicate possession, as in, for example, 'John's brother' or 'John and Susan's house', the word de (of) is used. There is no equivalent of the English 'apostrophe s', e.g.
le frère de John, la maison de John et Susan.

✳ demonstratives (this, that)

The demonstrative pronoun 'this' or 'that' is cela, which is commonly shortened to ça. Demonstrative adjectives used with a noun (as in 'this book') are:

	MASCULINE	FEMININE
this, that	ce	cette
these, those	ces	ces

To distinguish between 'this' and 'that', i.e. something close by and something further away, -ci or -là is added to the noun, e.g. ce livre-ci, ce livre-là.

✳ subject pronouns (I, you, he, she, etc)

I	je (or j' before a verb beginning with a vowel or h)
you *(informal)*	tu
he/she	il/elle
we	nous
you *(plural and formal)*	vous
they	ils (m), elles (f)

'You' In English there is only one way of addressing people – using the word 'you'. In French there are two ways – one is more polite/formal, the other more casual/informal.

Tu is the informal way, and it is used between friends and relatives and people of the same age group, and to children. Tu is used with the second person singular of the verb.

Vous is both the formal way to address someone and the plural of 'you'. It is used with the second person plural of the verb. Most of the phrases in this book use the formal way of saying 'you'.

basic grammar

✳ object pronouns

Direct object pronouns are the equivalent of 'me', 'him', 'it', 'us' etc, e.g.
je le parle bien (I speak it well)
elle les aime (she loves them)

Indirect object pronouns are the equivalent of 'to/for me', 'to/for him', 'to/for us' etc. For example:
pourriez-vous lui donner un message? (could you give (to) him/her a message?)

The full list is:

DIRECT OBJECT		INDIRECT OBJECT	
me	nous	me	nous
te	vous	te	vous
le, la	les	lui	leur

They generally come before the verb. When two object pronouns are used together, the direct object comes first, e.g. je le lui donnerai (I will give it to him/her).

✳ emphatic pronouns

These are used after prepositions, e.g.
à moi (to me), pour toi (for you)
and after commands, e.g.
donnez-moi les clés (give me the keys)

The pronouns are:

PRONOUNS	
moi	nous
toi	vous
lui, elle	eux, elles

basic grammar

✳ verbs

French verbs have different endings according to (i) the subject of the verb, (ii) the tense. There are three main groups of verbs, with different sets of endings for each group.

In dictionaries verbs are listed in the infinitive form, which ends in -er, -ir or -re (these are the three groups). Below are the endings for the present tense of these three groups:

	-ER	-IR	-RE
	parler	**finir**	**vendre**
je	parle	finis	vends
tu	parles	finis	vends
il/elle	parle	finit	vend
nous	parlons	finissons	vendons
vous	parlez	finissez	vendez
ils/elles	parlent	finissent	vendent

The French present tense translates both the English 'I...' and 'I am ...-ing' forms, e.g. je parle means both 'I speak' and 'I am speaking'.

✳ reflexives

Reflexive verbs are listed in dictionaries with the reflexive pronoun se, e.g.
se laver (to wash oneself), s'appeler (to be called).

The reflexive pronouns are:

PRONOUNS	
me	nous
te	vous
se	se

e.g. je me lave, tu te laves, il/elle se lave, etc.

✳ irregular verbs

Some common verbs are irregular. They include:

ÊTRE	AVOIR	ALLER	FAIRE
(to be)	(to have)	(to go)	(to do, to make)
je suis	j'ai	je vais	je fais
tu es	tu as	tu vas	tu fais
il/elle est	il/elle a	il/elle va	il/elle fait
nous sommes	nous avons	nous allons	nous faisons
vous êtes	vous avez	vous allez	vous faites
ils/elles sont	ils/elles ont	ils/elles vont	ils/elles font

VENIR	POUVOIR	VOULOIR
(to come)	(to be able)	(to want)
je viens	je peux	je veux
tu viens	tu peux	tu veux
il/elle vient	il/elle peut	il/elle veut
nous venons	nous pouvons	nous voulons
vous venez	vous pouvez	vous voulez
ils/elles viennent	ils/elles peuvent	ils/elles veulent

✳ other verb tenses

A few verbs in other tenses that you may find useful:

être	I was/have been	j'ai été
(to be)	we were/have been	nous avons été
	I was/used to be	j'étais
	we were/used to be	nous étions
avoir	I had/have had	j'ai eu
(to have)	we had/have had	nous avons eu
	I had/used to have	j'avais
	we had/used to have	nous avions

aller	I went	je suis allé(e)
(to go)	we went	nous sommes allé(e)s
	I used to go	j'allais
	we used to go	nous allions
faire	I did, I made	j'ai fait
(to do, to make)	we did, we made	nous avons fait
	I used to do/make	je faisais
	we used to do/make	nous faisions
venir	I came/have come	je suis venu(e)
(to come)	we came/have come	nous sommes venu(e)s
	I came/used to come	je venais
	we came/used to come	nous venions

As in English, you can talk about the future by using 'I am going to...' using the verb aller, followed by an infinitive, e.g. demain je vais jouer au tennis (tomorrow I am going to play tennis); nous allons visiter Rouen (we are going to visit Rouen). French also has a future tense with another set of verb endings.

✳ negatives

To make a verb negative, put ne before it and pas after it. Ne is shortened to n' before a verb beginning with a vowel or h, e.g.

Je n'ai pas d'enfants. (I don't have any children.)
Je ne comprends pas. (I don't understand.)
Monsieur Dupont n'est pas là. (Mr Dupont isn't in.)

Other words are used instead of pas to mean 'nothing', 'no one', 'never' etc, e.g.

Je ne connais personne. (I know no one, *or*
I don't know anyone.)

Il ne va jamais à l'école. (He never goes to school.)

✳ questions

There are different ways of forming questions in French. Starting with a statement such as vous avez une chambre (you have a room), you can make a question (do you have a room?) as follows:

By adding Est-ce que at the beginning,
e.g. Est-ce que vous avez une chambre?

Or by changing the intonation of the voice – making it rise at the end of the sentence, e.g.
Vous avez une chambre?

(These are the most usual ways.)

Also by changing the word order – that is, swapping the positions of the subject pronoun and the verb, e.g.
Avez-vous une chambre?

English – French dictionary

French nouns are given with their gender in brackets: (m) for masculine and (f) for feminine, (m/f) for those nouns that can be either gender. Other abbreviations: (m/pl) – masculine plural; (f/pl) – feminine plural; (adj.) – adjective.

Where adjectives have different endings or forms for masculine and feminine, the masculine is given first, e.g. bleu(e) (i.e. bleu for masculine, bleue for feminine), courageux/euse (i.e. courageux, courageuse), fou, folle. See **basic grammar**, page 149, for further explanation.

There's a list of **car parts** on page 58 and **parts of the body** on page 141. See also the **menu reader** on page 87, and **numbers** on page 14.

A

a, an un, une *uñ, ewn*

abbey abbaye (f) *abayee*

about *(relating to)* à propos de, sur *a prohpoh duh, sewr*
(approximately) environ *oñveerawñ*

above au-dessus, ci-dessus, en haut *oh duhsew, si duhsew, oñ oh*

abroad à l'étranger *a laytroñjay*

abscess abcès (m) *abse*

to accept *(take)* accepter, recevoir *axeptay, ruhsuhvwar*

accident accident (m) *axeedoñ*

accommodation logement (m), chambre (f) *lojmoñ, shoñbr*

account *(bank)* compte (bancaire) (m) *kawñt (boñkair)*

ache douleur (f) *dooluhr*

across à travers *a traver*
(opposite) en face *oñ fas*

to act jouer *jooay*

actor acteur/trice *akturh/trees*

adaptor adaptateur (m) *adaptatuhr*

addicted dépendant(e) *daypoñdoñ(t)*

address adresse (f) *adres*

admission entrée (f) *oñtray*
» **admission charge** droits (m/pl) d'entrée *drwa doñtray*

adopted adopté(e) *adoptay*

adult adulte (m/f) *adewlt*

advance avance (f) *avoñs*
» **in advance** en/par avance *oñ/par avoñs*

advanced *(level)* (niveau) avancé(e) *(neevoh) avoñsay*

advertisement, advertising publicité (f) *pewbleeseetay*

aerial antenne (f) *oñten*

aeroplane avion (m) *avyawñ*

to afford se permettre *suh permetr*
» **I can't afford it** je ne peux pas me permettre *juh nuh puh pa muh permetr*

afraid effrayé(e) *efreyay*
» **I'm afraid** j'ai peur *jay puhr*
after après *apre*
afternoon après-midi (m/f) *apremeedee*
aftershave après-rasage (m) *aprerazaj*
afterwards après *apre*
again encore *oñkor*
against contre *kawñtr*
age âge (m) *aj*
agency agence (f) *ajoñs*
ago il y a *eelya*
to agree être d'accord *etr dakor*
AIDS SIDA (m) *seeda*
air air (m) *er*
» **by air, air mail** par avion *par avyawñ*
air conditioning climatisation (f),
air conditionné (m) *kleemateezasyawñ,*
er kawñdeesyonay
air force armée de l'air (f) *armay duh ler*
airline compagnie aérienne (f)
kawñpanee aayryen
airport aéroport (m) *aayropor*
aisle couloir (m) *koolwar*
alarm alarme (f) *alarm*
» **alarm clock** réveil (m) *rayvey*
alcohol alcool (m) *alkol*
alcoholic *(content)* alcoolique
alkoleek (person) alcoolique (m/f)
alkoleek
alive vivant(e) *veevoñ(t)*
all tout, tous, toutes *too, toos, toot*
allergic to allergique à *alerjeek a*
to allow permettre *permetr*
allowed permis(e) *permee(z)*
all right *(OK)* d'accord, OK *dakor, okay*
alone seul(e) *suhl*
along le long de *luh lawñ duh*
already déjà *dayja*
also aussi *ohsee*
although bien que *byañ kuh*
always toujours *toojoor*
ambassador ambassadeur/drice
oñbasaduhr/drees
ambition ambition (f) *oñbeesyawñ*

ambitious ambitieux/se *oñbeesyeuh(z)*
ambulance ambulance (f) *oñbewloñs*
among parmi *parmee*
amount *(total)* montant (m) *mawñtoñ*
anaesthetic *(local)* anesthésie (locale)
(f) *anestaysee (lokal)* (general)
(générale) *jaynayral*
and et *e*
angry en colère *oñ koler*
animal animal (m) *aneemal*
ankle cheville (f) *shuhveey*
anniversary anniversaire (m) *aneeverser*
annoyed fâché(e) *fashay*
another un(e) autre *uñ (ewn) ohtr*
answer réponse (f) *raypawñs*
to answer répondre *raypawñdr*
antibiotic antibiotique (m) *oñteebyoteek*
antifreeze antigel (m) *oñteejel*
antique antiquité (f) *oñteekeetay*
antiseptic antiseptique (m) *oñteesepteek*
any *(some)* quelque(s) *kelkuh*
anyone *(someone)* quelqu'un *kelkuñ*
anything *(something)* quelque chose
kelkuh shohz
» **anything else?** autre chose? *ohtr*
shohz
anyway de toute façon *duh toot fasawñ*
anywhere n'importe où *nañport oo*
apart (from) à part *a par*
apartment appartement (m) *apartuhmoñ*
appendicitis appendicite (f) *apañdeeseet*
apple pomme (f) *pom*
appointment rendez-vous (m) *roñdayvoo*
approximately environ *oñveerawñ*
arch arche (f) *arsh*
archaeology archéologie (f) *arkayolojee*
architect architecte (m/f) *arsheetekt*
area zone, aire (f) *zohn, er*
argument dispute (f) *deespewt*
armbands *(swimming)* flotteurs (m/pl)
flotuhr
army armée (f) *armay*
around autour (de) *ohtoor (duh)*
to arrange *(fix)* arranger *aroñjay*

arrest arrestation (f) *arestasyawñ*
 » **under arrest** en état d'arrestation *oñ nayta darestasyawñ*
arrival arrivée (f) *areevay*
to **arrive** arriver *areevay*
art art (m) *ar*
 » **art gallery** galerie (f) d'art *galuhree dar*
 » **fine arts** beaux-arts (m/pl) *bohz ar*
arthritis arthrite (f) *artreet*
article article (m) *arteekl*
artificial artificiel(le) *arteefeesyel*
artist artiste (m/f) *arteest*
as *(like)* comme *kom*
ashtray cendrier (m) *soñdreeay*
to **ask** demander *duhmoñday*
aspirin aspirine (f) *aspeereen*
assistant assisant(e) *aseestoñ(t)*
asthma asthme (m) *asm*
at à *a*
atmosphere atmosphère (f) *atmosfer*
to **attack** attaquer *atakay*
 (mug) voler *volay*
attractive attirant(e) *ateeroñ(t)*
auction enchère (f) *oñsher*
aunt tante (f) *toñt*
author auteur (m) *ohtuhr*
automatic automatique *ohtomateek*
autumn automne (m) *ohtom*
avalanche avalanche (f) *avaloñsh*
to **avoid** éviter *ayveetay*
away loin *lwañ*
awful affreux/se *afruh(z)*

B

baby bébé (m) *baybay*
 » **baby food** nourriture (f) pour bébé *nooreetewr poor baybay*
 » **baby wipes** lingettes (f/pl) pour bébé *lañjet poor baybay*
baby's bottle biberon (m) *beebrawñ*
babysitter babysitter (m/f) *babeeseetur*
back *(reverse side)* dos (m), envers (m) *doh, oñver*

back dos (m) *doh*
 » **at the back** à l'arrière *a larryair*
backwards en arrière *oñ naryer*
bacon bacon (m) *baykon*
bad mauvais(e) *mohve(z)*
bag sac (m) *sak*
baggage bagage (m) *bagaj*
baker's boulangerie (f) *booloñjree*
balcony *(theatre etc.)* balcon (m) *balkawñ*
bald chauve *shohv*
ball *(large)* ballon (m), *(small)* balle (f) *balawñ, bal*
ballet ballet (m) *balay*
ballpoint pen stylo à bille (m) *steelo a beey*
banana banane (f) *banan*
band *(music)* groupe (m) *groop*
bandage bande (f), bandage (m) *boñd, boñdaj*
bank *(money)* banque (f) *boñk*
banker banquier (m) *boñkyay*
bar bar (m) *bar*
barber's coiffeur (m) *kwafurh*
bargain affaire (f) *afer*
baseball baseball (m) *bayzbohl*
basement sous-sol (m) *soosol*
basin *(sink)* évier (m), lavabo (m) *ayvyay, lavaboh*
basket panier (m) *panyay*
basketball basket (m) *basket*
bath bain (m) *bañ*
 » **to have a bath** prendre un bain *proñdr uñ bañ*
 » **to bathe** se baigner *baynyay*
bathing costume maillot de bain (m) *miyoh duh bañ*
bathroom salle de bains (f) *sal duh bañ*
battery pile (f) *peel* *(car)* batterie (f) *batree*
bay baie (f) *bay*
to **be** être *etr* (see grammar, page 156)
beach plage (f) *plaj*
beans haricots (m/pl) *areeko*

beard barbe (f) *barb*

beautiful beau, belle *boh, bel*

because parce que *parskuh*

bed lit (m) *lee*

bedroom chambre (f) *shoñbr*

bee abeille (f) *abey*

beef bœuf (m) *buhf*

beer bière (f) *byer*

before avant *avoñ*

to **begin** commencer *komoñsay*

beginner débutant(e) *daybewtoñ(t)*

beginning commencement *komoñsmoñ*

behind derrière *deryer*

beige beige *bej*

Belgian belge *belj*

Belgium Belgique (f) *beljeek*

to **believe** croire *krwar*

bell cloche (f) *klosh,* (door) sonnette (f) *sonet*

to **belong to** appartenir à *apartuhneer a*

below en bas *oñ ba* (beneath) sous *soo*

belt ceinture (f) *sañtewr*

bend virage (m) *veeraj*

bent tordu(e) *tordew*

berry baie (f) *bay*

berth couchette (f) *kooshet* (on ship) mouillage (m) *mooyaj*

besides en plus *oñ plews*

best meilleur(e) *meyuhr*

better mieux *myuh*

between entre *oñtr*

beyond au-delà (de) *oh duhla (duh)*

bib bavette (f) *bavet*

bicycle vélo (m) *vayloh*

big gros(se) *groh(s)*

bigger plus gros(se) *plew groh(s)*

bill addition (f) *adeesyawñ*

bin (rubbish) poubelle (f) *poobel*

  » **bin liners** sacs (m/pl) poubelle *sak poobel*

binding (ski) fixation (f) *feexasyawñ*

binoculars jumelles (f/pl) *jewmel*

bird oiseau (m) *wazoh*

birthday anniversaire (m) *aneeverser*

bishop évêque (m) *ayvek*

bit morceau (m) *morsoh*

  » **a bit** un peu *uñ puh*

to **bite** mordre *mordr*

black noir(e) *nwar*

  » **black and white** (film) noir et blanc *nwar e bloñ*

  » **black coffee** café noir (m) *kafay nwar*

blackcurrant cassis (m) *kasees*

blanket couverture (f) *koovertewr*

to **bleed** saigner *saynyay*

blind aveugle *avuhgl*

blister ampoule (f) *oñpool*

blocked (pipe etc.) bouché(e) *boushay* (road) bloqué(e) *blokay*

blonde blond(e) *blawñ(d)*

blood sang (m) *soñ*

blouse chemisier (m) *shumeesyay*

to **blow-dry** faire un brushing *fer uñ brushing*

blue bleu(e) *bluh*

blusher fard à joues (m) *far a joo*

to **board** embarquer *oñbarkay*

  » **boarding card** carte d'embarquement (f) *kart doñbarkuhmoñ*

boat bateau (m) *batoh*

  » **boat trip** voyage en bateau (m) *vwiyaj oñ batoh*

body corps (m) *kor*

to **boil** bouillir *booyeer*

boiled egg œuf cuit dur (m) *uhf kwee dewr*

boiler chauffe-eau (m) *shohfoh*

bomb bombe (f) *bawñb*

bone os (m) *os*

book livre (m) *leevr* (of train/bus tickets) carnet (m) *karnay*

to **book** réserver *rayzervay*

booking réservation (f) *rayzervasyawñ*

  » **booking office** (rail) bureau de réservations (m) *bewroh duh rayzervasyawñ,* (theatre) bureau de location (m), guichet (m) *bewroh duh lokasyawñ, geeshay*

bookshop librairie (f) *leebrayree*

boot *(shoe)* botte, bottine (f) *bot, boteen*

border *(edge)* bord (m) *bor*
　(frontier) frontière (f) *frawñtyer*

boring ennuyeux/se *oñnweeyuh(z)*

both *(tous/toutes)* les deux *(too/toot) lay duh*

bottle bouteille (f) *bootey*

bottle opener ouvre-bouteilles (m) *oovrbootey*

bottom fond (m) *fawñ*
　(body) derrière (m) *deryer*

bow *(ship)* avant (m) *avoñt*

bow *(knot)* nœud (m) *nuh*

bowl bol (m) *bol*

box boîte (f) *bwat* *(theatre)* loge (f) *loj*

box office guichet (m) *geeshay*

boy garçon (m) *garsawñ*

boyfriend petit ami (m) *puhteetamee*

bra soutien-gorge (m) *sootyañgorj*

bracelet bracelet (m) *braslay*

brain cerveau (m) *servoh*

branch *(bank etc.)* succursale (f) *sewkewrsal*

brand marque (f) *mark*

brandy cognac (m) *konyak*

brave courageux/se *koorajuh(z)*

bread pain (m) *pañ*
　» **bread roll** petit pain (m) *puhtee pañ*
　» **wholemeal bread** pain complet (m) *pañ kawñplay*

to **break** *(inc. limb)* casser *kasay*

to **break down** tomber en panne *tawñbay oñ pan*

breakdown truck dépanneuse (f) *daypanuhz*

breakfast petit déjeuner (m) *puhtee dayjuhnay*

to **breathe** respirer *respeeray*

bride mariée (f) *maryay*

bridegroom marié (m) *maryay*

bridge pont (m) *pawñ*

briefcase serviette (f) *serviet*

bright *(colour)* vif, vive *veef, vive*
　(light) clair(e) *kler*

to **bring** apporter *aportay*

British Britannique *breetaneek*

broad large *larj*

brochure brochure (f) *broshewr*

broken cassé(e) *kasay*

bronchitis bronchite (f) *brawñsheet*

brooch broche (f) *brosh*

broom balai (m) *balay*

brother frère (m) *frer*

brother-in-law beau-frère (m) *bohfrer*

brown marron *marawñ*

bruise bleu (m) *bluh*

brush brosse (f) *bros*

bucket seau (m) *soh*

buffet buffet (m) *bewfay*

to **build** construire *kawñstrweer*

builder constructeur (m) *kawñstrewktuhr*

building bâtiment (m) *bateemoñ*

building site chantier (m) *shoñtyay*

bulb *(light)* ampoule (f) *oñpool*

bull taureau (m) *tohroh*

bumper *(car)* pare-chocs (m) *parshok*

burn brûlure (f) *brewlewr*

to **burn** brûler *brewlay*

burnt *(food)* brûlé(e) *brewlay*

bus bus (m) *bews*
　» **by bus** en bus *en bews*

bus-driver chauffeur de bus (m) *shohfuhr duh bews*

bush buisson (m) *bweesawñ*

business entreprise (f) *oñtruhpreez*
　» **business trip** voyage d'affaires (m) *vwiyaj dafer*
　» **on business** pour affaires *poor afer*

businessman/woman homme (m) /femme (f) d'affaires *om/fam dafer*

business studies études commerciales (f/pl) *aytewd komersyal*

bus station gare de bus (f) *gar duh bews*

bus stop arrêt de bus (m) *aray duh bews*

busy occupé(e) *okewpay*

but mais *me*

butane gas butane (m) *bewtan*

butcher's boucherie (f) *booshree*

butter beurre (m) *buhr*

butterfly papillon (m) *papeeyawñ*

button bouton (m) *bootawñ*

to **buy** acheter *ashtay*

by *(author etc.)* par *par*

C

cabin cabine (f) *kabeen*

cable car téléphérique (m) *taylayfayreek*

café café (m) *kafay*

cake gâteau (m) *gatoh*

cake shop pâtisserie (f) *patisree*

calculator calculatrice (f) *kalkewlatrees*

call *(phone)* appel (téléphonique) (m) *apel (taylayfoneek)*

to **call** appeler *aplay*

 » **to be called** s'appeler *saplay*

calm calme *kalm*

camera appareil photo (m) *aparey fohtoh*

to **camp** camper *koñpay*

camp bed lit de camp (m) *lee duh koñ*

camping camping (m) *koñpeeng*

camping gas camping gaz (m) *koñpeeng gaz*

campsite terrain de camping (m) *teraň duh koñpeeng*

can *(to be able)* pouvoir *poovwar*

 » **I can** je peux *juh puh* *(to know how to)* savoir *savwar*

 » **I (don't) know how to...** je (ne) sais (pas)... *juh (nuh) say (pa)...*

can *(tin)* boîte de conserve (f) *bwat duh kawňserv (petrol)* bidon (m) *beedawñ*

to **cancel** annuler *anewlay*

cancer cancer (m) *koñser*

candle bougie (f) *boojee*

canoe canoë (m) *kanoay*

can opener ouvre-boîte (m) *oovruhbwat*

capital *(city)* capitale (f) *kapeetal*

captain *(boat)* capitaine (m) *kapeeten*

car voiture (f) *vwatewr*

 » **by car** en voiture *oñ vwatewr*

 » **car hire** location de voiture (f) *lokasyawñ duh vwatewr*

carafe carafe (f) *karaf*

caravan caravane (f) *karavan*

 » **caravan site** terrain de caravanes (m) *teraň duh karavan*

care: to take care faire attention *fer atoñsyoñ (see grammar, page 157)*

 » **I don't care** ça m'est égal *sa met egal*

career carrière (f) *karier*

careful prudent(e) *prewdoñ(t)*

careless négligeant(e) *naygleejoñ(t)*

car park parking (m) *parking*

carpet moquette (f) *moket*

carriage *(rail)* wagon (m) *vagawñ*

carrier bag sac (en plastique) (m) *sak (oñ plasteek)*

to **carry** porter *portay*

car wash lavage de voiture (m) *lavaj duh vwatewr*

case: in case au cas où *ohka oo*

cash liquide (m), espèces (f/pl) *leekeed, espes*

 » **to pay cash** payer en espèces *payay oñ nespes*

to **cash** encaisser *oñkaysay*

 » **cash desk** caisse (f) *kays*

cassette cassette (f) *kaset*

castle château (m) *shatoh*

cat chat(te) *sha(t)*

catalogue catalogue (m) *katalog*

to **catch** *(train/bus)* prendre *proñdr*

cathedral cathédrale (f) *kataydral*

Catholic catholique (m/f) *katoleek*

to **cause** causer *kohzay*

caution prudence (f) *prewdoñs*

cave grotte (f) *grot*

CD CD (m) *sayday*

 » **CD-ROM** CD-ROM (m) *saydayrom*

ceiling plafond (m) *plafawñ*

cellar cave (f) *kav*

cemetery cimetière (m) *seemtyer*

centimetre centimètre (m) *soñteemetr*

central central(e) *soñtral*

central heating chauffage central (m) *shohfaj soñtral*

centre centre (m) *soñtr*

century siècle (m) *syekl*

CEO PDG (m) *paydayjay*

certain certain(e) *sertañ (sertayn)*

certainly certainement *sertaynmoñ*

certificate certificat (m) *serteefeeka*

chain chaîne (f) *shayn*

chair chaise (f) *shayz*

  » **chair lift** télésiège (m) *taylaysyej*

chalet chalet (m) *shalay*

champagne champagne (m) *shoñpany*

change (small coins) monnaie (f) *monay*

to **change** (clothes) se changer *suh shoñjay* (money) changer de l'argent *shoñjay duh larjoñ* (trains) changer de train *shoñjay duh trañ*

changing room cabine d'essayage (f) *kabeen deseyaj*

chapel chapelle (f) *shapel*

charcoal charbon (m) *sharbawñ*

charge (money) prix (m) *pree*

charter flight vol charter (m) *vol sharter*

cheap bon marché *bawñ marshay*

to **check** vérifier *vayreefyay*

checked (pattern) à carreaux *a karoh*

check-in (desk) enregistrement *oñrujeestruhmoñ*

to **check in** enregistrer *oñrujeestray*

cheers! santé! *soñtay*

cheese fromage (m) *fromaj*

chef chef (m) *shef*

chemist pharmacien(ne) *farmasyañ/syen*

cheque chèque (m) *shek*

chess échecs (m/pl) *ayshek*

chewing gum chewing gum (m) *shweeng gom*

chicken poulet (m) *poolay*

chickenpox varicelle (f) *vareesel*

child enfant (m/f) *oñfoñ*

children enfants (m/pl) *oñfoñ*

chimney cheminée (f) *shuhmeenay*

china porcelaine (f) *porsuhlen*

chips pommes frites (f/pl) *pom freet*

chocolate chocolat (m) *shokola*

to **choose** choisir *shwazeer*

Christian chrétien(ne) *kraytyañ/tyen*

  » **Christian name** prénom (m) *praynawñ*

Christmas Noël *noel*

  » **Christmas Day** jour de Noël (m) *joor duh noel*

  » **Christmas Eve** réveillon de Noël (m) *rayveyawñ duh noel*

church église (f) *aygleez*

cigarette cigarette (f) *seegaret*

cinema cinéma (m) *seenayma*

circle cercle (m) *serkl* (theatre) balcon (m) *balkawñ*

city ville (f) *veey*

civil servant fonctionnaire (m/f) *fawñxyoner*

class classe (f) *klas*

classical music musique classique (f) *mewzeek klaseek*

to **clean** nettoyer *naytwiyay*

clean propre *propr*

cleaner femme de ménage (f) *fam duh maynaj*

cleansing lotion lotion démaquillante (f) *lohsyawñ daymakeeyoñt*

clear clair(e) *kler*

clerk employé(e) de bureau *oñplwiyay duh bewroh*

clever intelligent(e) *añteleejoñ(t)*

cliff falaise (f) *falez*

climate climat (m) *kleema*

to **climb** grimper *grañpay*

clinic clinique (f) *kleeneek*

cloakroom vestiaire (m) *vestyer*

clock horloge (f) *orloj*

close (by) proche *prosh*

to **close** fermer *fermay*

closed fermé(e) *fermay*

cloth tissu (m) *teesew*

clothes vêtements (m/pl) *vetmoñ*

clothes pegs pinces à linges (f/pl)
pañs a lañj

cloud nuage (m) *newaj*

cloudy nuageux *newajuh*

club club (m) *kluhb*

coach car (m) *kar (railway)* wagon (m)
vagoñ

coal charbon (m) *sharbawñ*

coarse *(texture)* grossier/ère *grosyay/sier*

coast côte (f) *koht*

coat manteau (m) *moñtoh*

coat-hanger cintre (m) *sañtr*

cocktail cocktail (m) *koktel*

coffee café (m) *kafay*

coin pièce (f) *pyes*

cold froid(e) *frwa(d)*

» **I'm cold** j'ai froid *jay frwa*

» **it's cold** il fait froid *eel fay frwa*

» **to have a cold** être enrhumé(e)
etr oñrewmay

collar col (m) *kol*

colleague collègue (m/f) *koleg*

to **collect** collecter *kolektay*

collection *(stamps etc.)* collection
(f) *kolexyawñ (postal/rubbish)*
enlèvement (m) *oñlevmoñ*

college collège (m) *kolej*

colour couleur (f) *kooluhr*

» **colour-blind** daltonien(ne)
daltonyañ/nyen

» **colour-fast** grand teint *groñ tañ*

comb peigne (m) *peny*

to **come** venir *vuhneer (see grammar, p156)*

» **to come back** revenir *ruhvuhneer*

» **to come in** entrer *oñtray*

» **to come off** *(e.g. button)* se détacher
suh daytashay

comedy comédie (f) *komaydee*

comfortable confortable *koñfortabl*

comic *(magazine)* bande dessinée (f)
boñd deseenay

commercial commercial(e) *komersyal*

common *(usual)* courant(e), fréquent(e)
kooroñ(t), fraykoñ(t) (shared)
commun(e) *komuñ/komewn*

company entreprise (f) *oñtruhpreez*

compared with comparé(e) à
kawñparay a

compartment compartiment (m)
kawñparteemoñ

compass compas (m) *kawñpa*

to **complain** se plaindre *suh plañdr*

complaint plainte (f) *plañt (official)*
réclamation (f) *rayklamasyoñ*

complete *(finished)* achevé(e) *ashuvay
(whole)* entier/ère *oñtyay/er*

complicated compliqué(e) *kawñpleekay*

compulsory obligatoire *obleegatwar*

computer ordinateur (m) *ordeenatuhr*

» **computer programme** programme
informatique (m) *program
añformateek*

» **computer science** informatique (f)
añformateek

concert concert (m) *kawñser*

concert hall salle de concert (f) *sal de
kawñser*

concussion commotion (f) *komosyawñ*

condition *(state)* condition (f)
kawñdeesyawñ

conditioner *(hair)* après-shampooing
(m) *apreshoñpwañ*

condom préservatif (m) *prayzervateef*

conference conférence (f) *kawñfayroñs*

to **confirm** confirmer *kawñfeermay*

conjunctivitis conjonctivite (f)
kawñjawñkteeveet

connection connexion (f) *konexyawñ*

conscious conscient(e) *kawñsyoñ(t)*

conservation sauvegarde (f), protection
(f) *sohvgard, protexyawñ*

conservative *(politics)* conservateur/
trice *kawñservatuhr/trees*

constipation constipation (f)
kawñsteepasyawñ

consulate consulat (m) *kawñsewla*

consultant consultant(e) *kawñsultoñ(t)*

contact lens lentille (f) *loñteey*

» **contact lens cleaner** nettoyant pour les lentilles (m) *naytwiyoñ poor lay loñteey*

continent continent (m) *kawñteenoñ*

contraceptive contraceptif (m) *kawñtrasepteef*

contract contrat (m) *kawñtra*

control *(passport)* contrôle (m) *kawñtrohl*

convenient pratique *prateek*

convent couvent (m) *koovoñ*

cook cuisinier (m) *kweezeenyay*

to cook faire cuire *fer kweer*

» **cooked** cuit(e) *kwee(t)*

cooker cuisinière (f) *kweezeenyer*

cool frais, fraîche *fre, fresh*

cool box glacière (f) *glasyer*

copy copie (f) *kopee*

cork bouchon (m) *booshawñ*

corkscrew tire-bouchon (m) *teerbooshawñ*

corner coin (m) *kwañ*

correct correct(e) *korekt*

corridor couloir (m) *koolwar*

cosmetics produits cosmétiques (m/pl) *prodwee kosmayteek*

to cost coûter *kootay*

cot lit d'enfant (m) *lee doñfoñ*

cotton *(material)* coton (m) *kotawñ* *(thread)* fil (m) *feel*

cotton wool ouate (f) *wat*

couchette couchette (f) *kooshet*

cough toux (f) *too*

to cough tousser *toosay*

to count compter *kawñtay*

counter *(post office)* comptoir (m) *kawñtwar*

country pays (m) *payee*

country(side) campagne (f) *koñpany*

» **in the country** à la campagne *a la koñpany*

couple *(pair)* couple (m) *koopl*

course *(lessons)* cours (m) *koor*

court *(law)* tribunal (m) *treebewnal* *(sport)* court (m)

cousin cousin(e) *koozañ (koozeen)*

cover *(lid)* couvercle (m) *kooverkl*

cow vache (f) *vash*

crab crabe (m) *krab*

cramp crampe (f) *kroñp*

crayon crayon (m) *krayawñ*

crazy fou, folle *foo, fol*

cream crème (f) *krem* *(lotion)* lotion (f) *losyawñ*

credit card carte de crédit (f) *kart duh kraydee*

cross croix (f) *krwa*

» **Red Cross** Croix Rouge *krwa rooj*

to cross *(road etc.)* traverser *traversay*

cross-country skiing ski de fond (m) *skee duh fawñ*

crossing *(sea)* traversée (f) *traversay*

crossroads carrefour (m) *carfoor*

crowd foule (f) *fool*

crowded bondé(e) *bawñday*

crown couronne (f) *kooron*

cruise croisière (f) *krwazyer*

crutch béquille (f) *baykeey*

to cry pleurer *pluhray*

crystal cristal (m) *kreestal*

cup tasse (f) *tas*

cure *(remedy)* remède (f) *ruhmed*

to cure guérir *gayreer*

curler *(hair)* rouleau (m) *rooloh*

current actuel(le) *aktuel*

curtain rideau (m) *reedoh*

curve courbe (f) *koorb*

cushion coussin (m) *koosañ*

customs douane (f) *dwan*

cut coupure (f) *koopewr*

to cut (off) couper *koopay*

» **to cut oneself** se couper *suh koopay*

cutlery couverts (m/pl) *koover*

cycling cyclisme (m) *seecleesm*

cyclist cycliste (m/f) *seecleest*

cystitis cystite (f) *seesteet*

D

daily quotidien(ne) *koteedyañ/en*
damage dégâts (m/pl) *dayga*
to damage abîmer *abeemay*
damp humide *ewmeed*
dance danse (f) *doñs*
to dance danser *doñsay*
danger danger (m) *doñjay*
dangerous dangereux/se *doñjruh(z)*
dark sombre *sawñbr*
darling chéri(e) *shayree*
date (day) date (f) *dat*
daughter fille (f) *feey*
daughter-in-law belle-fille (f) *belfeey*
day jour (m), journée (f) *joor, joornay*
» day after tomorrow après-demain *apreduhmañ*
» day before yesterday avant-hier *avoñtyer*
dead mort(e) *mor(t)*
deaf sourd(e) *soor(d)*
dealer marchand (m) *marshoñ*
dear (loved) cher/ère *sher*
death mort (f) *mor*
debt dette (f) *det*
decaffeinated décaféiné(e) *daykafayeenay*
to decide décider *dayseeday*
deck pont (m) *pawñ*
deckchair chaise longue (f) *shayz lawñg*
to declare déclarer *dayklaray*
deep profond(e) *profawñ(d)*
defect défaut (m) *dayfoh*
defective défaillant(e) *dayfiyoñ(t)*
definitely vraiment *vraymoñ*
degree (temperature) degré (m) *duhgray*
(university) diplôme (m) *deeplohm*
delay retard (m) *ruhtar*
delicate délicat(e) *dayleeka(t)*
delicious délicieux/se *dayleesyuh(z)*
to deliver livrer *leevray*
delivery livraison (f) *leevrayzawñ*
demonstration manifestation (f) *maneefestasyawñ*

denim jean (m) *jeen*
dentist dentiste (m/f) *doñteest*
denture appareil dentaire (m) *aparey doñter*
deodorant déodorant (m) *dayodoroñ*
to depart (bus, car, train) partir *parteer* (plane) décoller *daykolay*
department département (m) *daypartuhmoñ*
department store grand magasin (m) *groñ magazañ*
departure (bus, car, train) départ (m) *daypar* (plane) décollage (m) *daykolaj*
departure lounge salle d'embarquement (f) *sal doñbarkuhmoñ*
deposit caution (f) *kohsyawñ*
to describe décrire *daykreer*
description description (f) *deskreepsyawñ*
desert désert (m) *dayzer*
design dessin (m) *desañ* (dress) style (m) *steel*
to design dessiner *deseenay*
dessert dessert (m) *dayser*
destination destination (f) *desteenasyawñ*
detail détail (m) *daytiy*
to develop développer *dayvlopay*
diabetes diabète (m) *dyabet*
diabetic diabétique *dyabeteek*
to dial composer *kawñpohzay*
dialling code indicatif (m) *añdeekateef*
dialling tone tonalité (f) *tonaleetay*
diamond diamant (m) *dyamoñ*
diarrhoea diarrhée (f) *dyaray*
diary journal (m) *joornal*
dictator dictateur (m) *deektaturh*
dictionary dictionnaire (m) *deexyoner*
to die mourir *mooreer*
» ... died ... est mort(e) *ay mor(t)*
diesel diesel (m) *dyesel*
diet régime (m) *rayjeem*
different différent(e) *deefayroñ(t)*
difficult difficile *deefeeseel*

D

digital numérique *newmayreek*
» **digital camera** appareil photo numérique (m) *aparey fohtoh newmayreek*
dining room salle à manger (f) *sal a moñjay*
dinner dîner (m) *deenay*
diplomat diplomate (m/f) *deeplomat*
direct *(train)* direct(e) *deerekt*
direction direction (f) *deerexyawñ*
director directeur/trice *deerektuhr/trees*
directory annuaire (m) *anwer*
dirty sale *sal*
disabled handicappé(e) *oñdeekapay*
disc disque (m) *deesk,* *(computer)* disque (m), disquette (f) *deesk, deesket,* *(vinyl)* disque *deesk*
disco discothèque (f) *deeskotek*
discount remise (f) *ruhmeez*
dish plat (m) *pla*
dishwasher lave-vaisselle (m) *lav vaysel*
disinfectant désinfectant (m) *désañfektoñ*
dislocated démis(e), luxé(e) *daymee(z), lewxay*
disposable jetable *juhtabl*
» **disposable nappies** couches jetables (f/pl) *koosh juhtabl*
distance distance (f) *deestoñs*
distilled water eau déminéralisée (f) *oh daymeenayraleezay*
district quartier (m) *kartyay*
to **dive** plonger *plawñjay*
diversion déviation (f) *dayvyasyawñ*
diving plongée (f) *plawñjay*
divorced divorcé(e) *deevorsay*
dizzy pris(e) de vertiges *pree(z) duh verteej*
DJ DJ *deejay*
to **do** faire *fer*
doctor médecin (m) *maydsañ*
document document (m) *dokewmoñ*
dog chien(ne) *shyañ/en*
doll poupée (f) *poopay*

dollar dollar (m) *dolar*
donkey âne (m) *an*
door porte (f) *port*
double double *doobl*
double bed lit deux places (m) *lee duh plas*
dough pâte (f) *pat*
down *(movement)* en bas *oñ ba*
download téléchargement (m) *taylaysharjuhmoñ*
downstairs en bas *oñ ba*
drain égout (m) *aygoo*
drama drame (m) *dram*
draught *(air)* courant d'air (m) *kooroñ der*
draught beer bière pression (f) *byer presyawñ*
to **draw** *(curtains etc.)* tirer *teeray* *(picture)* dessiner *deseenay*
drawer tiroir (m) *teerwar*
drawing dessin (m) *desañ*
dress robe (f) *rob*
to **dress, get dressed** s'habiller *sabeeyay*
dressing *(medical)* pansement (m) *poñsmoñ, (salad)* vinaigrette (f) *vinaygret*
drink boisson (f) *bwasawñ*
to **drink** boire *bwar*
to **drip** *(tap)* goutter *gootay*
to **drive** conduire *kawñdweer*
driver conducteur/trice *kawñdewktuhr/ trees*
driving licence permis de conduire (m) *permee duh kawñdweer*
to **drown** se noyer *suh nwayay*
drug drogue (f) *drog*
» **drug addict** toxicomane (m/f) *toxeekoman*
drunk ivre *eevr*
dry sec, sèche *sek, sesh*
dry-cleaner's pressing (m) *preseeng*
dubbed doublé(e) *dooblay*
duck canard (m) *kanar*
dull *(weather)* couvert(e), gris *coovair(t), gree*

dumb muet(te) *meway/et*
dummy *(baby's)* sucette (f) *sewset*
dust poussière (f) *poosyer*
dustbin poubelle (f) *poobel*
dusty poussiéreux/se *poosyeruh(z)*
duty *(customs)* droit (m) *drwa*
duty free hors-taxe *ortax*
duvet couette (f) *kwet*
DVD DVD (m) *dayvayday*
  » **DVD-player** lecteur de DVD (m) *lektuhr duh dayvayday*
dyslexia dyslexie (f) *deeslexee*
dyslexic dyslexique *deeslexeek*

E

each chaque *shak*
ear oreille (f) *orey*
  » **earache** mal d'oreilles (m) *mal dorey*
eardrops gouttes pour les oreilles (f/pl) *goot poor layz orey*
earlier plus tôt *plew toh*
early tôt *toh*
to **earn** gagner *ganyay*
earring boucle d'oreille (f) *bookl dorey*
earth terre (f) *ter*
earthquake tremblement de terre (m) *troñbluhmoñ duh ter*
east est (m) *est*
  » **eastern** de l'est *duh lest*
Easter Pâques (f/pl) *pak*
easy facile *faseel*
to **eat** manger *moñjay*
economical économique *aykonomeek*
economics, economy économie (f) *aykonomee*
edible comestible *komesteebl*
egg œuf (m) *uhf*
either ... or... ou (bien) ... ou (bien)... *oo (byañ) ... oo (byañ)...*
elastic band élastique (m) *aylasteek*
election élection (f) *aylexyawñ*
electric électrique *aylektreek*
electrician électricien(ne) (m/f) *aylektreesyañ/yen*

electricity électricité (f) *aylektreeseetay (wiring etc.)* courant (m) *kooroñ*
electronic électronique *aylektroneek*
email e-mail, courrier électronique (m) *eemayl, kooray aylektroneek*
to **email** envoyer un e-mail *oñvwiyay uñ neemayl*
to **embark** *(boat)* embarquer *oñbarkay*
embarrassing gênant(e) *jenoñ(t)*
embassy ambassade (f) *oñbasad*
emergency urgence (f) *ewrjoñs*
emergency telephone téléphone de secours (m) *taylayfon duh suhkoor*
empty vide *veed*
to **empty** vider *veeday*
end fin (f) *fañ*
to **end** finir *feeneer*
energy énergie (f) *aynerjee*
engaged *(to be married)* fiancé(e) *feeoñsay, (occupied)* occupé(e) *okewpay*
engine moteur (m) *motuhr*
England Angleterre *oñgluhter*
English anglais(e) *oñglay(z)*
to **enjoy** s'amuser *samewzay*
enough assez *asay*
to **enter** entrer *oñtray*
entertainment divertissement (m) *deeverteesmoñ*
enthusiastic enthousiaste *oñtoozyast*
entrance entrée (f) *oñtray*
envelope enveloppe (f) *oñvlop*
environment environnement (m) *oñveeronmoñ*
environmentally friendly respectueux/se de l'environnement *respektewuh(z) duh loñveeronmoñ*
equal égal(e) *aygal*
equipment équipement (m) *aykeepmoñ*
escalator escalier roulant (m) *eskalyay rooloñ*
especially surtout *syoortoo*
essential essentiel(le) *esoñsyel*

estate agent agent immobilier (m) *ajoñ eemobeelyay*

even *(including)* même *mem (not odd)* pair *per*

evening soirée (f), soir (m) *swaray, swar*

every *(all)* tous/toutes *toos/toot (each)* chaque *shak*

everyone tout le monde *too luh mawñd*

everything tout *too*

everywhere partout *partoo*

exactly exactement *egzaktuhmoñ*

examination *(school etc.)* examen (m) *egzamañ*

example exemple (m) *egzoñpl*
» **for example** par exemple *par egzoñpl*

excellent excellent(e) *exeloñ(t)*

except sauf *sohf*

excess baggage excédent de bagages (m) *exaydoñ duh bagaj*

to **exchange** changer *shoñjay*

exchange rate taux de change (m) *toh duh shoñj*

exciting excitant(e) *exeetoñ(t)*

excursion excursion (f) *exkewrsyawñ*

excuse me pardon, excusez-moi *pardawñ, exkewzay mwa*

executive *(adj.)* exécutif/ve *egzaykewteef/v*

exercise exercice (m) *egzersees*

exhibition exposition (f) *expohzeesyawñ*

exit sortie (f) *sortee*

to **expect** s'attendre à *satoñdr à*

expensive cher, chère *sher*

experience expérience (f) *expayryoñs*

expert expert (m) *exper*

to **explain** expliquer *expleekay*

explosion explosion (f) *explohzyawñ*

export export (m) exportation (f) *expor, exportasyawñ*

to **export** exporter *exportay*

extension cable rallonge (f) *ralawñj*

external externe, extérieur(e) *extern, exteryer*

extra *(in addition)* en supplément *on sewplaymoñ*

eye œil (m), yeux (m/pl) *uhy, yuh*

eyebrow sourcil (m) *soorseel*

eyelash cil (m) *seel*

eyeliner eye-liner (m) *iyliyner*

eyeshadow ombre à paupières (f) *awñbr a pohpyer*

F

fabric tissu (m) *teesew*

face visage (m) *veezaj*
» **face cream** crème pour le visage (f) *krem poor luh veezaj*
» **face powder** poudre de riz (m) *poodr duh ree*

facilities installations (f/pl) *añstalasyawñ*

fact fait (m) *fet*
» **in fact** en fait *oñ fet*

factory usine (f) *ewzeen*

to **fail** *(exam/test)* échouer *ayshway*

to **faint** s'évanouir *sayvanweer*

fair *(haired)* blond(e) *blawñ(d) (just)* juste *jewst*

fair foire (f), fête (f) *fwar, fet*
» **trade fair** foire exposition (f) *fwar expohzeesyawñ*

faith foi (f) *fwa*

faithful fidèle *feedel*

fake faux, fausse *foh, fohs*

to **fall** tomber *tawñbay*

false faux, fausse *foh, fohs*

family famille (f) *fameey*

famous célèbre *saylebr*

fan *(air)* ventilateur (m) *voñteelatuhr (supporter)* fan (m) *fan*

fantastic fantastique *foñtasteek*

far *(away)* loin *lwañ*

fare prix (du billet) (m) *pree (dew beeyay)*

farm ferme (f) *ferm*

farmer fermier (m) *fermyay*

fashion mode (f) *mod*

fashionable/in fashion à la mode *a la mod*

fast rapide *rapeed*

fat *(adj.)* gros(se) *groh(s)*

fat *(noun)* graisse (f) *gres*

fatal fatal(e) *fatal*

father père (m) *per*

father-in-law beau-père (m) *bohper*

fault faute (f), erreur (f) *foht, eruhr*

faulty défectueux/euse *dayfektewuh/uhz*

favourite préféré(e) *prayfayray*

fax fax (m) *fax*

feather plume (f) *plewm*

fee prix (m) *pree*

to feed *(inc. baby)* nourrir *nooreer*

to feel se sentir *suh soñteer (ill/well)* se sentir bien/mal *suh soñteer byañ/mal*

female femelle *fuhmel*

feminine féminin(e) *faymeenañ/een*

feminist féministe *faymeeneest*

fence clôture (f) *klohtewr*

ferry ferry (m) *feree*

festival *(village etc.)* fête (f) *fet (film etc.)* festival (m) *festeeval*

to fetch aller chercher *alay shershay*

fever fièvre (f) *fyevr*

(a) few *(some)* quelques *kelk, (not many/ much)* (un) peu de *(uñ) puh duh*

fiancé(e) fiancé(e) *feeoñsay*

field champ (m) *shoñ*

to fight se battre *suh batr*

file *(documents)* fichier (m) *feeshyay (nail/DIY)* lime (à ongles) (f) *leem (a awñgl)*

to fill remplir *roñpleer*

filling *(dental)* plombage (m) *plawñbaj*

film *(cinema)* film (m) *feelm (for camera)* pellicule (f) *peleekewl*

film star star du cinéma (f) *star dew seenayma*

finance finance (f) *feenoñs*

to find trouver *troovay*

fine *(OK)* bien *byañ (penalty)* amende (f) *amoñd (weather)* beau, belle (f) *boh, bel*

finger doigt (m) *dwa*

finish finir *feeneer*

fire feu (m) *fuh*

fire brigade pompiers (m/pl) *pawñpyay*

fire extinguisher extincteur (m) *extañktuhr*

firewood bois de chauffage (m) *bwa duh shohfaj*

firework feu d'artifice (m) *fuh darteefees*

firm ferme *ferm*

firm *(company)* entreprise (f) *oñtruhpreez*

first premier/ère *pruhmyay/yer*

» **first aid** premiers soins (m/pl) *pruhmyay swañ*

» **first aid kit** trousse de pharmacie (f) *troos duh farmasee*

fish poisson (m) *pwasawñ*

to fish/go fishing pêcher/aller à la pêche *peshay/alay a la pesh*

fishing pêche (f) *pesh*

fishing rod canne à pêche (f) *kan a pesh*

fishmonger's poissonnier (m) *pwasonyay*

fit *(healthy)* en forme *oñ form*

to fit aller bien *alay byañ*

fitting room cabine d'essayage (f) *kabeen deseyaj*

to fix *(mend)* réparer *rayparay*

fizzy gazeux/euse *gazuh(z)*

flag drapeau (m) *drapoh*

flash *(camera)* flash (m) *flash*

flat *(apartment)* appartement (m) *apartuhmoñ*

flat *(level)* plat(e) *pla(t) (battery, tyre)* à plat *a pla*

flavour saveur (f) *savuhr (ice-cream)* parfum (m) *parfañ*

flaw défaut (m) *dayfoh*

flea market marché aux puces (m) *marshay oh pews*

flight vol (m) *vol*

flippers palmes (f/pl) *palm*

flood inondation (f) *eenawñdasyawñ*

floor étage (m) *aytaj*

» **on the first floor** au premier étage *oh pruhmyay aytay*

» **ground floor** au rez-de-chaussée *oh ray duh shohsay*

floppy disc disquette (f) *deesket*

flour farine (f) *fareen*

flower fleur (f) *fluhr*

flu grippe (f) *greep*

fluently *(language)* couramment *kooramon*

fluid liquide (m) *leekeed*

to **fly** voler *volay*

fly mouche (f) *moosh*

fly sheet feuille de vol (f) *fuhy duh vol*

fog brouillard (m) *brooyar*

» **it's foggy** il fait du brouillard *eel fay duh brooyar*

foil papier aluminium (m) *papeeay alewmeenyom*

folding *(chair etc.)* pliant(e) *pleeon(t)*

to **follow** suivre *sweevr*

following *(next)* suivant *sweevoñ*

food nourriture (f) *nooreetewr*

food poisoning intoxication alimentaire (f) *añtoxeekasyawñ aleemoñter*

foot pied (m) *pyay*

» **on foot** à pied *a pyay*

football football (m) *footbol*

footpath sentier (m) *soñtyay*

for pour *poor*

forbidden interdit(e) *añterdee(t)*

foreign étranger/ère *aytroñjay/er*

forest forêt (f) *fore*

to **forget** oublier *oobleeay*

to **forgive** pardonner *pardonay*

fork fourchette (f) *foorshet*

form formulaire (m) *formewler*

fortnight quinzaine (f) *kañzen*

forward en avant *oñ avoñ*

foundation *(make-up)* fond de teint (m) *fawñ duh tañ*

fountain fontaine (f) *fawñten*

fox renard (m) *ruhnar*

foyer hall (m) *ol*

fracture fracture (f) *fraktewr*

fragile fragile *frajeel*

freckles taches de rousseur (f/pl) *tash duh roosuhr*

free *(available/unoccupied)* libre *leebr*
(for free) gratuit(e) *gratwee(t)*

freedom liberté (f) *leebertay*

to **freeze** geler *juhlay*

freezer congélateur (m) *kawñjaylatuhr*

frequent fréquent(e) *fraykoñ(t)*

fresh frais, fraîche *fre, fresh*

fridge réfrigérateur (m), frigo (m) *rayfreejayratuhr, freegoh*

fried frit(e) *free(t)*

friend ami(e) *amee*

frightened effrayé(e) *efrayay*

fringe frange (f) *froñj*

frog grenouille (f) *gruhnooy*

from de, à partir de, de la part de *duh, a parteer duh, duh la par duh*

front: in front (of) devant *devoñ*

front door porte d'entrée (f) *port doñtray*

frontier frontière (f) *frawñtyer*

frost gel (m) *jel*

frozen *(water etc.)* gelé(e), *(food)* congelé(e) *juhlay, kawñjuhlay*

fruit fruit (m) *frwee*

to **fry** frire *freer*

frying pan poêle à frire (f) *pwel a freer*

fuel carburant (m) *karbewroñ*

full plein(e) *plañ/plen*

full board pension complète *poñsyawñ kawñplet*

full up *(booked up)* complet/ète *kawñplet/et*

to **have fun** s'amuser *samewzay*

funeral enterrement (m) *oñtermoñ*

funfair fête foraine (f) *fet foren*

funny *(amusing)* drôle *drohl (peculiar)* bizarre *beezar*

fur fourrure (f) *foorewr*

furniture meubles (m/pl) *muhbl*

futher on plus loin *plew lwuñ*

fuse fusible (m) *fewzeebl*

fusebox boîte à fusibles (f) *bwat a fewzeebl*

G

gallery galerie (f) *galree*

gambling jeu (m) *juh*

game jeu (m) *juh (match)* match (m) *match (hunting)* gibier (m) *jeebyay*

gangway passerelle (f) *pasrel*

garage *(for parking)* garage (m) *garaj*

garden jardin (m) *jardañ*

gardener jardinier (m), jardinière (f) *jardeenyay, jardeenyair*

garlic ail (m) *iy*

gas gaz (m) *gaz*

>> **gas bottle/cylinder** bouteille de gaz (f) *bootey duh gaz*

>> **gas refill** recharge de gaz (f) *ruhsharj duh gaz*

gate barrière (f) *baryer (airport)* porte (f) *port*

gay *(homosexual)* homosexuel (m) *ohmohsexwel*

gel *(hair)* gel (m) *jel*

general général(e) *jaynayral*

>> **in general** en général *oñ jaynayral*

generous généreux/se *jaynayruh(z)*

gentle doux/ce *doo(s)*

gentleman/men monsieur (m) messieurs (m/pl) *muhsyuh, maysyuh (gents)* toilettes pour hommes (f/pl) *twalet poor om*

genuine authentique *ortonteek*

geography géographie (f) *jayografee*

German allemand(e) *almoñ(d)*

Germany Allemagne *almany*

to get obtenir *obtuhneer*

to get off *(bus)* descendre *desoñdr*

to get on *(bus)* monter (dans) *mawñtay (doñ)*

to get through *(phone)* obtenir *obtuhneer*

gift cadeau (m) *kadoh*

gin gin (m) *jeen*

>> **gin and tonic** gin-tonic (m) *jeentoneek*

girl fille (f) *feey*

girlfriend petite amie (f) *puhteet amee*

to give donner *donay*

>> **to give back** rendre *roñdr*

glass verre (m) *ver*

glasses lunettes (f/pl) *lewnet*

global warming réchauffement de la planète (m) *rayshohfmoñ duh la planet*

gloves gants (m/pl) *goñ*

glue colle (f) *kol*

to go aller *alay (see grammar, page 156)*

>> **to go away** partir *parteer*

>> **to go down** descendre *desoñdr*

>> **to go in** entrer *oñtray*

>> **to go out** sortir *sorteer*

>> **to go round** *(visit)* rendre visite à *roñdr veezeet a*

>> **let's go!** allons-y! *alawñzee*

goal but *bewt*

goat chèvre (f) *shevr*

God Dieu (m) *dyuh*

goggles lunettes de plongée (f/pl) *lewnet duh plawñjay*

gold or (m) *or*

golf golf (m) *golf*

>> **golf clubs** clubs de golf (m/pl) *klub duh golf*

>> **golf course** terrain de golf (m) *terañ duh golf*

good bon(ne) *bawñ, bon*

>> **goodbye** au revoir *oh ruhvwar (casual)* salut *salew*

>> **good day** bonne journée *bon joornay*

>> **good evening** bonsoir *bawñswar*

>> **good morning** bonjour *bawñjoor*

>> **good night** bonne nuit *bon nwee*

Good Friday vendredi saint *voñdruhdee sañ*

goods marchandises (f/pl) *marshoñdeez*

government gouvernement (m) *goovernuhmoñ*

grammar grammaire (f) *gramer*

gramme gramme (m) *gram*

grandchildren petits-enfants (m/pl) *puhteezoñfoñ*

granddaughter petite-fille (f) *puhteet feey*

grandfather grand-père (m) *groñper*

grandmother grand-mère (f) *groñmer*

grandparents grands-parents (m/pl) *groñparoñ*

grandson petit-fils (m) *puhtee fees*

grandstand tribune (f) *treebewn*

grass herbe (f) *erb*

grateful reconnaissant(e) *ruhkonaysoñ(t)*

greasy graisseux/se *graysuh(z)*

great! super! génial! *sewper, jaynyal*

green vert(e) *ver(t)*

to greet accueillir *akuhyeer*

grey gris(e) *gree(z)*

grilled grillé(e) *greeyay*

grocer's épicier/ère *aypeesyay/er*

ground sol *sol*

ground floor rez-de-chaussée (m) *ray duh shohsay*

groundsheet tapis de sol (m) *tapee duh sol*

group groupe (m) *groop*

guarantee garantie (f) *garoñtee*

guest invité(e) *añveetay* (hotel) client(e) *kleeoñ(t)*

guest house pension (f) *poñsyawñ*

guide guide (m) *geed*

» **guided tour** visite guidée (f) *veezeet geeday*

guidebook guide (touristique) (m) *geed (tooreesteek)*

guilty coupable *koopabl*

guitar guitare (f) *geetar*

gun révolver (m), pistolet (m) *rayvolver, peestolay*

guy rope corde de tente (f) *kord duh toñt*

gymnastics gymnastique (f) *jeemnasteek*

H

habit habitude (f) *abeetewd*

hail grêle (f) *grel*

hair cheveux (m/pl) *shuhvuh*

hairbrush brosse à cheveux (f) *bros a shuhvuh*

haircut coupe de cheveux (f) *koop duh shuhvuh*

hairdresser coiffeur/se *kwafuhr(z)*

hairdryer sèche-cheveux (m) *sesh shuhvuh*

hairgrip pince à cheveux (f) *pañs a shuhvuh*

hairspray laque (f) *lak*

half moitié (f) *mwatyay*

half *(adj.)* demi(e) *duhmee*

half board demi-pension (f) *duhmeepoñsyawñ*

half past et demie *ay duhmee*

half price moitié prix *mwatyay pree*

hall *(in house)* entrée (f) *oñtray*

ham jambon (m) *joñbawñ*

hamburger hamburger (m) *oñmburger*

hammer marteau (m) *martoh*

hand main (f) *mañ*

» **hand cream** crème pour les mains (f) *krem poor lay mañ*

» **hand luggage** bagage à main (m) *bagaj a mañ*

» **hand-made** fait(e) à la main *fe(t) a la mañ*

handbag sac à main (m) *sak a mañ*

handicapped handicapé(e) *oñdeekapay*

handkerchief mouchoir (m) *mooshwar*

handle poignée (f) *pwanyay*

hangover gueule de bois (f) *guhl duh bwa*

to hang up (telephone) raccrocher *rakroshay*

to happen arriver, se passer *areevay, suh pasay*

happy heureux/se *uhruh(z)*

harbour port (m) *por*

hard dur(e) *dewr* (difficult) difficile *deefeeseel*

hard drive disque dur (m) *deesk dewr*

hard shoulder bande d'arrêt d'urgence (f) *boñd daray dewrjoñs*

hardware shop quincaillerie (f) *kañkiyree*

to **hate** détester *daytestay*

to **have** avoir *avwar (see grammar, p 156)*

hay foin (m) *fwañ*

hayfever rhume des foins (m) *rewm day fwañ*

he il *eel*

head tête (f) *tet*, *(boss)* patron (m) *patrawñ*

headache mal de tête (m) *mal duh tet*

headphones écouteurs (m/pl) *aykootuhr*

to **heal** guérir *gayreer*

health santé (f) *soñtay*

healthy sain(e) *sañ, sen*

to **hear** entendre *oñtoñdr*

hearing ouïe (f) *wee*

» **hearing aid** appareil acoustique (m) *aparey akoosteek*

heart cœur (m) *kuhr*

» **heart attack** crise cardiaque (f) *kreez kardyak*

heat chaleur (f) *shaluhr*

heater radiateur (m) *radyatuhr*

heating chauffage (m) *shohfaj*

heaven paradis (m) *paradee*

heavy lourd(e) *loor(d)*

heel talon (m) *talawñ*

height hauteur (f) *ohtuhr*

helicopter hélicoptère (m) *ayleekopter*

hell enfer (m) *oñfer*

hello salut *salew*

helmet *(motorbike)* casque (de moto) (m) *kask (duh mohtoh)*

help aide (f) *ayd*

» **help!** à l'aide! *a layd*

to **help** aider *ayday*

her la, elle, son/sa/ses *la, el, sawñ/sa/say*

herb herbe (f) *erb*

herbal tea tisane (f), infusion (f) *teezan, añfewzyawñ*

here ici *eesee*

hers le sien, la sienne, les siens, les siennes *luh syañ, la syen, lay syañ, lay syen*

hiccups: to have hiccups avoir le hoquet *avwar luh okay*

high haut(e) *oh(t)*

» **high chair** chaise haute (f) *shayz oht*

to **hijack** détourner *daytoornay*

hill colline (f) *koleen*

him le, lui *luh, lwee*

to **hire** louer *lway*

his son/sa/ses *sawñ/sa/say*

» **it's his** c'est à lui *set a lwee*

history histoire (f) *eestwar*

to **hit** frapper *frapay*

to **hitchhike** faire du stop *fer dew stop*

HIV VIH *vay ee ash*

» **HIV positive** séropositif/ve *sayroposeeteef/v*

hobby hobby (m) *obee*

to **hold** tenir *tuhneer*

hole trou (m) *troo*

holiday vacances (f/pl) *vakoñs*

» **on holiday** en vacances *oñ vakoñs*

» **public holiday** fête (f) *fet*

holy saint(e) *sañ(t)*

home maison (f) *mayzawñ*

» **at (my) home** chez moi *shay mwa*

» **at (your) home** chez vous *shay voo*

to **go home** aller à la maison *alay a la mayzawñ*

homeopathic homéopathique *omayopateek*

to be **homesick** avoir le mal du pays *avwar luh mal dew payee*

homosexual homosexuel(le) *ohmohsexwel*

honest honnête *onet*

honeymoon lune de miel (f) *lewn duh myel*

to **hope** espérer *espayray*

» **I hope so/not** j'espère que oui/non *jesper kuh wee/noñ*

horrible horrible *oreebl*

horse cheval (m) *shuhval*

hospital hôpital (m) *ohpeetal*

host hôte (m) *oht*

hot chaud(e) *shoh(d)*

» (spicy) épicé(e) *aypeesay*

hotel hôtel (m) *ohtel*

hour heure (f) *uhr*

» **half-hour** demi-heure (f) *duhmee uhr*

house maison (f) *mayzawñ*

housework ménage (m) *maynaj*

hovercraft aéroglisseur (m) *aayrohgleesuhr*

how? comment? *komoñ*

how long? combien de temps? *kombyañ duh toñ*

how many/much? combien? *kombyañ*

how much is it? c'est combien? *say kombyañ*

human humain(e) *ewmañ/men*

hungry: to be hungry avoir faim *avwar fañ*

to **hunt** chasser *shasay*

hunting chasse (f) *shas*

hurry: to be in a hurry être pressé(e) *etr presay*

hurt: it hurts ça fait mal *sa fe mal*

husband mari (m) *maree*

hut cabane (f) *kaban*

hydrofoil hydroptère (m) *eedropter*

hypermarket hypermarché (m) *eepermarshay*

I

I je *juh*

ice glace (f) *glas*

ice cube glaçon (m) *glasoñ*

ice rink patinoire (f) *pateenwar*

icy (road) verglacé(e) *verglasay*

idea idée (f) *eeday*

if si *see*

ill malade *malad*

illness maladie (f) *maladee*

imagination imagination (f) *eemajeenasyawñ*

to **imagine** imaginer *eemajeenay*

immediately tout de suite *too de sweet*

impatient impatient(e) *añpasyoñ(t)*

important important(e) *añportoñ(t)*

impossible impossible *añposeebl*

impressive impressionnant(e) *añpresyonoñ(t)*

in dans *doñ*

included compris(e) *kawñpree(z)*

income revenu (m) *ruhvuhnew*

independent indépendant(e) *añdaypoñdoñ(t)*

indigestion indigestion (f) *añdeejestyawñ*

indoors à l'intérieur *a lañtayryuhr*

infected infecté(e) *añfektay*

infection infection (f) *añfexyawñ*

infectious contagieux/se *kawñtajyuh(z)*

inflamed enflammé(e) *oñflamay*

inflammation inflammation (f) *añflamasyawñ*

influenza grippe (f) *greep*

information informations (f/pl), renseignements (m/pl) *añformasyawñ, roñsenymoñ*

» **information desk/office** accueil (m) *akuhy*

injection piqûre (f) *peekewr*

to **injure** se blesser *suh blesay*

» **injured** blessé(e) *blesay*

injury blessure (f) *blesewr*

ink encre (f) *oñkr*

innocent innocent(e) *eenosoñ(t)*

insect insecte (m) *añsekt*

» **insect bite** piqûre d'insecte (f) *peekewr dañsekt*

» **insect repellent** antimoustiques (m) *oñteemoosteek*

inside à l'intérieur, dedans *a lañtayryuhr, duhdoñ*

to **insist** insister *añseestay*

inspector inspecteur (m) *añspektuhr*

instead of au lieu de *oh lyuh duh*

instructor moniteur/trice

moneetuhr/trees
insulin insuline (f) *añsewleen*
insult insulte (f) *añsewlt*
insurance assurance (f) *asewroñs*
» **insurance document** papiers
d'assurance (m/pl) *papyay dasewroñs*
to **insure** assurer *asewray*
» **insured** assuré(e) *asewray*
intelligent intelligent(e) *añteleejoñ(t)*
interest *(money)* intérêts (m/pl) *añtayre*
interesting intéressant(e) *añtayresoñ(t)*
international international(e)
añternasyonal
internet internet (m) *añternet*
» **internet connection** connexion
internet (f) *conxyawñ añternet*
to **interpret** interpréter *añterpraytay*
interpreter interprète (m/f) *añterpret*
interval *(theatre etc.)* entracte (m)
oñtrakt
interview entrevue (f) *oñtruhvew*
into dans *doñ*
to **introduce** présenter *prayzoñtay*
invitation invitation (f) *añveetasyawñ*
to **invite** inviter *añveetay*
iodine iode (f) *yod*
Ireland Irlande *eerloñd*
Irish irlandais(e) *eerloñday(z)*
iron *(metal)* fer (m) *fer* *(for clothes)*
fer à repasser (m) *fer a ruhpasay*
to **iron** repasser *ruhpasay*
is *(see to be)* est *e*
» **is there?** est-ce qu'il y a? *eskeelya*
Islam Islam (f) *eezlam*
Islamic islamique *eeslameek*
island île (f) *eel*
it ça *sa*
itch démangeaison (f) *daymoñjaysawñ*

J

jacket veste (f) *vest*
jam confiture (f) *kawñfeetewr*
jar pot (m) *po*
jeans jean (m) *djeen*

jelly gelée (f) *juhlay*
jellyfish méduse (f) *maydewz*
Jesus Christ Jésus-Christ *jaysew kreest*
jetty jetée (f), digue (f) *juhtay, deeg*
jeweller's bijouterie (f) *beejootree*
Jewish juif/ve *jweef/v*
job travail (m), emploi (m)
traviy, oñplwa
to **jog** faire du jogging *fer dew jogging*
joke blague (f) *blag*
journalist journaliste (m/f) *joornaleest*
journey voyage (m) *vwiyaj*
judge juge (m) *jewj*
jug carafe (f), pichet (m) *karaf, peeshay*
juice jus (m) *jew*
to **jump** sauter *sohtay*
jumper pull (m) *pewl*
jump leads câbles de démarrage (m/pl)
kabl duh daymaraj
junction *(road)* croisement (m)
krwazmoñ
just *(only)* seulement *suhlmoñ*

K

to **keep** garder *garday*
kettle bouilloire (f) *booywar*
key clé (f) *klay*
» **key ring** porte-clés (m) *portuhklay*
kidney *(food)* rognon (m) *ronyoñ*
(body) rein (m) *rañ*
to **kill** tuer *tway*
kilo(gramme) kilo (m) *keelo*
kilometre kilomètre (m) *keelometr*
kind *(sort)* genre (m) *joñr*
(generous) gentil(le) *joñtee(y)*
king roi (m) *rwa*
kiss baiser (m) *bayzay*
to **kiss** embrasser *oñbrasay*
kitchen cuisine (f) *kweezeen*
knee genou (m) *juhnoo*
knickers culotte (f), slip (m) *kewlot, sleep*
knife couteau (m) *kootoh*
to **knit** tricoter *treekotay*
knitting tricot (m) *treekoh*

» **knitting needle** épingle à tricoter (f)
aypañgl a treekotay

to **knock** frapper *frapay*

knot nœud (m) *nuh*

to **know** *(someone)* connaître *konetr*
(something) savoir *savwar*

» **I know him/her** je/la connais *juh
luh/la konay*

to **know how to** savoir *savwar*

» **I (don't) know (how to)** je (ne) sais
(pas) *juh (nuh) say (pa)*

L

label étiquette (f) *ayteeket*

ladder échelle (f) *ayshel*

ladies mesdames (f/pl) *maydam*

lady dame (f) *dam*

lager bière blonde (f) *byer blawñd*

lake lac (m) *lak*

lamb *(meat)* agneau (m) *anyoh*

lamp lampe (f) *loñp*

land terre (f) *ter*

to **land** atterrir *atereer*

landlord/lady propriétaire (m/f)
propreeayter

language langue (f) *loñg*

large grand(e) *groñ(d)*

last dernier/ère *dernyay, dernyer*

to **last** durer *dewray*

late tard *tar*

later plus tard *plew tar*

laugh rire (m) *reer*

to **laugh** rire *reer*

launderette laverie (f) *lavree*

laundry linge (m) *lañj*

law loi (f) *lwa*, *(study subject)* droit (m)
drwa

lawyer avocat(e) (m/f) *avoka(t)*

laxative laxatif (m) *laxateef*

lead plomb (m) *plawñ*

» **lead-free** sans-plomb *soñ plawñ*

leaf feuille (f) *fuhy*

leaflet dépliant (m) *daypleeoñ*

to **lean out** se pencher *suh poñshay*

to **learn** apprendre *aproñdr*

learner débutant(e) *daybewtoñ(t)*

least: at least au moins *oh mwañ*

leather cuir (m) *kweer*

to **leave** *(to go away)* partir *parteer*
(message) laisser *laysay*

lecturer professeur d'université (m)
profaysuhr dewneeverseetay

left gauche (f) *gohsh*

» **to/on the left** à gauche *a gohsh*

left luggage *(office)* bagages en
consigne (m/pl) *bagaj oñ kawñseeny*

legal légal(e) *laygal*

lemon citron (m) *seetrawñ*

lemonade limonade (f) *leemonad*

to **lend** prêter *praytay*

length longueur (f) *lawñguhr*

lens *(camera)* objectif (m) *objekteef*

lesbian lesbienne (f) *lesbyen*

less moins *mwañ*

lesson leçon (f) *luhsawñ*

to **let** *(allow)* permettre *permetr*
(rent) louer *looay*

letter lettre (f) *letr*

letterbox boîte à lettres (f) *bwat a letr*

lettuce laitue (f) *laytew*

leukemia leucémie (f) *luhsaymee*

level *(height, standard)* niveau (m)
neevoh *(flat)* plat(e) *pla(t)*

level crossing passage à niveau (m)
pasaj a neevoh

library bibliothèque (f) *beebleeotek*

licence *(driving)* permis (m) *permee*

to **lie down** s'allonger *salawñjay*

life vie (f) *vee*

lifebelt bouée de sauvetage (f) *booay
duh sohvtaj*

lifeboat canot de sauvetage (m) *kanoh
duh sohvtaj*

lifeguard maître-nageur (m) *metr najuhr*

lifejacket gilet de sauvetage (m) *geelay
duh sohvtaj*

lift ascenseur (m) *asoñsuhr*

light lumière (f) *lewmyer*

light bulb ampoule (f) *oñpool*

light *(coloured)* clair(e) *kler*

    (weight) léger/ère *layjay/jer*

to **light** *(fire)* allumer *alewmay*

lighter *(cigarette)* briquet (m) *breekay*

lighter fuel essence à briquet (m) *esoñs a breekay*

lightning éclair (m) *aykler*

like *(similar to)* comme *kom*

to **like** *(food, people)* aimer *aymay*

  » **I like** j'aime *jem*

  » **to like doing something** aimer faire quelque chose *aymay fer kelkuhshohz*

likely probable *probabl*

limited limité(e) *leemeetay*

line ligne (f) *leeny*

lion lion (m) *lyawñ*

lipstick rouge à lèvres (m) *rooj a levr*

liqueur liqueur (f) *leekuhr*

liquid liquide *leekeed*

list liste (f) *leest*

to **listen** écouter *aykootay*

litre litre (m) *leetr*

litter ordures (f/pl) *ordewr*

little peu *puh*

  » **a little** un peu *uñ puh*

to **live** vivre *veevr*

  » *(dwell)* habiter *abeetay*

liver foie (m) *fwa*

living-room salon (m) *salawñ*

loan prêt (m) *pre*

local local(e) *lokal*

lock serrure (f) *serewr*

to **lock** fermer à clé *fermay a klay*

locker casier (m) *kazyay*

London Londres *lawñdr*

lonely solitaire *soleeter*

long long(ue) *lawñg*

long-distance longue distance *lawñg deestoñs*

  » **long-distance call** appel longue distance (m) *appel lawñg deestoñs*

look regard (m) *ruhgar*

to **look (at)** regarder *ruhgarday*

to **look for** chercher *shershay*

lorry camion (m) *kamyawñ*

lorry-driver routier (m) *rootyay*

to **lose** perdre *perdr*

lost property office bureau des objets trouvés (m) *bewroh dayz objay troovay*

a lot *(of)* beaucoup (de) *bohkoo (duh)*

lotion lotion (f) *losyawñ*

lottery loto (m) *lohtoh*

loud bruyant(e) *brweeyoñ(t)*

lounge salon (m) *salawñ*

love amour (m) *amoor*

to **love** aimer *aymay*

low bas(se) *ba(s)*

lower plus bas *plew ba*

lucky: to be lucky avoir de la chance *avvar duh la shoñs*

luggage baggage (m) *bagaj*

lump *(swelling)* grosseur (f) *grosuhr*

lunch déjeuner (m) *dayjuhnay*

M

machine machine (f) *masheen*

mad fou, folle *foo, fol*

madam madame (f) *madam*

magazine magazine (m) *magazeen*

mail courrier (m) *kooryay*

main principal(e) *prañseepal*

make *(brand)* marque (f) *mark*

to **make** faire *fer* *(see grammar, page 156)*

make-up maquillage (m) *makeeyaj*

male mâle (m) *mal*

man homme (m) *om*

manager responsable (m), manager (m) *respawñsabl, manadjer*

managing director directeur général (m) *direktuhr jaynayral*

many beaucoup (de) *bohkoo (duh)*

  » **not many** peu (de) *puh (duh)*

map carte (f) *kart*

marble marbre (m) *marbr*

margarine margarine (f) *margareen*

market marché (m) *marshay*

married marié(e) *maryay*

» **to get married** se marier *suh maryay*
mascara mascara *maskara*
masculine masculin(e) *maskewlañ/een*
mask masque (m) *mask*
mass (church) messe (f) *mes*
match (game) match (m) *match*
matches allumettes (f/pl) *alewmet*
material tissu (m) *teesew*
matter: it doesn't matter ça ne fait rien *sa nuh fay ryañ*
» **what's the matter?** qu'est-ce qui se passe? *keskee suh pas*
mattress matelas (m) *matla*
mature (cheese) affiné(e) *afeenay*
me me, moi *muh, mwa*
meadow prairie (f) *prayree*
meal repas (m) *ruhpa*
mean: what does this mean? qu'est-ce que ça veut dire? *keskuh sa vuh deer*
measles rougeole (f) *roojol*
» **German measles** rubéole (f) *rewbayol*
to **measure** mesurer *muhzewray*
measurement mesure (f) *muhzewr*
meat viande (f) *vyoñd*
» **cold meats** charcuterie (f) *sharkewtree*
mechanic mécanique *maykaneek*
medical médical(e) *maydeekal*
medicine (subject) médecine (f) *maydseen* (drug) médicament (m) *maydeekamoñ*
medieval médiéval(e) *maydyayval*
Mediterranean Méditerranée (f) *maydeeteranay*
medium (size) moyen(ne) *mwayañ/en* (steak) à point *a pwañ* (wine) demi-sec *duhmeesek*
meeting réunion (f) *rayewnyawñ*
member membre (m) *moñbr*
memory souvenir (m), mémoire (f) *soovneer, maymwar*
» **memory card** (for camera) carte mémoire (f) *kart maymwar*
men hommes (m/pl) *om*
to **mend** réparer *rayparay*

menu carte (f) *la kart* (set menu) menu (m) *muhnew*
message message (m) *maysaj*
metal métal (m) *maytal*
metre mètre (m) *metr*
microwave oven four micro-ondes (m) *foor meekro awñd*
midday midi (m) *meedee*
middle milieu (m) *meelyuh*
middle-aged moyen-âge (m) *mwayenaj*
midnight minuit (m) *meenwee*
migraine migraine (f) *meegren*
mild doux, douce *doo, doos*
milk lait (m) *lay*
mill moulin (m) *moolañ*
mind: I don't mind ça m'est égal *sa met aygal*
mine: it's mine c'est à moi *set a mwa*
minibus minibus (m) *meeneebews*
mini-disc mini-disc (m) *meeneedeesk*
minister ministre (m) *meeneestr*
minute minute (f) *meenewt*
mirror miroir (m) *meerwar*
miscarriage fausse-couche (f) *fohskoosh*
Miss mademoiselle (f) *madmwazel*
to **miss** (bus etc.) manquer *moñkay*
mist brume (f) *brewm*
mistake erreur (f) *eruhr*
» **to make a mistake** se tromper *suh trawñpay*
mixed mixte (salad) composé(e) *meext, kompozay*
mixture mélange (m) *mayloñj*
mobile (phone) (téléphone) portable (taylayfon) *portabl*
model modèle (m) *model*
modem modem (m) *modem*
modern moderne *modern*
moisturiser crème hydratante (f) *krem eedratoñt*
moment moment (m) *momoñ*
monastery monastère (m) *monaster*
money argent (m) *arjoñ*
month mois (m) *mwa*

monthly mensuel(le) *moñswel*

monument monument (m) *monewmoñ*

moon lune (f) *lewn*

moped mobylette (f) *mobeelet*

more plus *plews*

morning matin (m) *matañ*

mortgage emprunt immobilier (m) *oñpruñ eemobeelyay*

mosque mosquée (f) *moskay*

mosquito moustique (f) *moosteek*

mosquito net moustiquaire (f) *moosteeker*

most (of) la plupart (de) *la plewpar (duh)*

mother mère (f) *mer*

mother-in-law belle-mère (f) *belmer*

motor moteur (m) *motuhr*

motorbike moto (f) *mohtoh*

motorboat bateau à moteur (m) *batoh a motuhr*

motor racing course automobile (f) *koors ohtohmohbeel*

motorway autoroute (f) *ohtohroot*

mountain montagne (f) *mawñtany*

mountaineering alpinisme (m) *alpeeneesm*

moustache moustache (f) *moostash*

to move bouger *boojay*

» to move house déménager *daymaynajay*

Mr Monsieur (m) *muhsyuh*

Mrs Madame (f) *madam*

much beaucoup (de) *bohkoo (duh)*

mug (cup) grande tasse (f) *groñd tas*

to mug (someone) agresser *agraysay*

to murder assassiner *asaseenay*

museum musée (m) *mewzay*

music musique (f) *mewzeek*

musical musical(e) (f) *mewzeekal*

musician musicien(ne) *mewzeesyañ/en*

Muslim musulman(e) *mewzewlmoñ/man*

must: you must... il faut (que)... *eel foh (kuh)*

my mon, ma, mes *mawñ, ma, may*

mystery mystère (m) *meester*

N

nail clou (m) *klew*, (finger/toe) ongle (m) *awñgl*

nail clippers/scissors coupe-ongles (m) *koopawñgl*

nail file lime à ongles (f) *leem a awñgl*

nail polish vernis à ongles (m) *vernee a awñgl*

nail polish remover dissolvant (m) *deesolvoñ*

naked nu(e) *new*

name nom (m) *nawñ*

napkin serviette (f) *servyet*

nappy couche (f) *koosh*

» disposable nappy couche jetable (f) *koosh juhtabl*

» nappy liner protège-couche (m) *protej koosh*

national national(e) *nasyonal*

nationality nationalité (f) *nasyonaleetay*

natural naturel(e) *natewrel*

naughty méchant(e) *mayshoñ(t)*

navy marine (f) *mareen*

navy blue bleu marine *bluh mareen*

near (to) près (de) *pre (duh)*

» nearby tout près *too pre*

nearest plus proche *plew prosh*

nearly presque *presk*

necessary nécessaire *nayseser*

necklace collier (m) *kolyay*

to need avoir besoin (de) *avwar buhswañ (duh)*

needle aiguille (f) *aygweey*

negative (photo) négatif (m) *naygateef*

neighbour voisin(e) *vwazañ/zeen*

neither ... nor... ni ... ni... *nee ... nee...*

nephew neveu (m) *nuhvuh*

net filet (m) *feelay*

never jamais *jamay*

new nouveau/elle *noovoh/noovel*

» New Year Nouvel An (m) *noovel oñ*

news informations (f/pl)

añformasyawñ

newspaper journal (m) *joornal*

newspaper kiosk kiosque à journaux (m) *kyosk a joornoh*

next prochain(e) *proshañ/en*

next to près de *pre duh*

nice *(person)* sympathique *(place etc.)* joli(e) *johlee*

niece nièce (f) *nyes*

night nuit (f) *nwee*

nightclub boîte de nuit (f) *bwat duh nwee*

nightdress chemise de nuit (f) *shuhmeez duh nwee*

no non *noñ*

nobody personne *person*

noise bruit (m) *brwee*

noisy bruyant *brweeyoñ*

non-alcoholic sans alcool *soñz alkol*

none aucun(e) *ohkuñ/kewn*

non-smoking non fumeur *noñ fewmuhr*

normal normal(e) *normal*

» **normally** normalement *normalmoñ*

north nord (m) *nor*

nosebleed saignement de nez (m) *saynyuhmoñ duh ne*

not ne ... pas *nuh ... pa*

note *(bank)* billet (m) *beeyay*

notepad bloc-notes (m) *bloknot*

nothing rien *ryañ*

» **nothing else** rien d'autre *ryañ dohtr*

now maintenant *mañtuhnoñ*

nowhere nulle part *newl par*

number nombre (m) *nawñbr*

nurse infirmier/ère *añfeermyay/myer*

nursery slope piste pour débutants (f) *peest poor daybewtoñ*

nut noix (f) *nwa (DIY)* écrou (m) *aykroo*

nylon nylon (m) *neelawñ*

O

oar rame (f) *ram*

object *(thing)* objet (m) *objay*

obvious évident(e) *ayveedoñ(t)*

occasionally de temps en temps

duh toñz oñ toñ

occupied occupé(e) *okewpay*

odd bizarre *beezar, (not even)* impair *añper*

of de *duh*

off *(TV, light)* éteint(e) *aytañ(t) (milk)* tourné(e) *toornay*

offended offensé(e) *ofoñsay*

offer offrir *ofreer*

» **special offer** promotion (f) *promosyawñ*

office bureau (m) *bewroh*

officer officier (m) *ofeesyay*

official officiel(le) *ofeesyel*

often souvent *soovoñ*

» **how often?** combien de fois? *kawñbyañ duh fwa*

oil huile (f) *weel*

OK OK *ok*

old vieux, vieille *vyuh, vyey*

olive olive (f) *oleev*

olive oil huile d'olive (f) *weel doleev*

on sur *sewr (switched on)* allumé(e) *alewmay (engine)* en marche *oñ marsh*

once une fois *ewn fwa*

only seulement *suhlmoñ*

open ouvert(e) *oover(t)*

to open ouvrir *oovreer*

opera opéra (m) *opayra*

operation opération (f) *opayrasyawñ*

opinion opinion (f), avis (m) *opeenyawñ, avee*

» **in my opinion** à mon avis *a mawñ avee*

opposite en face de *oñ fas duh*

optician opticien(ne) *opteesyañ/syen*

or ou *oo*

orange orange (f) *oroñj*

order commande (f) *komoñd*

to order commander *komoñday*

ordinary ordinaire *ordeener*

to organise organiser *organeezay*

original original(e) *oreejeenal*

other autre *ohtr*

our notre, nos *nohtr, noh*

outdoors, outside dehors, à l'extérieur *duhor, a lextayryuhr*
ours: it's ours c'est à nous *set a new*
over dessus *duhsew*
overcast couvert(e) *koover(t)*
to overtake doubler *dooblay*
to owe devoir *duhvwar*
owner propriétaire (m/f) *propreeayter*
ozone friendly qui préserve la couche d'ozone *ki prayzerv la koosh dozohn*
ozone layer couche d'ozone (f) *koosh dozohn*

P

package tour voyage organisé (m) *vwiyaj organeezay*
packet paquet (m) *pakay*
paddle *(canoeing)* pagaie (f) *pagay*
padlock cadenas (m) *kadna*
page page (f) *paj*
pain douleur (f) *dooluhr*
painful douloureux/se *doolooruh(z)*
painkiller calmant (m) *kalmoñ*
paint, painting peinture (f) *pañtewr*
to paint peindre *pañdr*
painter peintre (m) *pañtr*
pair paire (f) *per*
palace palais (m) *palay*
pale pâle *pal*
pants pantalon (m), slip (m) *poñtalawñ, slip*
paper papier (m) *papyay*
paraffin paraffine (f) *parafeen*
parcel paquet (m) *pakay*
pardon? pardon? *pardawñ*
parents parents (m/pl) *paroñ*
park parc (m) *park*
to park se garer *suh garay*
parking parking (m) *parking*
  » parking meter parcmètre (m) *parkmetr*
parliament parlement (m) *parluhmoñ*
part pièce (f) *pyes*
partly en partie *oñ partee*

partner partenaire (m/f) *partuhner*
  (business) associé(e) *asosyay*
party fête (f) *fet*, *(political)* parti (m) *partee*
to pass *(salt etc.)* passer *pasay*
  (test, exam) réussir (à) *rayesseer a*
passenger passager/ère *pasajay/jer*
passport passeport (m) *paspor*
  » passport control contrôle des passeports (m) *kawñtrohl day paspor*
past passé (m) *pasay*
  » in the past dans le passé *doñ luh pasay*
pasta pâtes (f/pl) *pat*
pastry pâte (f) *pat*
path sentier (m) *soñtyay*
patient *(hospital)* patient(e) (m/f) *pasyoñ(t)*
pavement trottoir (m) *trotwar*
to pay payer *payay*
  » to pay cash payer comptant *payay kawñtoñ*
peace paix (f) *pay*
peanut cacahouète (f) *kakawet*
pedal pédale (f) *paydal*
pedal-boat pédalo (m) *paydaloh*
pedestrian piéton (m) *pyaytawñ*
pedestrian crossing passage clouté (m) *pasaj klootay*
to peel peler *puhlay*
pen stylo (m) *steeloh*
pencil crayon (m) *krayawñ*
penfriend correspondant(e) *korespawñdoñ*
penicillin pénicilline (f) *payneeseeleen*
penknife canif (m) *kaneef*
pension retraite (f) *ruhtret*
pensioner retraité(e) *ruhtretay*
people gens (m/pl) *joñ*
pepper poivre (m) *pwavr*
per par *par*
perfect parfait(e) *parfay/fet*
performance représentation (f) *ruhprayzoñtasyawñ*

(cinema) séance (f) *sayoñs*

perfume parfum (m) *parfuñ*

perhaps peut-être *puhtetr*

period *(menstrual)* règles (f/pl) *regl*

» **period pains** règles douloureuses (f/pl) *regl doolooruhz*

permit permis (m) *permee*

to **permit** permettre *permetr*

personal personnel(le) *personel*

petrol essence (f) *esoñs*

petrol can bidon d'essence (m) *beedawñ desoñs*

petrol station station-service (f) *stasyawñ servees*

petticoat jupon (m) *jewpawñ*

photo photo (f) *fohtoh*

photocopy photocopie (f) *fohtohkopee*

to **photocopy** photocopier *fohtohkopyay*

photographer photographe (m/f) *fohtohgraf*

phrase book guide de conversation (m) *geed duh kawñversasyawñ*

physics physique (f) *feeseek*

piano piano (m) *pyanoh*

to **pick** *(choose)* choisir *shwazeer* *(flowers etc.)* cueillir *kuhyeer*

picnic pique-nique (m) *peekneek*

picture photo (f), peinture (f), tableau (m), *fohtoh, pañtewr, tabloh*

piece morceau (m) *morsoh*

pier jetée (f) *juhtay*

pig cochon (m) *koshawñ*

pill pilule (f) *peelewl*

» **the pill** la pilule (f) *la peelewl*

pillow oreiller (m) *oreyay*

pillowcase taie d'oreiller (f) *tay doreyay*

pilot pilote (m) *peelot*

pilot light veilleuse (f) *vayuhz*

pin épingle (f) *aypañgl*

pink rose *rohz*

pipe *(smoking)* pipe (f) *peep* *(drain)* tuyau (m) *tweeyoh*

place endroit (m) *oñdrwa (seat)* place (f) *plas*

plain ordinaire *ordeener*

plan plan (m) *ploñ*

plane avion (m) *avyawñ*

plant plante (f) *plant*

plaster *(sticking)* sparadrap (m) *sparadra*

plastic plastique (m) *plasteek*

plastic bag sac en plastique (m) *sak oñ plasteek*

plate assiette (f) *asyet*

platform quai (m) *kay*

play *(theatre)* pièce (de théâtre) (f) *pyes (duh tayatr)*

to **play** jouer *jooay*

pleasant agréable *agrayabl*

please s'il vous plaît *seelvooplay*

pleased content(e) *kawñtoñ(t)*

plenty (of) assez (de) *asay (duh)*

pliers pince (f) *pañs*

plug *(bath)* bouchon (de la baignoire) (m) *booshawñ (duh la baynywar)* *(electrical)* prise (électrique) (f) *preez aylektreek*

plumber plombier (m) *plawñbyay*

pneumonia pneumonie (f) *pnuhmonee*

pocket poche (f) *posh*

point point (m) *pwañ*

poison poison (m) *pwazawñ*

poisonous *(animals)* vénimeux/se *vayneemuh(z) (plants)* vénéneux/se *vaynaynuh(z) (gas)* toxique *toxeek*

police police (f) *polees*

police car voiture de police (f) *vwatewr duh polees*

police station poste de police (m) *post duh polees*

polish cirage (m) *seeraj*

polite poli(e) *polee*

political politique *poleeteek*

politician politicien(ne) *poleeteesyañ/syen*

politics politique (f) *poleeteek*

polluted pollué(e) *polway*

pollution pollution (f) *polewsyawñ*

pool *(swimming)* piscine (f) *peeseen*

poor pauvre *pohvr*

pop *(music)* pop (f) *pop*

Pope Pape (m) *pap*

popular populaire *popewler*

pork porc (m) *por*

port *(harbour)* port (m) *por*
   (wine) porto (m) *portoh*

portable portable (m) *portabl*

porter portier (m) *portyay*

portrait portrait (m) *portray*

positive *(sure)* positif/ve *pozeeteef/eev*

possible possible *poseebl*

  » **as soon as possible** dès que possible
   de kuh poseebl

  » **if possible** si possible *see poseebl*

possibly éventuellement *ayvoñtuelemoñ*

post *(mail)* courrier *kooreay*

to **post** poster *postay*

postbox boîte à lettres (f) *bwate à letres*

postcard carte postale (f) *kart postal*

postcode code postal (m) *kod postal*

poster affiche (f) *afeesh*

post office bureau de poste (m) *buroh
   duh post*

to **postpone** reporter *ruhportay*

pot pot (m) *po*

potato pomme de terre (f) *pom duh ter*

  » **potato crisps** chips (f/pl) *sheeps*

pottery poterie (f) *potree*

potty *(child's)* pot (de bébé) (m) *po
   (duh baybay)*

pound *(sterling)* livre (f) *leevr*

to **pour** verser *versay*

powder poudre (f) *poodr*

powdered milk lait en poudre (m) *lay oñ
   poodr*

power pouvoir (m) *poovwar*
   (electrical) courant (m) *kooroñ*

power cut panne de courant (f) *pan duh
   kooroñ*

pram landeau (m) *loñdoh*

to **prefer** préférer *prayfayray*

pregnant enceinte *oñsoñt*

to **prepare** préparer *prayparay*

prescription ordonnance (f) *ordonoñs*

present *(gift)* cadeau (m) *kadoh*

press *(newspapers)* presse (f) *pres*

to **press** presser *presay*

pretty joli(e) *jolee*

price prix (m) *pree*

priest prêtre (m) *pretr*

prime minister premier ministre (m)
   pruhmyay meeneestr

prince prince (m) *prañs*

princess princesse (f) *prañses*

print *(photo)* tirage (m) *teeraj*

to **print** imprimer *añpreemay*

prison prison (f) *preezawñ*

private privé(e) *preevay*

prize prix (m) *pree*

probably probablement *probabluhmoñ*

problem problème (m) *problem*

profession profession (f) *profesyawñ*

professor professeur (m) *profesuhr*

profit bénéfice (m) *baynayfees*

programme *(computer)* programme (m)
   program, (TV, radio) émission (f)
   aymeesyoñ, (theatre) programme
   (m) *program*

prohibited interdit(e) *añterdee(t)*

to **promise** promettre *promettr*

to **pronounce** prononcer *pronawñsay*

properly correctement *korektuhmoñ*

property propriété (f) *propryaytay*

protestant protestant(e) *protestoñ(t)*

public public (m) *pewbleek*
   (adj.) public, publique *pewbleek*

public holiday jour férié (m) *joor fayryay*

to **pull** tirer *teeray*

to **pump up** gonfler *gawñflay*

puncture crevaison (f) *kruhvezawñ*

pure pur(e) *pewr*

purple violet(te) *vyolay/et*

purse porte-monnaie (m) *portuhmonay*

to **push** pousser *poosay*

push-chair poussette (f) *pooset*

to **put down** poser *pozay*

to **put on** *(clothes)* mettre *metr*

pyjamas pyjama (m) *peejama*

Q

quality qualité (f) *kaleetay*
quarter quart (m) *kar*
quay quai (m) *kay*
queen reine (f) *ren*
question question (f) *kestyawñ*
queue queue (f) *kuh*
quick rapide *rapeed*
quickly vite *veet*
quiet silencieux/se *siloñsyuh(z)*
quite *(fairly)* plutôt, assez *plewtoh,
    asay (completely)* complètement
    kompletuhmoñ

R

rabbi rabbin (m) *rabañ*
rabbit lapin (m) *lapañ*
rabies rage (f) *raj*
racecourse champ de courses (m),
    hippodrome (m) *shoñp de koors,
    heepodrohm*
racing courses (m/pl) *koors*
racket *(tennis)* raquette (f) *raket*
radio radio (f) *radyoh*
radioactive radioactif/tive
    radyohakteef/eev
radio station station de radio (f)
    stazyawñ duh radyoh
raft radeau (m) *radoh*
railway chemin de fer (m) *shemañ duh fer*
railway station gare (ferroviaire) (f) *gar
    (fayrovyer)*
rain pluie (f) *plwee*
    » **it's raining** il pleut *eel pluh*
raincoat imperméable (m) *añpermayabl*
to **rape** violer *vyohlay*
rare rare *rar (steak)* bleu *bluh*
rash *(spots)* rougeur (f) *roojuhr*
rate *(speed)* vitesse (f) *veetes
    (tariff)* tarif (m) *tareef*
raw cru(e) *krew*
razor rasoir (m) *razwar*

razor blade lame de rasoir (f)
    lam duh razwar
to **reach** atteindre *atañdr*
to **read** lire *leer*
reading lecture (f) *lektewr*
ready prêt(e) *pre/prayt*
real *(authentic)* véritable *vayreetabl*
rear arrière (m) *aryer*
reason raison (f) *rayzawñ*
receipt reçu (m) *ruhsew*
receiver *(telephone)* combiné (m)
    kawñbeenay
reception réception (f) *raysepsyawñ*
receptionist réceptionniste (m/f)
    rayseptyoneest
recipe recette (f) *ruhset*
to **recognise** reconnaître *ruhkonetr*
to **recommend** recommander *ruhkomoñday*
record *(audio)* disque (m) *deesk*
to **record** enregistrer *oñruhgeestray*
to **recover** *(from an illness)* se remettre de
    suh ruhmet duh
red rouge *rooj*
    » **Red Cross** Croix Rouge *krwa rooj*
reduction réduction (f) *raydewxyawñ*
to **refill** recharger *ruhsharjay*
refrigerator réfrigérateur (m), frigo (m)
    rayfreejayratuhr, freegoh
refugee réfugié(e) *rayfewjyay*
refund remboursement (m)
    roñboorsuhmoñ
to **refund** rembourser *roñboorsay*
region région (f) *rayjyawñ*
to **register** *(luggage etc.)* enregistrer
    oñruhjeestray
registered *(letter)* lettre recommandée
    (f) *(letr) ruhkomañday*
registration document *(car)* carte grise
    (f) *kart greez*
registration number *(car)* numéro
    d'immatriculation (m) *newmayroh
    deematreekewlasyañ*
relatively relativement *ruhlateevmoñ*
religion religion (f) *ruhleejyawñ*
to **remain** rester *restay*

to remember se rappeler *suh rapuhlay*
» I remember... je me rappelle...
juh muh rappel
» do you remember...? est-ce que
vous vous rappelez...? *es kuh voo voo
rapuhlay...*
to remove enlever *oñluhvay*
(tooth) arracher *arashay*
rent loyer (m) *lwiyay*
to rent louer *looay*
to repair réparer *rayparay*
to repeat répéter *raypaytay*
reply réponse (f) *raypawñs*
to reply répondre *raypawñdr*
report rapport (m) *rapor*
to report rendre compte *roñdr kawñt*
to rescue secourir *suhkooreer*
reservation (hotel etc.) réservation (f)
rayservasyawñ
to reserve réserver *rayzervay*
reserved réservé(e) *rayzervay*
responsible responsable *respawñsabl*
to rest se reposer *suh ruhpohzay*
restaurant restaurant (m) *restohroñ*
result résultat (m) *raysewlta*
retired retraité(e) *ruhtraytay*
return retour (m) *ruhtoor* (ticket)
aller-retour (m) *alay-ruhtoor*
to return retourner *ruhtoornay* (give back)
rendre *roñdr*
reverse-charge call appel en PCV (m)
apel oñ paysayvay
ribbon ruban (m) *rewboñ*
rice riz (m) *ree*
rich riche *reesh*
to ride (horse/bike) aller à (cheval/vélo)
alay à (shuhval/vayloh)
right droite (f) *drwat*
» on/to the right à droite *a drwat*
» to be right avoir raison *avwar rayzawñ*
» you're right vous avez raison *vooz
avay rayzawñ*

ring (jewellery) bague (f) *bag*
ripe mûr(e) *mewr*
river rivière (f) *reevyer*
road (main) route (f) *root*
roadworks travaux (m/pl) *travoh*
roast rôti(e) *rotee*
to rob voler *volay*
robbery vol (m) *vol*
roof toit (m) *twa*
room (house) pièce (f) *pies*
(hotel) chambre (f) *shawñbr*
(space) place (f) *plas*
rope corde (f) *kord*
rose rose (f) *roz*
rotten pourri(e) *pooree*
rough (surface) rugueux/se *rewguh(z)*
(sea) gros(se) *gro(s)*
round rond(e) *rawñ(d)*
roundabout rond-point (m) *rawñpwañ*
row (theatre etc.) rang (m) *roñ*
to row ramer *ramay*
rowing boat canot (m) *kanoh*
royal royal(e) *rwiyal*
rubber caoutchouc (m) *kaootshoo*
rubbish ordures (f/pl) *ordewr*
rucksack sac à dos (m) *sak a doh*
rude impoli(e) *añpolee*
ruins ruines (f/pl) *rween*
ruler (for measuring) règle (f) *regl*
rum rhum (m) *rom*
to run courir *kooreer*
rush hour heures de pointe (f/pl) *uhr
duh pwañt*

S

sad triste *treest*
safe (strongbox) coffre-fort (m) *kofruhfor*
safe sûr(e) *sewr*
safety pin épingle de sûreté (f) *aypañgl
duh sewrtay*
sail voile (f) *vwal*
to sail faire de la voile *fer duh la vwal*
sailing voile (f) *vwal*
sailing boat voilier (m) *vwalyay*

sailor matelot (m) *matloh*

saint saint(e) *sañ(t)*

salad salade (f) *salad*

sale (bargains) soldes (m/pl) *sold*

sales rep commercial (m) *komersyal*

salmon saumon (m) *sohmawñ*

salt sel (m) *sel*

salty salé(e) *salay*

same même *mem*

sample échantillon (m) *ayshoñteeyawñ*

sand sable (m) *sabl*

sandals sandales (f/pl) *soñdal*

sandwich sandwich (m) *sandwich*

sandy sablonneux/se *sablonuh(z)*

sanitary towels serviettes hygiéniques (f/pl) *servyet eejyayneek*

sauce sauce (f) *sohs*

saucepan casserole (f) *kasrol*

saucer soucoupe (f) *sookoop*

sauna sauna (m) *sohna*

to save (money) économiser *aykonomeezay*

to say dire *deer*

scales balance (f) *baloñs*

scarf écharpe (f) *aysharp* (head) foulard (m) *foolar*

scene scène (f) *sen*

scenery paysage (m) *payeesaj*

scent senteur (f) *soñtuhr*

school école (f) *aykol*

science science (f) *syoñs*

scissors ciseaux (m/pl) *seezoh*

scooter scooter (m) *skooter*

score: what's the score? quel est le score? *kell ay luh scor*

Scotland Ecosse (f) *aykos*

Scottish écossais(e) *aykosay(z)*

scratch rayure (f) *rayewr*

to scratch rayer *rayyay*

screen écran (m) *aykroñ*

screw vis (f) *vees*

screwdriver tournevis (m) *toornuhvees*

sculpture sculpture (f) *skewltewr*

sea mer (f) *mer*

seafood fruits de mer (m/pl) *frwee duh mer*

seasick mal de mer (m) *mal duh mer*

season saison (f) *sayzawñ*

season ticket carte d'abonnement (f) *kart dabonmoñ*

seat siège (m) *syej*

seatbelt ceinture de sécurité (f) *sañtewr duh saykewreetay*

second second(e), deuxième *suhgawñ(d), duhzyem*

second seconde (f) *suhgawñd*

secret secret (m) *suhkray*

secretary secrétaire (m/f) *suhkrayter*

sedative sédatif (m) *saydateef*

to see voir *vwar*

to seem paraître *paretr*

self-catering avec cuisine *avek kweezeen*

self-service libre-service (m) *leebr servees*

to sell vendre *voñdr*

to send envoyer *oñvwyay*

senior citizen personne âgée (f) *person ajay*

sensible raisonnable *raysonabl*

sentence phrase (f) *fraz*

separate, separated séparé(e) *sayparay*

serious grave *grav*

to serve servir *serveer*

service (charge) service (m) *servees* (church) office (m) *ofees*

several plusieurs *plewzyuhr*

to sew coudre *koodr*

sewing couture (f) *kootewr*

sex (gender) sexe (m) *sex* (intercourse) rapports sexuels (m) *rapor sexewel*

shade (not sunny) ombre (f) *awñbr*

shadow ombre (f) *awñbr*

shampoo shampooing (m) *shoñpwañ*

sharp aiguisé(e), pointu(e) *aygeezay, pwañtew*

shave rasage (m) *razaj*

to shave se raser *suh razay*

shaving cream/foam crème/mousse à raser (f) *krem/moos a razay*

she elle *el*

sheep mouton (m) *mootawñ*

sheet drap (m) *dra*

shelf étagère (f) *aytajer*

shell (egg, nut) coquille (f) *kokeey*
(seashell) coquillage (m) *kokeeyaj*

shelter abri (m) *abree*

shiny brillant(e) *breeyoñ(t)*

ship navire (m) *naveer*

shirt chemise (f) *shuhmeez*

shock (electrical) décharge (électrique)
(f) *daysharj (aylektreek)*
(emotional) choc (m) *shok*

shocked choqué(e) *shokay*

shoe(s) chaussure(s) (f) *shohsewr*

shoelace lacet (m) *lasay*

shoe polish cirage (m) *seeraj*

shoe repairer's cordonnier (m) *kordonyay*

shoe shop magasin de chaussures (m)
magazañ duh shohsewr

shop magasin (m) *magazañ*

shop assistant vendeur/se *voñduhr/duhz*

shopping: to go shopping faire des
courses *fer day koors*

shopping centre centre commercial
(m) *soñtr komersyal*

short court(e) *koor(t)*

shorts short (m) *short*

shout cri (m) *kree*

show spectacle (m) *spektakl*

to show montrer *mawñtray*

shower douche (f) *doosh*

shut fermé(e) *fermay*

to shut fermer *fermay*

shutter volet (m) *volay*

sick malade *malad*
» **to be sick** être malade *etr malad*
» **to feel sick** se sentir mal
se soñteer mal

sick bag sac vomitoire (m) *sak
vomeetwar*

side côté (m) *kotay*

sight (vision) vue (f) *vew* (tourist)
attraction (f), site (m) *atraxyawñ, seet*

sightseeing tourisme (m) *tooreesm*

sign panneau (m) *panoh*

to sign signer *seenyay*

signal signal (m) *seenyal*

signature signature (f) *seenyatewr*

silent silencieux/se *seeloñsyuh(z)*

silk soie (f) *swa*

silver argent (m) *arjoñ*

SIM card carte SIM (f) *kart seem*

similar semblable *soñblabl*

simple simple *sañpl*

since depuis *duhpwee*

to sing chanter *shoñtay*

single (room, ticket) simple *sañpl*
(unmarried) célibataire *sayleebater*

sink évier (m) *ayvyay*

sir monsieur *muhsyuh*

sister sœur (f) *suhr*

sister-in-law belle-sœur (f) *belsuhr*

to sit (down) s'asseoir *saswar*

size (clothes, shoes) taille (f) *tiy*

skates (ice) patins (m/pl) *patañ* (roller)
patins à roulettes (m/pl) *patañ a roolet*

to skate patiner *pateenay*

ski ski (m) *skee*

to ski skier *skeeay*

ski boots chaussures de ski (f/pl)
shohsewr duh skee

skiing ski (m) *skee*
» **downhill skiing** ski de descente (m),
ski alpin (m) *skee duh desoñt, skee
alpañ*
» **cross-country skiing** ski de fond (m)
skee duh fawñ

ski-lift remonte-pente (m) *remawñt poñt*

skimmed milk lait écrémé (m) *lay
aykraymay*

skin peau (f) *poh*

ski pole bâton de ski (m)
batawñ duh skee

skirt jupe (f) *jewp*

ski-slope piste de ski (f) *peest duh skee*

sky ciel (m) *syel*

to sleep dormir *dormeer*

sleeper/sleeping-car voiture-lit (f) *vwatewr lee*

sleeping bag sac de couchage (m) *sak duh kooshaj*

sleeve manche (f) *moñsh*

slice tranche (f) *troñsh*

sliced tranché(e) *troñshay*

slim mince *mañs*

slippery glissant(e) *gleesoñ*

slow lent(e) *loñt (uhmoñ)*

slowly lentement *loñtuhmoñ*

small petit(e) *puhteet*

smell odeur (f) *oduhr*

to smell (of) sentir *soñteer* sentir le... *soñteer luh...*

smile sourire (m) *sooreer*

smoke fumée (f) *fumay*

to smoke fumer *fumay*

smooth lisse *lees*

to sneeze éternuer *ayternway*

snorkel masque de plongée (m) *mask duh plawñjay*

snow neige (f) *nej*

to snow neiger *nayjay*

» it's snowing il neige *eel nej*

snow chains chaînes (f/pl) *shen*

so si *see (therefore)* ainsi, comme ça *añsee, kom sa*

soap savon (m) *savawñ*

sober sobre *sobr*

social worker assistante sociale *aseestoñt sosyal*

sociology sociologie (f) *sosyolojee*

sock chaussette (f) *shohset*

socket prise (f) *preez*

soft doux, douce *doo, doos*

soft drink boisson non-alcoolisée (f) *bwasawñ nawñalkoleezay*

software logiciel (m) *lojeesyel*

soldier soldat (m) *solda*

sold out complet/ète *kawñplay/plet*

solicitor notaire (m) *noter*

solid solide *soleed*

some quelques *kelkuh*

somehow d'une manière ou d'une autre *dewn manyer oo dewn ohtr*

someone quelqu'un *kelkuñ*

something quelque chose *kelkeshohz*

sometimes parfois, quelquefois *parfwa, kelkuhfwa*

somewhere quelque part *kelkuhpar*

son fils (m) *fees*

song chanson (f) *shoñsawñ*

son-in-law beau-fils (m) *bohfees*

soon bientôt *byañtoh*

» as soon as possible aussitôt que possible *ohseetoh kuh poseebl*

sore throat mal de gorge (m) *mal duh gorj*

sorry pardon *pardañ*

» I'm sorry (je suis) désolé(e) *(juh swee) dayzolay*

sort sorte (f), genre (m) *sort, joñr*

sound son (m) *sawñ*

soup soupe (f) *soop*

south sud (m) *sewd*

souvenir souvenir (m) *soovuhneer*

space espace (m) *espas*

spade pelle (f) *pel*

spare de rechange *duh ruhshoñj*

spare time temps libre (m) *toñ leebr*

spare tyre roue de secours (f) *roo duh suhkoor*

sparkling mousseux/se *moosuh(z)*

to speak parler *parlay*

special spécial(e) *spaysyal*

» special offer promotion (f) *promosyawñ*

specialist spécialiste (m/f) *spaysyaleest*

speciality spécialité (f) *spaysyaleetay*

spectacles lunettes (f/pl) *lewnet*

speed vitesse (f) *veetes*

speed limit limitation de vitesse (f) *leemeetasyawñ duh veetes*

to spend (money) dépenser *daypoñsay* (time) passer *pasay*

spice épice (f) *aypees*

spicy épicé(e) *aypeesay*

spirits alcools (m/pl) *alkol*

splinter écharde (f) *ayshard*

to **spoil** abîmer *abeemay*

sponge *(bath)* éponge (f) *aypawñj*

spoon cuiller (f) *kweeyer*

sport sport (m) *spor*

spot bouton (m) *bootawñ*

    (place) endroit (m) *oñdrwa*

to **sprain** se fouler *suh foolay*

sprained foulé(e) *foolay*

spray vaporisateur (m) *vaporeezatuhr*

spring *(season)* printemps (m) *prañtoñ*

square place (f) *plas*, *(shape)* carré (m) *karay*

stadium stade (m) *stad*

stain tache (f) *tash*

stainless steel inox (m) *eenox*

stairs escaliers (m/pl) *eskalyay*

stalls *(theatre)* strapontins (m/pl) *strapawñtañ*

stamp *(postage)* timbre (m) *tañbr*

stand *(stadium)* tribune (f) *treebewn*

stapler agrafeuse (f) *agrafuhz*

star étoile (f) *aytwal*

start commencement (m), départ (m) *komoñsmoñ, daypar*

to **start** commencer *komoñsay*

starter *(food)* entrée (f) *oñtray*

station gare (f) *gar*

stationer's papetier/ère *papuhtyay/tyer*

statue statue (f) *statew*

to **stay** *(live)* habiter *abeetay*

    (remain) rester *restay*

to **steal** voler *volay*

steam vapeur (f) *vapuhr*

steamer cocotte-minute (f) *kokot meenewt*

steel acier (m) *asyay*

steep raide *rayd*

step *(footstep)* pas (m) *pa*

    (stairs) marche (f) *marsh*

stepbrother demi-frère (m) *duhmeefrer*

stepfather beau-père (m) *bohper*

stepmother belle-mère (f) *belmer*

stepsister demi-sœur (f) *duhmeesuhr*

stereo poste (m) *post*

stick baguette (f) *baget*

to **stick: it's stuck** c'est collé(e) *se kolay*

sticky poisseux/se *pwasuh(z)*

sticky tape scotch (m) *skotsh*

stiff rigide *reejeed*

still *(yet)* encore, toujours *oñkor, toojoor*

still *(non-fizzy)* plat(e) *pla(t)*

sting piqûre (f) *peekewr*

to **sting** piquer *peekay*

stock exchange bourse (f) *boors*

stockings bas (m/pl) *ba*

stolen volé(e) *volay*

stomach estomac (m) *estoma*

  » **upset stomach** estomac dérangé (m) *estoma dayroñjay*

stomach ache mal d'estomac (m) *mal destoma*

stone pierre (f) *pyer*

stop *(bus)* arrêt (m) *aray*

to **stop** arrêter *araytay*

  » **stop!** arretez! *araytay!*

stopcock robinet d'arrêt (m) *robeenay daray*

story histoire (f) *eestwar*

stove poêle (m) *pwal*

straight droit(e) *drwa*

straight on tout droit *too drwa*

strange étrange *aytroñj*

stranger étranger/ère *aytroñjay/jer*

strap lanière (f) *lanyer*

straw *(drinking)* paille (f) *piy*

stream ruisseau (m) *rweesoh*

street rue (f) *rew*

stretcher brancard (m) *broñkar*

strike grève (f) *grev*

  » **on strike** en grève *oñ grev*

string ficelle (f) *feesel*

stripe rayure (f) *rayyewr*

striped rayé(e) *rayyay*

strong fort(e) *for(t)*

student étudiant(e) *aytewdyoñ(t)*

studio *(radio/TV)* studio (m) *stewdyoh*

to **study** étudier *aytewdyay*

stupid stupid(e) *stewpeed*

style style (m) *steel*

subtitles sous-titres (m/pl) *sooteetr*

suburb banlieue (f) *boñlyuh*

to **succeed** réussir *rayewseer*

success succès (m) *sewxay*

suddenly soudain *soodañ*

sugar sucre (m) *sewkr*

sugar lump morceau de sucre (m) *morsoh duh sewkr*

suit *(man's)* costume (m) *kostewm*

» *(woman's)* tailleur (m) *tiyuhr*

suitcase valise (m) *valeez*

summer été (m) *aytay*

sun soleil *soley*

to **sunbathe** se faire bronzer *suh fer brawñzay*

sunburn coup de soleil (m) *koo duh soley*

sunglasses lunettes de soleil (f/pl) *lewnet duh soley*

sunshade parasol (m) *parasol*

sunstroke insolation (f) *añsolasyawñ*

suntan bronzage (m) *brawñzaj*

» **suntan lotion** crème solaire (f) *krem soler*

» **suntan oil** huile bronzante (f) *weel brawñzoñt*

supermarket supermarché (m) *sewpermarshay*

supper souper (m) *soopay*

supplement supplément (m) *sewplaymoñ*

suppose: I suppose so/not je suppose que oui/non *juh sewpohz kuh wee/noñ*

suppository suppositoire (m) *sewpohzeetwar*

sure sûr(e) *sewr*

surface surface (f) *sewrfas*

surname nom (m) *nawñ*

surprise surprise (f) *sewrpreez*

surrounded by entouré(e) de *oñtooray duh*

to **sweat** transpirer *troñspeeray*

sweater pull (m) *pewl*

sweatshirt sweat-shirt (m) *swetshuhrt*

to **sweep** balayer *balayyay*

sweet doux, douce *doo, doos*

sweetener édulcorant (m) *aydewlkoroñ*

sweets bonbons (m/pl) *bawñbawñ*

swelling grosseur (f), bosse (f) *grosuhr, bos*

to **swim** nager *najay*

swimming nage (f) *naj*

swimming pool piscine (f) *peeseen*

swimming trunks slip de bain (m) *sleep duh bañ*

swimsuit maillot de bain (m) *miyoh duh bañ*

switch interrupteur (m) *añterewptuhr*

to **switch off** éteindre *aytoñdr*

to **switch on** allumer *alewmay*

swollen enflé(e) *oñflay*

symptom symptôme (m) *sañptohm*

synagogue synagogue (f) *seenagog*

system système (m) *seestem*

T

table table (f) *tabl*

tablet comprimé (m) *kawñpreemay*

table tennis ping pong (m) *ping pong*

tailor tailleur (m) *tiyuhr*

to **take** prendre *proñdr* (exam) passer *pasay*

taken (seat) occupé(e) *okewpay*

to **take off** (clothes) enlever *oñluhvay* (plane) décoller *daykolay*

to **talk** parler *parlay*

tall grand(e) *groñd*

tampons tampons (m/pl) *toñpawñ*

tap robinet (m) *robeenay*

tape (sticky) scotch (m) *skotsh* (cassette) cassette (f) *kaset*

tape measure mètre (m) *metr*

tape recorder magnétophone (m) *manyaytofon*

taste goût (m) *goo*

to **taste** goûter *gootay*

tax impôt (m) *añpoh*

taxi taxi (m) *taxee*

taxi rank station de taxis (f) *stasyawñ duh taxee*

tea thé (m) *tay*

teabag sachet de thé (m) *sashay duh tay*

to **teach** enseigner *oñsenyay*

teacher professeur (m) *profesuhr*

team équipe (f) *aykeep*

teapot théière (f) *tayyer*

tear *(rip)* déchirure (f) *daysheerewr* *(cry)* larme (f) *larm*

  » **in tears** en larmes *oñ larm*

teaspoon cuiller à café (f) *kweeyer a kafay*

teat *(for baby's bottle)* tétine (f) *tayteen*

tea-towel torchon (de vaisselle) (m) *torshawñ (duh vaysel)*

technical technique *tekneek*

technology technologie (f) *teknolojee*

teenager adolescent(e) *adolesoñ(t)*

telegram télégramme (m) *taylaygram*

telephone téléphone (m) *taylayfon*

to **telephone** téléphoner *taylayfonay*

telephone card carte téléphonique (f) *kart taylayfoneek*

telephone directory annuaire téléphonique (m) *anwer taylayfoneek*

telephone kiosk cabine téléphonique (f) *kabeen taylayfoneek*

television télévision (f) *taylayveezyawñ*

to **tell** raconter, dire *rakawñtay, deer*

temperature température (f) *toñpayratewr*

  » **to have a temperature** avoir de la fièvre *avwar duh la feeyevr*

temporary provisoire *proveezwar*

tennis tennis (m) *taynees*

tennis court court de tennis (m) *koor duh taynees*

tent tente (f) *toñt*

tent peg piquet de tente (m) *peekay duh toñt*

tent pole montant de tente (m) *mawñtoñ duh toñt*

terminal *(airport)* aérogare (m) *aayrogar*

terminus terminus (m) *termeenews*

terrace terrasse (f) *teras*

terrible terrible *tereebl*

terrorist terroriste (m/f) *teroreest*

text message SMS (m) *es em es*

to **text** envoyer un SMS *oñviyay uñ es em es*

than que *kuh*

thank you (very much) merci (beaucoup) *mersee (bohkoo)*

that (one) celui (-ci) *suhlwe (see)*

the le, la, les *luh, la, lay*

theatre théâtre (m) *tayatr*

their leur, leurs *luhr, luhr*

theirs: it's theirs c'est à eux *set a uh*

them eux, elles *uh, el*

then ensuite, alors *oñsweet, alor*

there là *la*

  » **there is/are** il y a *eelya*

therefore donc *dawñk*

thermometer thermomètre (m) *termometr*

these ces *say*

they ils, elles *eel, el*

thick épais(se) *aype(s)*

thief voleur/se *voluhr(z)*

thin mince *mañs*

thing chose (f) *shohz*

to **think** penser *poñsay* *(believe)* croire *krwar*

third troisième *trwazyem*

thirsty: to be thirsty avoir soif *avwar swaf*

this ce, cet, cette *suh, set, set*

this one celui-ci, celle-ci *selweesi, selsi*

those ces *say*

thread fil (m) *feel*

throat lozenges/pastilles pastilles pour la gorge (f/pl) *pasteey poor la gorj*

through à travers *a traver*

to **throw** lancer *loñsay*

to **throw away** jeter *juhtay*

thumb pouce (m) *poos*

thunder tonnerre (m) *toner*

ticket billet (m) *beeyay* *(bus, metro)* ticket (m) *teekay*

ticket office guichet (m) *geeshay*

tide *(high/low)* marée (f) *maray*

tidy propre *propr*

tie cravate (f) *kravat*

to tie attacher, nouer *atashay, nooay*

tight *(clothes)* serré(e), étroit(e) *seray, aytrwa*

tights collants (m/pl) *koloñ*

till *(until)* jusqu'à *jewska*

time temps (m) *toñ*, *(on clock)* heure (f) *uhr*

timetable *(train)* horaire (m) *orayr*

tin boîte (f) *bwat*

tinned en boîte *oñ bwat*

tin opener ouvre-boîte (m) *oovruhbwat*

tip *(in restaurant etc.)* pourboire (m) *poorbwar*

tired fatigué(e) *fateegay*

tissues kleenex (m) *kleenex*

to à *a*

toast pain grillé (m), toast (m) *pañ greeyay, tohst*

tobacco tabac (m) *taba*

tobacconist's bureau de tabac (m) *buroh duh taba*

toboggan toboggan (m) *tobogoñ*

today aujourd'hui *aujoordwee*

toiletries articles de toilette (m/pl) *arteekl duh twalet*

toilet paper papier hygiénique (m) *papyay eejjayneek*

toilets toilettes (f/pl) *twalet*

toll péage (m) *payaj*

tomato tomate (f) *tomat*

tomorrow demain *duhmañ*

tongue langue (f) *loñg*

tonight ce soir *suh swar*

too *(also)* aussi *ohsee*
    (excessively) trop *tro*

tool outil (m) *ootee*

tooth dent (f) *doñ*

toothache mal de dent (m) *mal duh doñ*

toothbrush brosse à dents (f) *bros a doñ*

toothpaste dentifrice (m) *doñteefrees*

toothpick cure-dent (m) *kewrdoñ*

top *(mountain)* sommet (m) *some*
    » **on top of** sur, dessus *sewr, duhsew*

torch torche (f) *torsh*

torn déchiré(e) *daysheeray*

total total (m) *total*

totally totalement *totalmoñ*

to touch toucher *tooshay*

tough *(meat)* dur(e) *dewr*

tour visite (f) *veezeet*

to tour visiter *veezeetay*

tourism tourisme (m) *tooreesm*

tourist touriste (m/f) *tooreest*

tourist office office de tourisme (m) *ofees duh tooreesm*

to tow remorquer *ruhmorkay*
    » **tow rope** câble de remorquage (m) *kabl duh ruhmorkaj*

towards vers *ver*

towel serviette (f) *servyet*

tower tour (f) *toor*

town ville (f) *veel*
    » **town centre** centre-ville (m) *soñtruhveel*
    » **town hall** hôtel de ville (m), mairie (f) *ohtel duh veel, mayree*

toy jouet (m) *jooay*

track piste (f) *peest*

traditional traditionnel(le) *tradeesyonel*

traffic circulation (f) *seerkewlasyawñ*

traffic jam embouteillage (m) *oñbooteyaj*

traffic lights feux (m/pl) *fuh*

trailer remorque (f) *ruhmork*

train train (m) *trañ*
    » **by train** en train *oñ trañ*

trainers baskets (f/pl) *basket*

tram tram (m) *tram*

tranquilliser calmant (m) *kalmoñ*

to translate traduire *tradweer*

translation traduction (f) *tradewxyawñ*

to travel voyager *vwiyajay*

travel agency agence de voyage (f) *ajoñs duh vwiyaj*

travellers' cheques chèques de voyage (m/pl) *shek duh vwiyaj*

travel sickness mal des transports (m) *mal day troñspor*

tray plateau (m) *platoh*

treatment traitement (m) *traitmoñ*

tree arbre (m) *arbr*

trip voyage (m) *vwiyaj*
trousers pantalon (m) *poñtalawñ*
trout truite (f) *trweet*
true vrai(e) *vray*
  » **that's true** c'est vrai *se vray*
to **try (on)** essayer *esayyay*
T-shirt T-shirt (m) *teeshuhrt*
tube *(pipe)* tuyau (m) *tweeyoh*
  (underground) métro (m) *maytro*
tuna thon (m) *tawñ*
tunnel tunnel (m) *tewnel*
turn: it's my turn c'est mon tour
  se mawñ toor
to **turn** tourner *toornay*
to **turn off** fermer *fermay*
  (light) éteindre *aytañdr*
  (engine) arrêter *aretay*
to **turn on** allumer *alewmay* (tap) ouvrir
  ewvreer (engine) mettre en marche
  metr oñ marsh
twice deux fois *duh fwa*
twin beds lits jumeaux (m/pl) *lee jewmoh*
twins jumeaux (m/pl) *jewmoh*
twisted tordu(e) *tordew*
type *(sort)* sorte (f) *sort*
to **type** taper *tapay*
typical typique *teepeek*

U

UBS lead câble USB (m)
  kabl ewesbay
ugly laid(e) *lay(d)*
ulcer ulcère (m) *ewlser*
umbrella parapluie (m) *paraplwee*
uncle oncle (m) *awñkl*
uncomfortable inconfortable
  añkawñfortabl
under sous *soo*
underground *(tube)* métro (m) *maytro*
underpants slip (m) *slip*
underpass passage souterrain (m) *pasaj
  sootayrañ*
to **understand** comprendre *kawñproñdr*
underwater sous l'eau *soo loh*
underwear sous-vêtement (m)
  soovetmoñ

to **undress** se déshabiller *se dayzabeeay*
unemployed au chômage, sans emploi
  oh shohmaj, soñz oñplwa
unfortunately malheureusement
  maluhruhzmoñ
unhappy mécontent(e) *maykawñtoñ(t)*
uniform uniforme (m) *ewneeform*
university université (f) *ewneeverseetay*
unleaded petrol essence sans plomb (f)
  esoñs soñ plawñ
unless à moins que/de *a mwañ kuh/duh*
unpack déballer *daybalay*
unpleasant désagréable *dayzagrayabl*
to **unscrew** dévisser *dayveesay*
until jusqu'à *jewska*
unusual inhabituel(le), étrange
  eenabeetwel, aytroñj
unwell souffrant(e) *soofroñ(t)*
up en haut *oñ oh*
upper supérieur(e) *sewpayryuhr*
upstairs en haut *oñ oh*
urgent urgent(e) *ewrjoñ(t)*
urine urine (f) *ewreen*
us nous *noo*
to **use** utiliser *ewteeleezay*
useful utile *ewteel*
useless inutile *eenewteel*
usually normalement *normalmoñ*

V

vacant libre *leebr*
vacuum cleaner aspirateur (m)
  aspeeratuhr
valid valable *valabl*
valley vallée (f) *valay*
valuable de grande valeur, précieux/se
  duh groñd valuhr, praysyuh(z)
valuables objets de valeur (m/pl) *objay
  duh valuhr*
van camionnette (f) *kamyonet*
vanilla vanille (f) *vaneey*
vase vase (m) *vaz*
VAT TVA (f) *tayvaya*
vegan végétalien(ne) *vayjaytalyañ/yen*
vegetables légumes (m/pl) *laygewm*
vegetarian végétarien(ne)

vayjaytaryañ/yen
vehicle véhicule (m) *vayeekewl*
very très *tre*
vest maillot de corps (m) *miyoh duh kor*
vet vétérinaire (m/f) *vaytayreener*
video vidéo (f) *veedayo*
view vue (f) *vew*
villa villa (f) *veela*
village village (m) *veelaj*
vinegar vinaigre (m) *veenegr*
vineyard vignoble (m) *veenyobl*
virgin vierge (f) *vyerj*
» **Virgin Mary** Vierge Marie (f) *vyerj maree*
visa visa (m) *viza*
visit visite (f) *veezeet*
to visit *(tourist site)* visiter *veezeetay*
visitor visiteur/se *veezeetuhr(z)*
vitamin vitamine (f) *veetameen*
voice voix (f) *vwa*
volleyball volley-ball (m) *volaybohl*
voltage tension (f) *toñsyawñ*
to vote voter *votay*

W

wage salaire (m) *saler*
waist taille (f) *tiy*
waistcoat gilet (m) *jeelay*
to wait (for) attendre *atoñdr*
waiter serveur (m) *savwar*
waiting room salle d'attente (f) *sal datoñt*
waitress serveuse (f) *servuhz*
Wales pays de Galles (m) *payyee duh gal*
walk promenade (f) *promnad*
to walk, go for a walk marcher, se promener *marshay, suh promnay*
walking stick canne (f) *kan*
wall *(inside)* mur (m) *mewr*
wallet portefeuille (m) *portuhfuhy*
to want vouloir *voolwar*
war guerre (f) *ger*
warm chaud(e) *shohd*
to wash laver *lavay*
washable lavable *lavabl*
wash-basin lavabo (m) *lavaboh*
washing lessive (f) *leseev*
washing machine machine à laver (f)

masheen a lavay
washing powder lessive (f) *leseev*
washing-up vaisselle (f) *vaysel*
washing-up liquid liquide vaisselle (m) *leekeed vaysel*
wastepaper basket corbeille à papier (f) *korbey a papyay*
watch *(clock)* montre (f) *mawñtr*
to watch regarder *ruhgarday*
water eau (f) *oh*
waterfall cascade (f) *kaskad*
water heater chauffe-eau (m) *shohfoh*
waterproof imperméable *añpermayabl*
water-skiing ski nautique (m) *skee nohteek*
wave vague (f) *vag*
wax cire (f) *seer*
way *(path)* chemin (f) *shuhmañ*
we nous *noo*
weather temps (m) *toñ*
» **what's the weather like?** quel temps fait-il? *kel toñ fetil*
weather forecast prévisions météorologiques (f/pl) *prayveezyawñ maytayorolojeek*
web *(internet)* web (m) *web*
web designer concepteur/trice web *kawñseptuhr/trees web*
wedding mariage (m) *maryaj*
week semaine (f) *suhmen*
weekday jour de semaine (m) *joor duh suhmen*
weekend week-end (m) *weekend*
weekly hebdomadaire *ebdomader*
to weigh peser *puhzay*
weight poids (m) *pwa*
welcome bienvenu(e) *byañvenew*
well bien *byañ*
» **as well** aussi *ohsee*
well done *(steak)* bien cuit(e) *byañ kwee(t)*
Welsh gallois(e) *galwa(z)*
west ouest (m) *ooest*
western *(film)* western (m) *western*

wet mouillé(e) *mooyay*

wetsuit combinaison de plongée (f) *kawñbeenayzawñ duh plawñjay*

what quoi *kwa*

what? quoi? *kwa*

what is...? qu'est-ce que c'est...? *keskuhsay*

wheel roue (f) *roo*

wheelchair fauteuil roulant (m) *fohtuhy rooloñ*

when quand *koñ* (what time?) à quelle heure? *a kel uhr*

where où *oo*

which lequel, laquelle, lesquels, lesquelles *luhkel, lakel, laykel, laykel*

white blanc(he) *bloñ(sh)*

who? qui? *kee*

whole entier/ière *oñtyay/yer*

why? pourquoi? *poorkwa*

» **why not?** pourquoi pas? *poorkwa pa*

wide large *larj*

widow veuve (f) *vuhv*

widower veuf (m) *vuhf*

wife femme (f), épouse (f) *fam, aypooz*

wild sauvage *sohvaj*

to win gagner *ganyay*

wind vent (m) *voñ*

windmill moulin à vent (m) *moolañ a voñ*

window fenêtre (f) *fuhnetr* (shop) vitrine (f) *veetreen*

to windsurf faire de la planche à voile *fer duh la ploñsh a vwal*

windy: it's windy il y a du vent *eeleeya doo voñ*

wine vin (m) *vañ*

wine merchant/shop marchand de vins (m) *marshoñ duh vañ*

wing aile (f) *el*

winter hiver (m) *eever*

with avec *avek*

without sans *soñ*

woman femme (f) *fam*

wonderful merveilleux/se *mervayyuh(z)*

wood bois (m) *bwa*

wool laine (f) *len*

word mot (m) *moh*

work travail (m) *traviy*

to work (job) travailler *traviyay* (function) marcher *marshay*

world monde (m) *mawñd*

world (adj.) mondial(e) *mawñdeeal*

worse pire *peer*

worth: it's worth... ça vaut... *sa voh*

» **it's not worth it** ça n'en vaut pas la peine *sa noñ voh pa la pen*

wound blessure (f) *blesewr*

to wrap (up) emballer *oñbalay*

to write écrire *aykreer*

writer écrivain (m) *aykreevañ*

writing pad bloc-notes (m) *bloknot*

writing paper papier à lettres (m) *papyay a letr*

wrong faux, fausse *foh, fohs*

X

X-ray radiographie (f) *radyografee*

Y

yacht yacht (m) *yoht*

to yawn bâiller *bayay*

year an (m), année (f) *oñ, anay*

yellow jaune *john*

yes oui *wee*

yesterday hier *eeyer*

yet déjà *dayja*

yoghurt yaourt (m) *yaoort*

you (formal) vous *voo* (informal singular) tu *tew*

young jeune *juhn*

your ton, ta, tes, votre, vos *tawñ, ta, tay, vohtr, voh*

yours: it's yours c'est à vous *set a voo*

youth hostel auberge de jeunesse (f) *ohberj duh juhnes*

Z

zip fermeture éclair (f) *fermuhtewr aykler*

zoo zoo (m) *zoh*

French – English dictionary

Words for food and drink are given in the menu reader, page 87. See also the **'You may see...'** lists in the individual subject sections of the phrase book.

A

à to, at
à... heures at... o'clock
à... kilomètres/minutes ...kilometres/ minutes away
abonnement (m) season ticket
absolument absolutely
accepter to accept
accident (m) accident
accord: être d'accord to agree
accueil (m) welcome, reception
achat (m) purchase
achats (m/pl) shopping
acheter to buy
acier (m) steel
activité (f) activity
actuel(le) present, current
actuellement at present
addition (f) bill
adresse (f) address
adulte (m/f) adult
aéroglisseur (m) hovercraft
aéroport (m) airport
affaires (f/pl) business, things, belongings
affreux/euse awful, dreadful
âge (m) age
» quel âge avez-vous? how old are you?
agence (f) agency
agenda (m) diary
agité(e) rough *(sea)*
agneau (m) lamb
agréable pleasant
aider to help
aigre sour
aiguille (f) needle
ail (m) garlic

aimer to like
ainsi thus, like this, in this way
air (m) air
» en plein air in the open air
alentours (m/pl) surrounding area, outskirts
aliment (m) food
aller to go
aller-retour (m) return (ticket)
aller simple (m) single, one way (ticket)
allumer to light, to switch/turn on
allumettes (f/pl) matches
alors then
ambassade (f) embassy
amende (f) fine
amer, amère bitter
ami(e) (m/f) friend
ampoule (f) (light) bulb
amuse-gueule (m) appetiser
an (m) year
ancien(ne) old
âne (m) donkey
anglais(e) English
animé(e) busy, lively
année (f) year
anniversaire (m) anniversary, birthday
annonce (f) advertisement
annuaire (m) (telephone) directory
antenne (f) aerial
antigel (m) anti-freeze
antiquités (f/pl) antiques
appareil (m) appliance, machine
appareil photo (m) camera
appartement (m) apartment, flat
appel (m) call
appeler to call

s'appeler to be called
» comment vous appelez-vous? what is your name?
apprendre to learn
approprié(e) suitable
approximativement approximately
appuyer (sur) to push, press
après after(wards), later on
» apr. J-C (après Jésus-Christ) AD
après-midi (m) afternoon
après-shampooing (m) (hair) conditioner
araignée (f) spider
arbitre (m) referee
arbre (m) tree
argent (m) money, silver
armoire (f) cupboard
arracher to pull/take out, extract
arrêt (m) stop, (taxi) rank
arrêter to stop
arrhes (f/pl) deposit
arrière rear
» en arrière backwards
arrivée (f) arrival
arriver (à) to arrive (at), reach
art (m) art
articulation (f) joint (body)
artisanat (m) craft goods
ascenseur (m) lift
assez enough, quite, fairly, quite a lot
assiette (f) plate
assis(e) sitting (down)
associé(e) (m/f) member, partner
assurance (f) insurance
atelier (m) workshop
attaquer to attack
attendre to wait (for)
attention beware, take care, look out!
au (à + le), aux (à + les) at/to the
auberge (f) hotel, hostel
au-delà (de) beyond
au-dessous (de) under, below
au-dessus (de) above
augmenter to increase
aujourd'hui today

au revoir goodbye
aussi also, as well, too
autant que as much/many as
autobus (m) bus
autocar (m) coach
automne (m) autumn
autoroute (f) motorway
auto-stop (m) hitch-hiking
autour (de) around
autre another, other
» autre chose? anything else?
autrefois in the past, once
autrement otherwise
avance: à l'avance in advance
avant before, front
» en avant forward(s)
» av. J-C (avant Jésus-Christ) BC
avantage (m) advantage
avec with
avenir (m) future
avertir to tell, inform, to warn
aveugle blind
avion (m) aeroplane
avis (m) opinion, notice, warning
avocat (m) lawyer
avoir to have

B

bagages (m/pl) luggage, baggage
bague (f) ring
baguette (f) loaf of bread (French stick)
baie (f) bay, berry
baignoire (f) bath(tub)
bain (m) bath
baiser (m) kiss
baisser to lower, to turn down (volume)
balade (f) walk, stroll
baladeur (m) personal stereo
balai (m) broom
balcon (m) balcony, circle (theatre)
balle (f) ball
ballon (m) ball, balloon
bande dessinée (f) comic strip
bande magnétique (f) (recording) tape

banque (f) bank

barbe (f) beard

bas, basse low, short

» en bas down, downstairs, below

bas (m/pl) stockings

bateau (m) boat

bâtiment (m) building

bâton (m) stick, pole

batterie (f) car battery

beau, belle beautiful, handsome, lovely, fine

beaucoup very (much), a lot

» beaucoup de a lot of, many

beau-fils (m) son-in-law, stepson

beau-frère (m) brother-in-law, stepbrother

beau-père (m) father-in-law, stepfather

beauté (f) beauty

beaux-parents (m/pl) in-laws

bébé (m) baby

belge Belgian

belle (see beau)

belle-fille (f) daughter-in-law, stepdaughter

belle-mère (f) mother-in-law, stepmother

belle-sœur (f) sister-in-law, stepsister

besoin: avoir besoin de to need

bête stupid, silly

biberon (m) baby's bottle

bibliothèque (f) library

bicyclette (f) bicycle

bien well, fine

» bien entendu of course

» bien que although

» bien sûr of course

bientôt soon

» à bientôt see you later

bienvenu(e) welcome

billet (m) ticket, banknote

bizarre strange, odd

blanc, blanche white

» en blanc blank

blanchisserie (f) laundry

blessé(e) injured, wounded

bleu (m) bruise

bleu(e) blue, very rare *(steak)*

bleu marine navy blue

bloc(-notes) notepad, writing pad

bloqué(e) blocked, jammed

blouse (f) overall, white coat

boire to drink

bois (m) wood

boisson (f) drink

boîte (f) box, tin, can

boîte aux lettres (f) letterbox, postbox

boîte de nuit (f) nightclub

bol (m) bowl, basin

bombe (f) bomb, aerosol, spray can

bon, bonne good

» bon appétit! enjoy your meal!

bonbons (m/pl) sweets

bonde (f) plug *(bath)*

bondé(e) crowded

bonjour good day, good morning, good afternoon

bonne (see bon)

bonsoir good evening

bord (m) edge, border

» à bord aboard

botte (f) boot

bouche (f) mouth

bouclé(e) curly

bouger to move

bougie (f) candle, spark plug

bouilli(e) boiled

bourse (f) stock exchange

bout (m) end

bouteille (f) bottle

bouton (m) button, switch

branche (f) branch

bras (m) arm

bref, brève brief, short

bricolage (m) DIY

brillant(e) shiny, bright

brillant (m) lip gloss

briller to shine

briquet (m) (cigarette) lighter

B
C

bronzé(e) (sun-)tanned
brosse (f) brush
brouillard (m) fog
bruit (m) noise
brûler to burn
brun(e) brown, dark *(hair/skin)*
bureau (m) office
bureau de poste (m) post office
bureau de tabac (m) tobacconist's
but (m) goal, aim, purpose

C

ça this, that
cabine (f) cabin, cubicle
câble USB (m) USB lead
cacher to hide
cadeau (m) gift, present
cadre (m) frame, setting, scope,
   executive, manager
café (m) cafe, coffee
cafetière (f) coffee pot
cahier (m) exercise book
caisse (f) box, cash desk
caisse d'épargne (f) savings bank
camion (m) lorry
camionnette (f) van
campagne (f) country(side)
camper to camp
canne (f) walking stick
canoë (m) canoe
canot (m) boat
caoutchouc (m) rubber
car because
carnet (m) (note)book
carré (m) square
carreaux: à carreaux (m) check(ed)
   (material)
carrefour (m) crossroads, junction
carrière (f) career
carte (f) map, card, menu
carte postale (f) postcard
carte SIM (f) SIM card
carton (m) cardboard, carton
cas (m) case

» en cas de in case of
» en tout cas in any case
casse-croûte (m) snack
casser to break
casserole (f) saucepan
cause: à cause de because of
cave (f) cellar
caverne (f) cave
CD (m) CD
CD-ROM (m) CD Rom
ce/cet, cette this, that
ceci this
ceinture (f) belt
cela this, that
célibataire single, unmarried
celle (see celui)
celle-ci, celle-là (see celui-ci, celui-là)
celles (see ceux)
celles-ci, celles-là
   (see ceux-ci, ceux-là)
celui, celle the one
celui-ci, celle-ci this one
celui-là, celle-là that one
cendrier (m) ashtray
centre (m) centre, middle
cependant however
certainement certainly
ces these, those
c'est it/that/he/she is
» c'est-à-dire that's to say, in
   other words
» c'est ça! that's right!
cette (see ce)
ceux, celles the ones
ceux-ci, celles-ci these ones
ceux-là, celles-là those ones
chacun(e) each (one), every (one)
chaîne (f) chain
chaise (f) chair
chaleur (f) heat
chambre (f) room
chambre à coucher (f) bedroom
champ (m) field
chance (f) luck

» bonne chance! good luck!
changer to change
chanson (f) song
chanter to sing
chapeau (m) hat
chaque each, every
charbon (m) coal
charcuterie (f) cooked meats
chariot (m) trolley
charmant(e) charming, lovely
chat, chatte cat
château (m) castle
chaud(e) hot
» il fait chaud it's hot *(weather)*
» avoir chaud to be hot
chauffage (m) heating
chauffeur (m) driver
chaussée (f) carriageway, road surface
chaussette (f) sock
chaussure (f) shoe
chef (m) chef, boss, head, chief
chemin (m) path, lane, way, route
chemin de fer (m) railway
chemise (f) shirt
chemisier (m) blouse
cher, chère expensive, dear
chercher to look for, to search
cheval (m) horse
cheveux (m/pl) hair
chèvre (f) goat
chez... at ...'s house
chien, chienne dog
chiffon (m) cloth, rag
chiffre (m) figure, number
choix (m) choice, range
chômage (m) unemployment
chose (f) thing
chute d'eau (f) waterfall
cicatrice (f) scar
Cie (compagnie) (f) company
ciel (m) sky, heaven
cigarette (f) cigarette
cinéma (m) cinema
cirage (m) shoe polish

circulation (f) traffic
ciseaux (m/pl) scissors
cité (f) city
clair(e) clear, light (coloured), pale
clé/clef (f) key, spanner
client(e) customer, client
climat (m) climate
climatisation (f) air conditioning
cloche (f) bell
clou (m) nail
cœur (m) heart
coiffeur/euse hairdresser
coin (m) corner
col (m) collar, (mountain) pass
colère (f) anger
colis (m) parcel
collant (m) tights
colle (f) glue
collier (m) necklace, dog collar
colline (f) hill
combien? how much? how many?
» combien de temps? how long? how
   much time?
combinaison (f) combination, wetsuit,
   flying suit, petticoat, slip
comme as, like
» comme ça thus, like this/that
» comme d'habitude as usual
commencer to begin
comment? how? pardon?
commissariat (de police) (m) police
   station
commun(e) common
compagnie (f) company
complet, complète full (up)
complètement completely
comprendre to understand
compris(e) included
compte (m) account
compteur (m) meter
concepteur/trice web web designer
concours (m) competition
conducteur/trice driver
conduire to drive

confiture (f) jam
confortable comfortable
congé (m) holiday, day off, leave
congrès (m) conference, congress
connaître to know, be acquainted with
conseiller to advise
conserve (f) tinned food
conserver to keep
conte (m) story
contenu (m) contents
content(e) content(ed), pleased
contraceptif (m) contraceptive
contre against
coquille (f) shell
corde (f) rope, string
corps (m) body
correspondance (f) connection,
   correspondence
costume (m) suit, costume
côte (f) rib, chop, hill, coast
côté (m) side
» à côté de beside, next to
coton (m) cotton
coton hydrophile (m) cotton wool
couches (f/pl) nappies
couleur (f) colour
couloir (m) corridor
coup (m) blow, hit, shot
coup de soleil (m) sunburn
couper to cut, to cut off
cour (f) courtyard, court
courageux/euse brave
couramment fluently
courant (m) power, current
courant d'air (m) draught
courir to run
couronne (f) crown
cours (m) course, lesson
course (f) race
» faire des courses (f/pl) to go shopping
court(e) short
cousin(e) cousin
couteau (m) knife
coûter to cost

couture (f) sewing
couvercle (m) top, lid
couvert(e) covered
couverts (m/pl) cutlery, place settings
couverture (f) blanket
couvrir to cover
cracher to spit
cravate (f) tie
crayon (m) pencil
crème (f) cream, lotion
cri (m) shout, cry
crime (m) crime
croire to think, believe
croisière (f) cruise
croix (f) cross
cru(e) raw
cuiller (f) spoon
cuir (m) leather
cuire to cook
cuisine (f) cooking, kitchen

D

d'abord (at) first
d'accord agreed, fine, very well
daim (m) suede
dame (f) lady
danger (m) danger
dans in, inside
danser to dance
davantage (any) more, (any) longer
de of, from, about
debout standing (up)
début (m) beginning
débutant(e) beginner
déchiré(e) torn
décider to decide
découvrir to discover
décrire to describe
dedans inside
degré (m) degree (temperature)
dégustation (f) tasting, sampling
dehors outside
déjà already, now
déjeuner (m) lunch

demain tomorrow
demander to ask (for)
demi(e) half
demi-frère (m) stepbrother
demi-sœur (f) stepsister
dent (f) tooth
départ (m) departure
dépêchez-vous! dépêche-toi! hurry up!
dépenser to spend
dépliant (m) brochure
depuis since
dernier, dernière last, latest
derrière behind
des (de + les) of the
dès from, since
désagréable unpleasant
désavantage (m) disadvantage
descendre to come/go down,
    to get off (bus etc.), to stay
    (at a hotel), to take down
désirer to want, desire
dessin (m) drawing, design, pattern
dessin animé (m) cartoon film
dessous underneath
dessus on top, above
deux two
» les deux both
deuxième second
devant in front (of)
dévisser to unscrew
devoir to have to
d'habitude usually
diapositive (f) slide (photo)
différent(e) different
difficile difficult
dîner (m) dinner
dire to say, to tell
» disons let's say
discussion (f) discussion, argument
disque (m) disc, record
disque dur (m) hard drive (computer)
divers(e) varied, various
doigt (m) finger
doigt de pied (m) toe

dois: je dois I must, have to
domaine (m) estate, property
dommage (m) damage
» quel dommage! what a pity!
donc so
donner to give
dont whose, of which
dormir to sleep
dossier (m) file
douane (f) customs
douce (see doux)
douche (f) shower
douleur (f) pain, ache
doute (m) doubt
» sans doute no doubt, doubtless
doux, douce sweet, soft, mild, gentle
drap (m) sheet
droite (f) right
» à droite on/to the right
droits (de douane) (m/pl) (customs) duty
drôle funny, amusing
du (de + le) of/from the
dur(e) hard, tough
durant during
durer to last
DVD (m) DVD

E

eau (f) water
échantillon (m) sample
école (f) school
écouter to listen (to)
écran (m) screen
écrire to write
efficace effective
effectivement really, in fact, exactly
effrayé(e) frightened
égal(e) equal, the same, even
» ça m'est égal it's all the same to me,
    I don't care
église (f) church
égratignure (f) scratch
élastique (m) rubber band, elastic
élève (m/f) pupil

élevé(e) high
elle she, her, it
elle-même herself
elles they, them (f)
e-mail, courrier électronique (m) email
émail (m) enamel
embarquement (m) boarding,
    embarcation
embêter to bother, annoy
embouteillage (m) traffic jam
embrasser to kiss
emploi (m) use
employer to use, employ
emporter to take away
en in, to, some, any
encaisser to cash (cheque)
enceinte pregnant
enchanté(e) delighted, pleased to
    meet you
encore still, yet
» encore une fois again, once more
endroit (m) place
énergie (f) energy, power
enfant (m/f) child
enfer (m) hell
enfin at last
ennuyé(e) bored
énorme enormous
enregistrer to record; to register,
    to check in
enrhumé: être enrhumé(e) to have a cold
enseigner to teach
ensemble together
ensuite then
entendre to hear
entier, entière whole
entouré(e) (de) surrounded (by)
entracte (m) interval (theatre)
entre among, between
entrée (f) entrance, way in, admission,
    ticket, starter (food)
entrer to enter, go in
entrevue (f) interview
enveloppe (f) envelope

envers: à l'envers upside down,
    inside out, back to front
environ about, around
environnement (m) environment
envoyer to send
» envoyer un SMS to text
épais(se) thick
épice (f) spice
épingle (f) pin
épuisé(e) exhausted, sold out,
    out of stock
équipage (m) crew
équipe (f) team
équipement (m) equipment
escalier (m) stairs, staircase
espace (m) space, area
espèce (f) sort, kind
espérer to hope (for), to expect
essayer to try
essence (f) petrol
est: il/elle est he/she/it is
est (m) east
estomac (m) stomach
et and
étage (m) floor, storey
étagère (f) shelf
état (m) state
été (m) summer
éteindre to switch/turn off
étoile (f) star
étonnant(e) surprising, amazing
étrange strange, odd
étranger, étrangère foreigner
» à l'étranger abroad
être to be
étroit(e) narrow, tight
étude (f) study
étudiant(e) (m/f) student
EU (États-Unis) United States
euro (m) euro
eux them
eux-mêmes themselves
excusez-moi excuse me, pardon me
exemple (m) example

expliquer to explain
exposition (f) exhibition
exprès deliberately, on purpose

F

face: en face (de) facing, opposite
fâché(e) annoyed
facile easy
façon (f) way, manner
» de toute façon anyway
faible weak
faim: avoir faim to be hungry
faire to do, to make
fait (m) fact
famille (f) family
fatigué(e) tired
faubourgs (m/pl) outskirts
fausse (see faux)
fausse couche miscarriage
faut: il faut you have to, you must,
   it is necessary to
faute fault
fauteuil (m) armchair
fauteuil roulant (m) wheelchair
faux, fausse false, fake
félicitations! congratulations!
femme (f) woman, wife
fenêtre (f) window
fer (m) iron
ferme (f) farm
fermer to close
fermeture (f) closing, closure, catch,
   fastener
fermeture éclair (f) zip
fête (f) festival, holiday
feu (m) fire
feuille (f) leaf, sheet of paper
feux (m/pl) traffic lights
ficelle (f) string, stick of French bread
fichier (m) file (computer)
fièvre (f) fever, (high) temperature
fil (m) thread
filet (m) net
fille (f) girl, daughter

fils (m) son
fin (f) end
finalement finally, in the end
finir to end
fleur (f) flower
fleuve (m) river
foire (f) fair
fois (f) time
» à la fois at the same time
folie (f) madness (see fou)
fond (m) back, end, bottom
fontaine (f) fountain
forêt (f) forest
forme (f) form, shape, figure
formulaire (m) form
fort(e) strong, loud, great
fou, folle crazy, mad
four (m) oven
four à micro-ondes (m) microwave oven
fourchette (f) fork
frais, fraîche fresh, cool
français(e) French
frapper to hit, to strike, to knock
fréquemment frequently, often
fréquent(e) frequent
frère (m) brother
frigidaire (m) refrigerator
frigo (m) fridge
frit(e) fried
froid(e) cold
» il fait froid it's cold (weather)
» avoir froid to be cold
fromage (m) cheese
frontière (f) border, frontier
fruit (m) fruit
fruits de mer (m/pl) seafood, shellfish
fumée (f) smoke
fumer to smoke

G

gagner to earn, to win, to gain
galerie (f) gallery, roof rack
gant (m) glove
garçon (m) boy, waiter
garde: de garde on duty

garder to keep, to look after
gare (f) station
gauche left
» à gauche on/to the left
gazon (m) lawn, grass
gens (m/pl) people
gentil(le) kind
gérant (m) manager
gérante (f) manageress
gestion (f) management
gilet (m) waistcoat
gitan(e) gypsy
glace (f) ice, ice cream, mirror
glaçon (m) ice cube
glissant(e) slippery
gomme (f) rubber *(eraser)*
gonfler to inflate
gorge (f) throat
gourmand(e) greedy
goût (m) taste
goûter (m) (afternoon) tea
goutte (f) drop, drip
gouvernement (m) government
grand(e) big, large, great
Grande-Bretagne Great Britain
grand magasin (m) department store
grand-mère (f) grandmother
grand-père (m) grandfather
gras, grasse fat, fatty, greasy
gratuit(e) free
grave serious
grève (f) strike
grippe (f) flu
gris(e) grey, dull
groom (m) bellboy
gros, grosse fat, big, large
grosseur (f) size, bulk, lump
grossier, grossière rude
grotte (f) cave
guerre (f) war
guichet (m) ticket office
guide (m) guide-book
guide (m/f) guide

H

habitude (f) custom, habit
haut(e) high, tall
» en haut up, upstairs, above
hebdomadaire weekly
herbe (f) grass, herb
hésiter to hesitate
heure (f) hour
heures d'affluence/de pointe
 (f/pl) rush hour
heureux/euse happy, fortunate
hier yesterday
histoire (f) history, story
hiver (m) winter
homme (m) man
horaire (m) timetable
horloge (f) clock
hors (de) out (of)
hôte (m) host, landlord, guest
hôtel (m) hotel
hôtel de ville (m) town hall
hôtesse (f) hostess, air stewardess
huile (m) oil
humide damp, wet

I

ici here
ignorer to be unaware of, not to know
il he, it
île (f) island
ils they
il y a there is/are
» il n'y en a pas there isn't/aren't any
» il y a ... (ans) ...(years) ago
imperméable (m) raincoat
impoli(e) rude
importer to import, to matter
» n'importe qui/où no matter who/
 where, anyone/where
impôt (m) tax
impressionnant(e) impressive
imprévu(e) unexpected
incendie (m) fire
inconnu(e) unknown, strange
inconvénient (m) disadvantage, drawback

inférieur(e) lower, bottom
informatique (f) computer science/ studies, information technology
inquiet, inquiète worried
insolation (f) sunstroke
insolite unusual
instantané(e) instant
instituteur, institutrice (primary school) teacher
interdit(e) prohibited, forbidden
intérêts (m/pl) interest *(money)*
intérieur(e) interior
» à l'intérieur inside, indoors
internet (m) internet
introduire to introduce, to insert
inutile useless, unnecessary
issue (f) exit
ivre drunk

J

j' (je) I
» j'ai I have
jamais never, ever
jambe (f) leg
jambon (m) ham
jardin (m) garden
jaune yellow
je I
jean (m) jeans
jeter to throw (away)
» à jeter disposable
jeu (m) game, gambling, set, collection
jeune young
jeunesse (f) youth
joli(e) pretty, nice, lovely
jouer to play, to gamble
jouet (m) toy
jour (m) day
jour férié (m) (public) holiday
journal (m) newspaper
journaliste (m/f) journalist
journée (f) day
jupe (f) skirt
jus (m) juice

jusqu'à until, as far as
juste fair, just, correct, tight

L

l' (le or la) the
la the, her, it
là there
là-bas (over) there, down there
lac (m) lake
là-haut up there
laid(e) ugly
laine (f) wool
laisser to leave, to let, allow
lait (m) milk
lame (f) blade
lampe (f) lamp, light
lancer to throw
langue (f) tongue, language
laquelle (see lequel)
large broad, wide
lavabo (m) wash-basin
laver to wash
le the, him, it
lecture (f) reading
léger, légère light
lendemain (m) day after
lent(e) slow
lentement slowly
lentille (f) lens
lequel, laquelle which (one)
les the, them
lesquels, lesquelles which (ones)
lessive (f) washing powder, detergent, washing
leur (to/for) them
leur(s) their
le/la leur theirs
lever to lift, raise
librairie (f) bookshop
libre free, unoccupied, vacant, for hire
lieu (m) place
» au lieu de instead of
» avoir lieu to take place
ligne (f) line, (bus/underground) route

lime (f) file *(tool)*
lire to read
lisse smooth
lit (m) bed
livre (f) pound *(weight)*
livre (m) book
locataire (m/f) tenant
logement (m) accommodation
logiciel (m) software
loi (f) law
loin far (away)
Londres London
long, longue long
» le long de along
longtemps (for) a long time, (for) long
lorsque when
lotion (f) lotion
louer to rent, hire
lourd(e) heavy
lui him, her, it
lui-même himself
lumière (f) light
lune (f) moon
lunettes (f/pl) glasses, spectacles
luxe: grand luxe (m) luxury

M

M (Monsieur) Mr
m' (me) me
ma (see mon)
machine (f) machine
Madame (f) Mrs, madam
Mademoiselle (f) Miss
magasin (m) shop
magnétoscope (m) video recorder
maillot de bain (m) bathing costume, swimsuit
main (f) hand
maintenant now
maire (m) mayor
mairie (f) town hall
mais but
maison (f) house, home
maître (m) teacher

maîtresse (f) teacher
majorité (f) majorité
mal badly
» avoir mal à... to have a pain in...
» pas mal (de) quite a lot (of)
malade (f) ill
malgré despite, in spite of
malheur (m) misfortune
malheureusement unfortunately
malle (f) trunk
manche (f) sleeve
la Manche (f) English Channel
manger to eat
manière (f) way, manner
manifestation (f) demonstration (protest)
manquer to miss, to be lacking
manteau (m) coat
maquillage (m) make-up
marchand(e) dealer, merchant
marche (f) step, stair
» en marche moving, working
marché (m) market
» bon marché cheap
marcher to walk, to work, to function
mari (m) husband
mariage (m) wedding
marié(e) married
marque (f) make, brand
marron brown
marteau (m) hammer
matelas (m) mattress
matériel (m) equipment, materials
matière (f) subject, material, matter
matin (m) morning
mauvais(e) bad
me (to) me
méchant(e) naughty
médecin (m) doctor
médecine (f) medicine
médicament (m) medicine, drug
meilleur(e) better, best
mélange (m) mixture
membre (m) member, limb
même same, even

ménage (m) housework, household, couple
ménagère (f) housewife
mensuel(le) monthly
mer (f) sea
merci (beaucoup/bien) thank you (very much)
mère (f) mother
merveilleux/euse marvellous, wonderful
mes my
Mesdames ladies
messe (f) mass
Messieurs gentlemen
mesure (f) measurement, size
métier (m) occupation, trade, job
mettre to put (on)
meublé(e) furnished
meubles (m/pl) furniture
midi (m) midday, noon
Midi (m) South of France
le mien, la mienne mine
mieux better, best
milieu (m) middle, environment
mince slim
minuit (m) midnight
miroir (m) mirror
mi-temps (f) half-time
mixte mixed
Mlle (Mademoiselle) (f) Miss
Mme (Madame) (f) Mrs
mode (f) fashion
modem (m) modem
moi me
moi-même myself
moins less, minus
» au moins at least
mois (m) month
moitié (f) half
mollah (m) mullah
mon, ma my
monde (m) world
monnaie (f) currency, coin, change
monsieur (m) gentleman
Monsieur Mr, sir

montagne (f) mountain(s)
montant (m) amount
monter to go up, to take up, to climb, to ride
montre (f) (wrist) watch
montrer to show
morceau (m) piece, bit
mort(e) dead
mosquée (f) mosque
mot (m) word, note
moto (f) motorbike
mouche (f) fly
mouchoir (m) handkerchief
mouillé(e) wet
moulin (m) mill
mouton (m) sheep
moyen(ne) medium, average
moyens (m/pl) means
mur (m) wall
mûr(e) mature, ripe
musulman(e) Muslim

N

n' (ne) not
nager to swim
natation (f) swimming
navire (m) ship
né(e) born
neige (f) snow
ne ... jamais never
ne ... pas not
ne ... rien nothing
n'est-ce pas? isn't that so? isn't it?
nettoyer to clean
» nettoyer à sec to dry clean
neuf, neuve new
neveu (m) nephew
nez (m) nose
ni ... ni neither ... nor
nièce (f) niece
noce (f) wedding
Noël Christmas
noir(e) black
nom (m) name

nom de famille (m) surname

non no, not

nord (m) north

nos our

notre our

le/la nôtre ours

nouer to tie

nourriture (f) food

nous we, us

nous-mêmes ourselves

nouveau, nouvelle new

» de nouveau again

nouvelles (f/pl) news

nu(e) naked, nude

nuage (m) cloud

nuit (f) night

nul(le) no, useless, void

nulle part nowhere

numérique digital

numéro (m) number

numéro d'immatriculation (m) registration number (car)

O

objet (m) object

obtenir to obtain, get

occasion (f) occasion, bargain

» d'occasion second hand

occupé(e) occupied, taken, engaged, busy

odeur (f) smell

œil (m) eye

œuf (m) egg

œuvre (f) work (art etc.)

offrir to offer, to give (as a gift)

oiseau (m) bird

ombre (f) shade, shadow

on one, people, you

oncle (m) uncle

onde (f) wave

ongle (m) nail (finger/toe)

or (m) gold

orchestre (m) orchestra, stalls (theatre)

ordinateur (m) computer

ordonnance (f) prescription

ordures (f/pl) rubbish

oreille (f) ear

oreiller (m) pillow

orteil (m) toe

os (m) bone

ou or

ou (bien) ... ou (bien) either ... or

où? where?

oublier to forget

ouest (m) west

oui yes

outre: en outre besides, as well

ouvert(e) open

ouverture (f) opening

ouvre-boîtes (m) tin/can opener

ouvre-bouteilles (m) bottle opener

ouvrier (m) workman

ouvrir to open

P

pain (m) bread

paix (f) peace

pâle pale

panaché (m) shandy

panaché(e) mixed

pancarte (f) notice, sign

panier (m) basket

panne: en panne (f) broken, broken down, out of order

panneau (m) sign

pantalon (m) trousers

papier (m) paper

Pâques (m) Easter

par by, for, per, through, via

» par exemple (p.ex.) for example (e.g.)

paraître to appear, to seem

» il paraît (que)... it seems (that)...

parapluie (m) umbrella

parc (m) park

parce que because

pardon sorry, pardon, excuse me

pareil(le) same, similar

parent, parente relation, relative

paresseux/euse lazy

parfois sometimes

par hasard by chance

parler to speak, to talk

parmi among

part: à part apart (from), extra

parti (m) party *(political)*

particulier, particulière private, particular, specific

partie (f) part

partir to leave, depart

» à partir de (starting) from

partout everywhere

passage à niveau (m) level crossing

passage clouté (m) pedestrian crossing

passager/ère passenger

passé(e) past

passer to pass, to spend (time), to happen

passionnant(e) exciting

patins (m/pl) skates

pâtisserie (f) (small) cake, pastry, cake shop

patron (m) owner, boss, pattern *(dressmaking etc.)*

patronne (f) owner, boss

pauvre poor

payer to pay (for)

pays (m) country

paysage (m) scenery, countryside

PDG (le président directeur général) (m) managing director, president

péage (m) toll

peau (f) skin, hide, leather, rind, peel

pêche (f) peach, fishing

peigne (m) comb

peine: à peine hardly, scarcely

» ce n'est pas la peine it's not worth it

peintre (m) painter

peinture (f) paint, painting

pellicule (f) film *(photo)*

pelouse (f) lawn

pendant during

» pendant ce temps meanwhile

» pendant que while

penser to think

pension (f) pension, boarding school

pente (f) slope

perdre to lose, to miss

perdu(e) lost

père (m) father

permis (m) licence, permit

permis de conduire (m) driving licence

permis(e) allowed

personne no one, nobody, anyone

personne (f) person

peser to weigh

petit(e) small, little

petit déjeuner (m) breakfast

petite-fille (f) granddaughter

petit-fils (m) grandson

petit pain (m) bread roll

petits-enfants (m/pl) grandchildren

peu little, not much

» peu de few, little

» un peu a bit, a little

peuple (m) people, populace

peur: avoir peur to be afraid

peut-être perhaps, maybe

peux: je peux I can

pichet (m) pitcher, jug

pièce (f) piece, component, room, coin, play *(theatre)*

pièce de rechange (f) spare part

pied (m) foot

pierre (f) stone

piéton (m) pedestrian

pile (f) pile, battery

pilule (f) pill

piqûre (f) prick, sting, bite *(insect)*, injection

pire worse, worst

piscine (f) swimming pool

piste (f) runway, track, course, (ski-)run

placard (m) cupboard

place (f) square, place, seat

plafond (m) ceiling

plage (f) beach

plaisanterie (f) joke
planche (f) plank, board
planche à voile (f) sailboard, windsurfing
plancher (m) floor
plante (f) plant
plat (m) dish, course, flat, level
plateau (m) tray
plein(e) full (up)
pleurer to cry
pleut: il pleut it's raining
plier to fold, to bend
plomb (m) lead
plombier (m) plumber
plongeoir (m) diving board
plonger to dive
pluie (f) rain
plupart most, majority
plus more, plus
plusieurs several
plutôt rather
poche (f) pocket
poêle (f) frying pan
poêle (m) stove
poids (m) weight
poignée (f) handle, handful
poignet (m) wrist
poing (m) fist
point (m) point, stitch
» à point medium (steak)
pointe (f) point, tip
pointure (f) size (shoe)
poisson (m) fish
poivre (m) pepper
poli(e) polite
police (f) police
politique (f) politics
pollué(e) polluted
pompiers (m/pl) fire brigade
pont (m) bridge, ramp, deck
porc (m) pig, pork
port (m) port, harbour, docks
(téléphone) portable (m) mobile (phone)
porte (f) door, gate
portefeuille (m) wallet

porte-monnaie (m) purse
porter to carry, to wear
poser to put (down)
poste (f) post, mail
poste (m) post, job, set (radio/TV),
    extension (telephone)
poste de police (m) police station
pot (m) pot, jar, jug, (child's) potty
poubelle (f) dustbin
pouce (m) thumb
poudre (f) dust, powder
poulet (m) chicken
poupée (f) doll
pour for
pourboire (m) tip
pourquoi? why?
pourri(e) rotten
pourtant however
pousser to push
poussette (f) push-chair
pouvoir to be able
pouvoir (m) power
précieux/euse precious
préférer to prefer
premier, première first
prendre to take, catch, get, to have
prénom (m) first name, Christian name
préparer to prepare, get ready
près (de) close (to), near
présenter to present, to introduce
presque almost, nearly
pressé(e) in a hurry, (freshly) squeezed
prêt(e) ready
prêt (m) loan
prêtre (m) priest
prière de... please...
printemps (m) spring
prise (f) plug, socket
privé(e) private
prix (m) price, prize
problème (m) problem
prochain(e) next
proche close
professeur (m) professor, teacher

profond(e) deep

promenade walk, ride

propos: à propos de about, on the subject of

propre clean, (one's) own

propriétaire (m/f) owner

public, publique public

puis then

puisque since

puissant(e) powerful

Q

quai (m) platform, quay

qualité (f) quality

quand when

» quand même still, even so, all the same

quant à as for

quart (m) quarter

quartier (m) district, quarter

que that, which, whom, what, than

quel(le)? what? which?

quelque some

quelque chose something, anything

quelquefois sometimes

quelque part somewhere

quelques some, a few

quelques-uns/unes some, a few

quelqu'un someone, anyone

queue (f) tail, queue

qui who, which

quitter to leave, to take off

quoi what

R

rabais (m) discount

raccrocher to hang up (telephone)

raconter to tell

raide steep

raison (f) reason

» avoir raison to be right

raisonnable sensible

randonnée (f) hike, ramble

rang (m) row, tier

rappel (m) reminder

rapport (m) relationship, connection, report

raser: se raser to shave

rasoir (électrique) (m) (electric) razor/shaver

ravi(e) delighted

rayé(e) striped

rayon (m) shelf, department, section (in shop)

réaliser to carry out, bring about

réalité (f) reality

récemment recently, lately

récent(e) recent

recette (f) recipe

recharge (f) refill

réclamation (f) complaint

reconnaissant(e) grateful

reçu (m) receipt

regarder to look (at), to watch

régime (m) diet

région (f) region, area

règle (f) ruler

règles (f/pl) (menstrual) period

regretter to regret, be sorry for

reine (f) queen

remboursement (m) refund

remède (m) remedy, cure

remise (f) delivery, reduction, postponement

remorquer to tow

remplir to fill (in)

rencontrer to meet

rendez-vous (m) appointment, date

rendre to give back, return

renseignements (m/pl) information

rentrer to go/come back (in)

réparer to repair

repas (m) meal

répéter to repeat

répondre to answer

réponse (f) reply

reportage (m) report

repos (m) rest

representation (f) performance
réseau (m) network
réservation (f) reservation, booking
réserver to reserve, book
rester to remain, stay
résultat (m) result
retard (m) delay
retour (m) return
retourner to return
retraité(e) retired
réveiller to wake
» se réveiller to wake up
réverbère (m) street lamp
revue (f) review, revue, magazine
rez-de-chaussée (m) ground floor
riche rich
rideau (m) curtain
rien nothing, anything
rire (m) laugh
rire to laugh
rivière (f) river
robe (f) dress
robinet (m) tap
roi (m) king
rond(e) round
rose pink
rôti(e) roast
roue (f) wheel
rouge red
rouge à lèvres (m) lipstick
rouille(e) rusty
rouler to roll, to go, to drive
route (f) (main) road, route
routier (m) lorry driver
ruban (m) ribbon, tape
rue (f) street
rugueux/euse rough
ruine (f) ruin
ruisseau (m) stream

S

SA (Société Anonyme) Limited, PLC
sa (see son)
sable (m) sand

sac (m) bag
sac à dos (m) rucksack
sac à main (m) handbag
saignant(e) rare *(steak)*
saigner to bleed
saint(e) holy, saint
sais: je sais I know
saison (f) season
salaire (m) wage
sale dirty
salé(e) salty, savoury
salle (f) room, lounge, (concert) hall
salle à manger (f) dining-room
salon (m) lounge, living-room
salut hello
sang (m) blood
sans without
» sans doute no doubt
santé (f) health
sauf except
sauter to jump
sauvage wild
sauver to rescue
savoir to know (how to)
savon (m) soap
scie (f) saw
se oneself, him/her/itself, themselves
séance (f) (cinema) performance,
    screening
seau (m) bucket
sec, sèche dry
sécher to dry
seconde (f) second
secours (m) help
séjour (m) stay
sel (m) salt
selon according to, depending on
semaine (f) week
sens (m) sense, meaning, direction
sensation (f) sensation, feeling
sensible sensitive
sentier (m) path
sentir to feel, to smell, to taste
sérieux/euse serious, dependable,

reliable

séropositif/tive HIV positive

serré(e) tight

serrure (f) lock

serveuse (f) waitress

service (m) service, service charge

serviette (f) towel, serviette, napkin, briefcase

serviettes hygiéniques (f/pl) sanitary towels

servir to serve, to be of use

ses his, her, its

seul(e) only, alone

seulement only

si if, whether, so, yes (emphatic)

SIDA (m) AIDS

siècle (m) century

le sien, la sienne his/hers/its

signaler to report

signer to sign

signifier to mean

silencieux/euse silent

s'il vous plaît please

simple simple

sinon otherwise, if not

sirop (m) syrup

skier to ski

slip (m) panties, underpants

SMS (m) text message

société (f) society, company

sœur (f) sister

soie (f) silk

soif: avoir soif to be thirsty

soi-même oneself

soir (m) evening

soirée (f) evening, party

soit ... soit either ... or

sol (m) ground, soil

soleil (m) sun, sunshine

son, sa his, her, its

sortie (f) exit, way out, departure

sortir to come/go out

soucoupe (f) saucer

soudain suddenly

soudain(e) sudden

soulier (m) shoe

soupe (f) soup

sourd(e) deaf

sourire (m) smile

sous under(neath)

sous-sol (m) basement

sous-vêtements (m/pl) underwear

souterrain(e) underground

soutien-gorge (m) bra

souvent often

sparadrap (m) sticking plaster

spécial(e) special, particular

spectacle (m) show, spectacle

St, Ste (Saint, Sainte) Saint

stade (m) stadium

station (f) (underground) station, resort

stationnement (m) parking

stationner to park

station-service (f) petrol station

store (m) (Venetian) blind

stylo (m) pen

stylo bille (m) ballpoint pen

succès (m) success

succursale (f) branch *(office, shop)*

sucette (f) lollipop, dummy

sucre (m) sugar

sud (m) south

suffit: ça suffit that's enough

suis: je suis I am

suisse Swiss

suivant(e) following, next

sujet (m) matter, subject, topic

supérieur(e) higher, upper, top, advanced

suppositoire (m) suppository

sur on, upon, about

sûr(e) sure, certain

surgelé(e) (deep) frozen

surprise (f) surprise

surtout above all, especially

survêtement (m) tracksuit

sus: en sus extra, in addition

suspendre to hang up

s.v.p. (s'il vous plaît) please

sympa, sympathique nice, charming, pleasant

T

t' (te) you

ta (see ton)

tabac (m) tobacco

tableau (m) picture, painting

tache (f) spot, stain

taie d'oreiller (f) pillowcase

taille (f) waist, size

taisez-vous! tais-toi! be quiet! shut up!

tant (de) so much (of), so many

tante (f) aunt

tapis (m) rug

tard late

tas (m) heap

tasse (f) cup

te you

tel, telle such

téléphérique (m) cable car

téléphone portable (m) mobile *(phone)*

tellement so (much)

témoin (m) witness

tempête (f) storm

temps (m) time, weather

» de temps en temps from time to time, occasionally

tenir to hold, to keep

tente (f) tent

terrain (m) ground, (playing) field, pitch

terrasse (f) terrace

terre (f) earth, land, ground

tes your

tête (f) head

théâtre (m) theatre

le tien, la tienne yours

timbre (m) stamp

tire-bouchon (m) corkscrew

tirer to pull, to shoot

tiroir (m) drawer

tissu (m) fabric

toi you

toilettes (f/pl) (public) toilets

toi-même yourself

toit (m) roof

tomber to fall (down/over)

ton, ta your

tonne (f) ton

tordu(e) twisted, sprained

tort: avoir tort to be wrong

tôt early

touche (f) key *(piano, keyboard)*

toucher to touch

toujours yet, still, always

tour (f) tower

tour (m) tour, trip, ride, turn

tourner to turn

tournevis (m) screwdriver

tous, toutes all

tout everything

tout(e) all, every

» tout à fait completely, quite

» tout de même all the same

» tout de suite immediately, right away

» tout droit straight on

» tout le monde everyone

toux (f) cough

traduction (f) translation

traduire to translate

train (m) train

» en train de in the process of

traiter to treat

tranchant(e) sharp

tranche (f) slice

tranquille calm, quiet

travail (m) work, job

travailler to work

travers: à travers through

traverser to cross

très very

triste sad, unhappy

troisième third

trompé(e) mistaken, wrong

trop too (much)

trottoir (m) pavement

trou (m) hole

trouver to find
tu you
tuer to kill
tuyau (m) pipe, hose
TVA (f) VAT
type (m) type, sort, kind, bloke, guy

U

UE, Union européenne (f) EU, European union
un, une a/an, one
unique unique, only
université (f) university
usine (f) factory
utile useful
utiliser to use

V

va: il/elle va he/she/it goes/is going
vacances (f/pl) holiday(s)
vache (f) cow
vague (f) wave *(water)*
vaincre to defeat, beat
vais: je vais I go/am going
vaisselle (f) crockery, washing up
valise (f) suitcase
vallée (f) valley
valoir to be worth
vapeur (f) steam
vapeur (m) steamship
vaut is worth
vélo (m) bike, bicycle
vendange (f) (grape) harvest, vintage
vendeur, vendeuse salesperson
vendre to sell
venir to come
vent (m) wind
vente (f) sale
verdure (f) greenery
vérifier to check
verre (m) glass, lens
vers towards, about
verser to pour, to pay (in)
vert(e) green

veste (f) jacket
vestiaire (m) cloakroom
vêtement (m) garment
vêtements (m/pl) clothes, clothing
veuf, veuve widower, widow
veut: ça veut dire it means
veux: je veux I want
viande (f) meat
vide empty
vie (f) life
vieux, vieille old
vif, vive live, alive, vivid, bright, sharp, acute *(pain)*
vignoble (m) vineyard
VIH (m) HIV
ville (f) town
vin (m) wine
violer to rape
violet(te) purple
virage (m) bend, curve
vis (f) screw
visage (m) face
visiter to visit
visser to screw
vite fast, quickly
vitesse (f) speed
vitre (f) pane, window *(car etc.)*
vitrine (f) shop window
vive (see vif)
vivre to live
voici here is/are
voie (f) lane *(on road)*, (railway) track
voilà there is/are, there you are
voile (f) sail, sailing
voir to see
voisin(e) neighbour
voiture (f) car, coach, carriage *(train)*
vol (m) flight, theft, robbery
voler to fly, to rob, to steal
vos your
votre your
le/la vôtre yours
voudrais: je voudrais I would like
vouloir to want

vous you, to you
vous-même, vous-mêmes yourself, yourselves
voyage (m) journey, trip
voyager to travel
vrai(e) true, real, genuine
vraiment really, very
vue (f) (eye)sight, look, view, sight

W

wagon (m) carriage *(train)*
web (m) web *(internet)*

Y

y there, it
yeux (m/pl) eyes

index

Now you're talking!

If you're keen to progress to a higher level, BBC Active offers a wide range of innovative products, from short courses and grammars to build up your vocabulary and confidence to more in-depth courses for beginners or intermediates. Designed by language-teaching experts, our courses make the best use of today's technology, with book and audio, audio-only and multi-media products on offer.

Independent, interactive study course
2 x PC CD-ROM; 144pp course book, 60-min audio CD; free online activities and resources

Get Into French is an interactive new language course for people on the go. Available as a complete course on CD-ROM, supported by a book, audio CD and website, its flexible approach puts you firmly in control of how, when and where you learn. Based around a virtual French town complete with hotel, restaurant, shops and more, it allows you to take part in on-screen conversations and improve your language skills in an environment second only to the real thing.
Also available: Get Into Spanish.

Short independent study course
128pp course book; 2 x 60-min CDs/cassettes; free online activities; 6-part television series on BBC TWO or DVD.

Short audio only course
2 x 70-min CDs/cassettes.

B B C ACTIVE

For further information on our language courses, or to buy online, visit www.bbcactive.com. For a catalogue, call our Languages Enquiry Line on 08705 210 292. BBC books are also available from bookshops, or from BBC shop on 08700 777 001 / www.bbcshop.com.